The Regulation of Boxing

The Regulation of Boxing

A History and Comparative Analysis of Policies Among American States

ROBERT G. RODRIGUEZ

Foreword by GEORGE KIMBALL

McFarland & Company, Inc., Publishers
Jefferson, North Carolina, and London

All photographs are from the author's collection unless otherwise credited.

LIBRARY OF CONGRESS CATALOGUING-IN-PUBLICATION DATA

Rodriguez, Robert G.
    The regulation of boxing : a history and comparative analysis of policies among American states / Robert G. Rodriguez ; foreword by George Kimball.
       p.   cm.
    Includes bibliographical references and index.

    ISBN 978-0-7864-3862-4
    softcover : 50# alkaline paper ∞

    1. Boxing — Law and legislation — United States — States.
2. Boxing — Safety regulations — United States — States.
3. Boxers (Sports) — Legal status, laws, etc. — United States — States.   4. Boxing — Safety regulations.   5. Boxers (Sports) — Legal status, laws, etc. I. Title.
KF3989.R63   2009
344.73'099 — dc22   2008046353

British Library cataloguing data are available

©2009 Robert G. Rodriguez. All rights reserved

No part of this book may be reproduced or transmitted in any form or by any means, electronic or mechanical, including photocopying or recording, or by any information storage and retrieval system, without permission in writing from the publisher.

On the cover: Boxing image ©2008 Clipart; Map image ©2008 Shutterstock.

Manufactured in the United States of America

McFarland & Company, Inc., Publishers
  Box 611, Jefferson, North Carolina 28640
    www.mcfarlandpub.com

To my children, Gabriela and Diego

Acknowledgments

This book is a revised and updated version of the doctoral dissertation I completed at the University of Kansas in 2005. Anyone who has earned a Ph.D. has had professors that should be thanked for their crucial guidance at various stages of their academic career. I would never have made it to KU if it hadn't been for the advice I received as an undergraduate from University of California at Irvine professor Caesar Sereseres and the Summer Academic Enrichment Program he coordinates. Dr. Sereseres and the SAEP were the key factors in my decision to pursue a graduate degree.

At the University of Kansas, I am indebted to several people who have taught and advised me throughout the years. Professor Chico Herbison served as my unofficial academic, professional and life advisor. Likewise, Dr. Ngondi Kamatuka, director of Educational Opportunity Programs at the university, has been my role model for over a decade. My doctoral dissertation committee was an outstanding conglomeration of several nationally recognized faculty members. Historian Bill Tuttle and political scientists Al Cigler and Burdett Loomis have each published books that are used in college classrooms throughout the United States, and Don Haider-Markel is one of the most productive faculty members in the political science department. Above all, I owe an eternal debt of gratitude to Dr. Mark Joslyn, my dissertation advisor. Words cannot accurately describe the profound appreciation I have for Dr. Joslyn's support, guidance and advice. My dissertation, and ultimately this book, would not have been possible without him.

With all of the academic, professional and personal advice I gained from the aforementioned individuals, it should be made clear that the road to completing this book has not been a solitary endeavor. University of Kansas college student and boxing fanatic Fernando Yaluk assisted me with the transcription of interviews, geography graduate student Yoshinori Nakazawa produced the outstanding maps and my colleague Allyson Flaster helped format the bibliography and notes.

My family has also been instrumental to my success. "Pirucho"

Rodriguez, an uncle who passed away in early 2008, imparted to me more wisdom than he could imagine. Among the gems he taught me early on was the importance of family, for I could have all the degrees, possessions and money in the world, yet if I had no one to share it with then I would have nothing. Most people born to Latin American parents with a minimal level of education and empty bank accounts never get the opportunity to advance in society. In my case, however, I had the good fortune to be born in a country where if you work hard and attain an education, you can progress professionally and economically. The American dream envisioned for my brothers (Edward and Mark) and me by our Argentine parents became our reality, and I want to thank my mother and father for making the decision to immigrate to the United States over forty years ago. My father, Marcos, deserves a special mention for introducing me to the magnificent sport of boxing, and my mother, Gladys, continues to inspire me from above. And finally, I wish to acknowledge my wife, Irina, who has been by my side since I embarked on my quest to earn my Ph.D.

TABLE OF CONTENTS

Acknowledgments	vii
Foreword by George Kimball	1
Preface	7
Introduction	13
1 • A History of Boxing Regulations	23
2 • Data Analysis	63
3 • Case Study: Boxing in Nevada	108
4 • Case Study: Boxing in Kansas	151
5 • An Alternative Model? Boxing in Argentina	163
Conclusion	190
Chapter Notes	205
Bibliography	213
Index	215

Foreword by George Kimball

One night last autumn I found myself at ringside for a club fight show at an ice rink outside Detroit. The first pro bout of the evening was supposed to commence at 8 P.M., and when 9 o'clock arrived with the gladiators nowhere in sight, the paying customers were growing restless. The public address announcer pleaded for patience and explained the problem: the ambulance and EMT crew required to be on hand were late in arriving but on their way.

This wasn't particularly unusual; over the years I've experienced similar delays for the same good reason at boxing venues around the world. What did make this occasion problematically puzzling was that the slate of professional bouts had been preceded by a pair of amateur contests that had already taken place, and there plainly had been no ambulance crew on site when *those* fights had taken place.

Amid conflicting explanations it seemed unclear whether this represented a grievous error on the part of the boxing commission or whether, as one ringside official lamely contended, a statutory loophole had exempted the amateur bouts from the safety requirement.

I didn't know the answer to that question, but I knew who would. I contacted Dr. Robert Rodriguez, and in short order he was back to me with confirmation that Michigan regulations should indeed have required an ambulance at the venue for the amateur bouts.

Now, some might think it odd that a Latin American studies professor in Lawrence, Kansas, would know more about another state's boxing regulations than the members of that state's commission themselves, but, as Rodriguez convincingly demonstrates in the pages of *The Regulation of Boxing*, we're talking about a sport in which the people running the show have been playing fast and loose with the rules pretty much since Cain TKO'd Abel and are not accustomed to being held accountable.

In the fall of 1999, Robert Rodriguez was in Kansas City when the late Randie Carver fought Kabary Salem, an Egyptian middleweight based in New York. Carver was a local favorite, unbeaten in 24 pro bouts, albeit against middling Midwestern opposition, while Salem had done most of his fighting at Connecticut's tribal casinos. In the tenth round of a scheduled 12-rounder, Salem, who had previously been cautioned for a couple of flagrant head-butts, landed an overhand right–straight left combination that put Carver on the mat.

Carver made several attempts to rise but never made it to his knees before collapsing. He remained on the canvas for a good 20 minutes before an ambulance arrived to take him to nearby North Kansas City Hospital, where he died of blunt head trauma two days later.

Whether more prompt medical attention would have made a difference remains unknown. Over the years I've witnessed a few of these unfortunate episodes myself. On the undercard of the 1980 Roberto Duran–Sugar Ray Leonard card in Montreal, a lightweight named Cleveland Denny was knocked into a coma by Gaetan Hart, and I watched Dr. Ferdie Pacheco, there as part of the ringside broadcast team, abandon his microphone and climb into the ring in full physician mode to aid the stricken boxer. I was also in Las Vegas when Jimmy Garcia collapsed in the ring at the conclusion of his 1995 bout against Gabriel Ruelas. Both Denny and Garcia received immediate medical attention, but it wasn't enough to save their lives.

Robert Rodriguez doesn't know whether the presence of an ambulance would have saved Randie Carver, either, but since there wasn't one, we'll never know. What was interesting was the explanation of the responsible authorities.

Tim Lueckenhoff, the chairman of the Missouri Office of Athletics, said that the law requiring an on-site ambulance was vague. The promoters had been in compliance with the letter, if not the spirit, of the law by relying on "medical personnel with appropriate resuscitation equipment" present at the venue and a "nearby" ambulance that arrived at least 15 minutes after it had been summoned.

What makes this explanation troublesome is that this is the same Tim Lueckenhoff who presently serves as the president of the Association of Boxing Commissions, which in the absence of a national body governing the sport presently functions as the closest we're likely to get to an umbrella organization overseeing boxing on a national scale.

In the pages of this book Rodriguez documents the bizarre discrepancies at play in regulating boxing in a nation that stages thousands of professional matches each year. A few states have no regulatory body at all, while at least one we can name has a boxing commission but no boxing. In some instances, the recognized commission might be a non-government agency thrown together by the promoters themselves — a case of the fox guarding the henhouse. And in far too many cases, governmentally appointed state boxing commissions are a dumping ground for patronage appointments, staffed by inept political hacks with little background in the sport. In almost all cases, the potential for corruption is profound.

When John McCain, a confirmed states rights advocate, emerges as a crusader for federal regulation of *anything*, you can probably take it that the situation must be dire indeed, but in fact the 2008 Republican presidential candidate has for many years been Washington's most prominent (and most successful) advocate of nationwide boxing reform, though by no means has it been a partisan issue. Between 1983 and 1994 then–New Mexico Representative Bill Richardson introduced no fewer than six boxing reform bills, all of which died on the vine, though usually after having been passed by the House.

Senator McCain took up the cudgel in 1994, and after a couple of false starts in which his measures met the same fate as had Richardson's, was able to push through legislation resulting in the Professional Boxing Safety Act, which President Bill Clinton signed into law in 1996, and the Muhammad Ali Boxing Reform Act, which was adopted in 2000. (McCain more recently authored an even more far-reaching bill providing for a federal regulatory authority, the fate of which presently rests in the hands of the Congress convening in 2008.)

Indeed, as the presidential debates unfolded over the autumn of 2007, one found oneself hoping that a panelist might slip in a boxing-related question that might have allowed Richardson and McCain an opportunity to give public currency to the issue. (Senator Barack Obama — who in his autobiographical *Dreams of My Father* recalls the boxing lessons he received from his Indonesian stepfather — also seems to have a more than passing interest in the subject, and might have also contributed to the dialogue.)

Most everyone seems to agree on the crying need for standardization of uniform rules and safety regulations that a national governing body would presumably be able to enforce, but as Rodriguez demonstrates here, the cooperation that would entail might meet with some resistance. State commissions can be relied upon to act primarily in their own self-interest. (Rhode Island, for instance, honored Nevada's suspension of heavyweight Joe Mesi right up until the minute that state's most influential boxing maven, Jimmy Burchfield, signed Mesi to a promotional contract, at which point the Rhode

Island commission unhesitatingly granted Mesi a license, despite overwhelming evidence that he had sustained a prior subdural hematoma.)

State regulatory bodies are often guided by economic motives, and sometimes, as in the case of Rodriguez's home state, that is the very reason for their creation. In his interview with Aaron Davis, the chairman of the Kansas Boxing Commission forthrightly admits that the KBC was established as an indirect result of a provision in the 1996 Professional Boxing Safety Act, which stipulated that in a jurisdiction lacking a boxing commission, "fights in such states require the supervision of another state's boxing commission that is subject to the guidelines of the Association of Boxing Commissions."

"What would happen," Davis told Rodriguez, "is Missouri or Colorado or other state commissions would come in, they would license the boxers, their state would get all the revenue and receive all the proceeds and fees, and Kansas would be left with nothing."

Think about that for a moment, and imagine the public reaction if, say, a Colorado state agency started licensing veterinarians in Lawrence, or a board appointed by the Missouri governor was put in charge of doling out taxicab licenses in Wichita.

And Marc Ratner, the former executive director of the Nevada State Athletic Commission, expressed his reservations about the funding of a national boxing commission to Rodriguez by noting, "I don't want anything that would take away anything from the state. Let's say that they took a dollar from every ticket to fund this thing. That might be money that comes out of the state of Nevada more than any other state. I don't want the State of Nevada to be penalized."

Not even the proponents of reform seem to be able to agree whether a national commission should be a federal regulatory agency (which would add yet another layer of bureaucracy, and potentially bring still more dim-witted politicians into the mix) or a federation, nationally recognized but devoid of federal funding and control.

With respect to the latter, Rodriguez cites the imperfect model of his ancestral homeland, where the *Federación Argentina de Boxeo* functions as a veritable fiefdom. A national regulatory body originally established by promoters, managers, and arena impresarios, the FAB is federally chartered but free of government oversight, a cozy arrangement whose potential for abuse would appear self-evident, particularly to those who can remember this country's experience with James A. Norris and the International Boxing Club.

In the detailed study he presents here, Dr. Rodriguez would appear to have a spiritual kinship with one of his Lawrence neighbors, Bill James, whose pioneering analysis over the past quarter-century eventually revolutionized the world of Major League Baseball. Although both men are obviously passionate about their respective sports, they generally restrain themselves in their advocacy, preferring to let the facts speak for themselves.

James could as easily have been talking about *The Regulation of Boxing* when he cited his own credo: "All of my work is driven entirely by questions. The statistics are simply a pathway between the question and the answer."

Arguments are fine for barroom conversations, but a simple rendition of undeniable facts can be far more persuasive. And if you ask enough of the right questions, you're apt to find the truth staring you in the face.

A winner of the Nat Fleischer Award for Excellence in Boxing Journalism, George Kimball is the author of *Four Kings: Leonard, Hagler, Hearns, Duran and the Last Great Era of Boxing* (2008).

Preface

My earliest boxing memories are short flashbacks of televised fights I watched as a young child. The first fight I consciously remember watching live was one of the Muhammad Ali–Leon Spinks bouts in 1978. I was just five years old at the time, but I can recall our family sitting in the kitchen watching the fight on a small 13-inch television that sat atop our refrigerator. I also recall watching the Roberto Duran–Sugar Ray Leonard fights that took place in June and November 1980. I remember asking my mother why she wanted Duran to win. Her response, "Because he helps poor people," is indelibly etched in my mind. I was a bit too young to fully comprehend the racial dynamics involved in the Larry Holmes–Gerry Cooney fight in 1982, but that was the first fight that I was able to watch multiple times, thanks to a bulky invention that made its way to our home called a VCR.

While the aforementioned fights along with a few others planted the seeds of appreciation I would develop for this sport, I can't say that I truly became a boxing fan until the night of October 29, 1987. Every boxing fan has one fight that had the most impact on him. For me, that fight was between Thomas Hearns and an Argentine fighter named Juan Domingo Roldan who fought for the vacant world middleweight championship. That exciting fight awoke something within me, and I have been hooked ever since. Soon thereafter, I bought my first boxing magazine and like so many other boys throughout history was taken to see my first boxing match by my father.

Most boxing fans can also remember the first fight they attended. For me, this life-altering event came on May 9, 1988, at the Great Western Forum in Inglewood, California. The main event was a US Boxing Association super middleweight title fight between Lindell Holmes and Steve Darnell. My father wanted to make it a memorable experience for me, so he bought us ringside seats at $35 a piece. It was such a significant evening that twenty years later those images come to mind with vivid clarity. Watching a fight in person is quite a different experience than watching it on television. If you sit ringside, droplets of blood, sweat, spit and water will make their way toward you. You can hear the incessant advice screamed by fans in the stands, and catcalls to the round-card girls. And if you're lucky, you may have the chance to meet the celebrities who always seem to turn up at the fights.

Boxing is a sport that attracts fans from all facets of society, from working-class immigrants, to famous actors, models, athletes, singers, politicians, and people of all races and nationalities. At the first boxing card I attended, I had the privilege of meeting Ike Williams, a legendary boxer who was the lightweight champion of the world between 1945 and 1951. From that moment forward, my passion for this sport became solidified, and I set out to learn as much as I could about the history of the sport while following contemporary boxers and events.

As fate would have it, soon after I started attending the fights, I became acquainted with an Argentine gentleman named Carlos Avilas, who was the Spanish media relations director for boxing at the Great Western Forum. He recognized my interest and enthusiasm for the sport and subsequently started providing my father and me with participant credentials and free tickets to the boxing matches that were held every two weeks at the Forum. When I was a college freshman in 1991, John Meyer, a friend in the advertising business informed me of a Spanish-language newspaper in Santa Ana, California, that needed a bilingual individual to write about boxing. Fitting the bill, I became a reporter for the *Unión Hispana* newspaper and started officially covering the fights in southern California and Las Vegas.

My work with *Unión Hispana* led to freelance writing jobs with other publications, and eventually, I also became involved in the photography side of the boxing reporting business. By the time I was twenty-one years old, I had published articles in national publications such as *USA Boxing News* and international magazines, including *The Ring Magazine*, the most recognized boxing publication in the world. For the next few years, I covered all of the most important boxing events in Las Vegas and southern California, and in the process I came to meet, photograph, report on, and interview many boxing legends as well as numerous celebrities.

In 1994, my pursuit of a graduate degree led me away from the boxing hotbed of California, to Lawrence, Kansas. In Kansas, I continued to follow boxing and cover sports events for the now defunct *Kansas City Sports Page*, but my attendance at boxing matches has been far more sporadic. Although I have occasionally made the trek to Los Angeles and Las Vegas for a few select fights, I have not seen many high-level boxing matches in the Midwest.

However, there was one fight I attended in Kansas City that would have a profound effect on me.

The inspiration for this book is a once up-and-coming Kansas City boxer named Randie Carver. Several years ago, Carver was supposed to have easily won a fight against unheralded Kabary Salem. Carver was the North American Boxing Federation champion and positioning himself to fight for a world title. On the tragic night of September 12, 1999, Salem knocked Carver out in the tenth round at Harrah's Casino in North Kansas City. Carver lost consciousness immediately after being counted out and underwent emergency brain surgery before dying two days later. I was among the thousands in attendance that night. Having attended hundreds of boxing matches since 1988 as a reporter, photographer, and a fan, I had seen just about every bizarre scenario imaginable, including a man in a para-glider crashing into the ring during a heavyweight championship fight between Evander Holyfield and Riddick Bowe. But I had never before witnessed a death in the ring, nor have I witnessed another since that ill-fated evening.

While death or serious injuries are inherent risks in a sport as violent as boxing, they rarely occur when those who regulate the sport take proper precautions. In Randie Carver's case, it seemed to me that the system of boxing regulations played a part in his death. My recollections of that unfortunate summer night are vivid to this day. Salem's roughhouse tactics (deliberate, in my view) marred the fight. Numerous head butts and holdings resulted in point deductions by referee Ross Strada. But Salem was not disqualified, and Carver, whose official cause of death was listed as blunt head trauma by the coroner's office, was visibly weakened as the fight went on. There were also rumors about Carver struggling to reach the 168-pound super middleweight limit, indicating that dehydration may have played a role in his death. Should the referee or ringside doctor have stopped the bout? It was a judgment call, and in an investigation conducted by the Missouri Office of Athletics in the Division of Professional Registration of the Department of Economic Development, the officials were not considered to be at fault.[1] Imagine that: the organization responsible for regulating the boxing match concluded that its officials were not at fault. The Kansas City Police Department investigation also concluded that the death was accidental due to the nature of the activity. In my judgment, there was more than enough reason to disqualify Salem well before the tenth round, and for that reason I was yelling for the referee to stop the fight from the stands.

I am convinced that the most damning evidence that the lack of standard professional boxing regulations was at least partially at fault in Carver's death was the lack of an ambulance present at the fight. At the time of 1999 fight, Missouri boxing matches should have followed the 1996 Professional Boxing Safety Act, a federal law requiring "an ambulance or medical personnel with appropriate resuscitation equipment continuously present on site."[2] "But the law does not specifically define what fulfills that requirement," said Tim Lueckenhoff, administrator of the Missouri Office of Athletics and president of the Association of Boxing Commissions.[3] Thus, if emergency medical equipment was on-site, or if the boxing venue was located in close proximity to a hospital, an ambulance would not necessarily have to be at the location of the event to comply with federal law. This was not even the first time that Missouri had to deal with this type of situation. In January 1999, just a few months prior to the Carver-Salem bout, Mexican boxer Fernando Maldonado collapsed in his dressing room after being knocked out in a boxing match held in St. Louis, Missouri. An ambulance was not on site. While Maldonado survived, he suffered brain damage and sued Gateway Hotel Holdings (the owner of the venue) for damages.[4]

In the case of the Carver-Salem bout, I watched the ambulance drive to the outdoor arena at least fifteen minutes after Carver was knocked out. Published reports indicate that Carver lay on the canvas for twenty minutes before paramedics took him to North Kansas City Hospital, which is located just a few minutes away from the casino where the event was held.[5] In the meantime, the ringside physician and others appeared to be trying to revive Carver, to no avail. How many of those precious minutes, and perhaps Carver's life, could have been saved if an ambulance was on site and he was immediately transported to the nearby hospital? We will never know the answer to that question, but it exemplifies the importance that professional boxing regulations may have on the health and safety of boxers.

For the record, Missouri eventually enacted an administrative rule requiring an ambulance and personnel on site in May 2002.[6] This rule came about after a Missouri jury awarded Fernando Maldonado $13.7 million in compensatory damages for the injuries he suffered in his 1999 boxing match where an ambulance was not present on site. That rule change came about just three years too late to help Maldonado or Carver.

In the aftermath of the Carver tragedy, I continued my quest to earn a doctoral degree at the University of Kansas by merging my interests in politics and sports. The idea of examining the disparity in regulations promulgated by the state athletic commissions as a dissertation topic came about through an informal conversation with a few University of Kansas political science professors on a fateful spring day in 2002. At that time, Mike Tyson, the tarnished former heavyweight champion, was searching for a state commission that would allow him to challenge Lennox Lewis for his championship belts. Nevada, Texas, Michigan and Colorado had denied Tyson a license to box based upon his notorious behavior in and out of the ring, and the pair eventually fought in Tennessee, a most-unlikely locale for a boxing event of that magnitude. The professors were curious to find out how this could happen. My response evolved into the book you are holding in your hands.

The federalist, republican nature of the United States government allows for states to regulate policy areas in a diverse fashion. Without federal oversight, or a national agency to regulate boxing, states will vary in their regulation of the sport, just as they have differences in any other policy area. While it is common knowledge that boxing regulations vary from state to state, the extent of this variance has not been documented in a single study at the national level. Thus, the purpose of this book is to analyze the most critical aspects of boxing regulations (those that relate to health and safety) in the United States.

Any analysis of current political issues requires context. Boxing regulations have developed over time, and at the outset of this book I provide a historical overview of boxing regulations from ancient times to the present day, with an emphasis on boxing in the United States. Utilizing the skills I honed as a graduate student, I created a survey that was distributed to all of the state athletic commissions in the United States. Three-fourths of the states with athletic commissions replied. The survey results reveal a great deal of consistency on several issues and frightening inconsistencies on others.

Following standard practices of political science research, I developed an index to capture the differences among state regulations. Then, through the guidance of theoretical works on state politics, I selected a set of factors that I considered would have an effect on the index. Once I collected all of the information available about the commissions' regulations and the factors that might account for their differences, I carried out several common statistical tests. These tests reveal some of the reasons for the variance in boxing regulations across the states that had commissions at the time of the study. As fate would have it, between the time I completed my initial study of boxing regulations in 2005 and the publication of this book, two state governments decided to create athletic commissions. This development provided me with the unique opportunity to test the statistical model that I created to see if it accurately predicts the level of boxing regulations in the states with newly formed commissions.

In addition to the statistical analysis, this book also includes in-depth case studies of athletic commissions to further illustrate the differences among the states. A case study of Nevada includes interviews with state athletic commission officials and a participant-observation of commission personnel performing their duties at a boxing event. A second case study examines Kansas, one of the two recently-established boxing commissions, through an exclusive interview with the boxing commissioner for that state. In addition, a foreign case study of Argentina, which has a centralized system of regulating boxing, is presented to provide an international example of regulating the sport.

Expert opinions introduced in this study come from long-time boxing analyst Thomas Hauser, former world champion Albert Davila, world renowned referee Joe Cortez, and former ringside physician Dr. Margaret Goodman. The study concludes with a discussion of the possible implications of the establishment of a federal boxing commission in the United States. Exclusive photographs illustrate the text; unless otherwise noted, all photographs are the property of the author.

INTRODUCTION

The United States is a federal republic, which allows for a wide disparity in the manner in which people are regulated since they are governed by laws established by both federal and state governmental elected officials. In some instances, the differences between state laws can have dire consequences on the governed. Professional boxing regulations are an example of how the lack of federal laws or a federal regulatory agency produces a potentially dangerous situation. Professional boxing does not possess uniform regulations, nor does it possess a national body that enforces the implementation of regulations in the United States.

Since a national boxing commission does not exist, international associations, individual countries, U.S. states, and U.S. territories govern the sport. There is a peak association (The Association of Boxing Commissions) that suggests uniform practices and shares information among state commissions, but it does not possess any oversight powers. At present, the participants in the sport (e.g., boxers, promoters, managers) are not organized. There is not a national professional boxers union, nor any national organization that carries out collective bargaining efforts on behalf of boxers for health care, pension plans or other types of benefits (although some individual states provide such benefits).

According to U.S. senator and Republican presidential candidate John McCain, "Professional boxing is the only major sport in the United States that does not have a strong, centralized association or league to establish and enforce uniform rules and practices."[1] As a result, there is tremendous disparity in the manner boxing is regulated throughout the fifty United States, its territories, the District of Columbia and on American Indian reservations. For example, the California State Athletic Commission[2] has overseen boxing within its borders for over eighty years and has actively enacted and enforced extensive boxing regulations to help ensure the safety and economic livelihood of boxers who exercise their occupation there. In contrast, the State of Kansas abolished its athletic commission in 1979, and until 2005 the sport

INTRODUCTION

had been regulated by a series of state laws passed in 1981 that provide the governing bodies of Kansas' cities and municipalities the authorization to regulate, supervise and license all professional boxing matches.[3] In 2004, however, the Kansas State Legislature passed a bill later signed by Governor Kathleen Sebelius to create a state athletic commission. In many states, the laws that remain on the books are thoroughly outdated. Given the disparities in the health and safety standards that regulate this sport and a lack of oversight ensuring the standards that protect professional boxers, a federal mechanism may be able to provide order and oversight powers.

This book is a study of how states vary in their regulation of a unique policy area. Specifically, the purpose is to analyze the differences between state boxing regulations in the United States. All 43 states that possessed a state athletic commission in 2004 are examined.[4] At present, there is only one limited study in existence that attempts to analyze these differences, a 2003 U.S. General Accounting Office Report entitled, "Professional Boxing: Issues Related to the Protection of Boxers' Health, Safety, and Economic Interests."[5] While the methods and findings of that study provide an excellent start to examine the variation of boxing regulations, it is limited in scope and its findings cannot be applied to the fifty states. Therefore, through this study I build upon the GAO report to answer the central question of how states differ in their regulation of professional boxing.

There is a wide degree of variance in the regulation of professional boxing. For example, California conducts neurological testing of boxers prior to participation in boxing matches, but relatively few other states do. Given the nature of the sport and the repeated blows to the head experienced by participants, it would seem important to include neurological testing in pre-fight medical evaluations to help minimize the possibilities of a participant suffering brain damage or death. A post-fight physical examination would also seem to be a standard practice given the possibility of neurological damage that a participant may have incurred during a fight and that may not be readily apparent. However, the extent of post-fight physical examinations varies. While federal law requires states to honor suspensions made in other states, a federal entity to enforce this practice is non-existent.

In terms of preserving safety standards for professional boxing, several variables can help minimize the risk of serious injury or death to participants. For example, preventing mismatches of boxers with clearly unequal talent is one method. An analysis of boxers' records is one way to carry this out. Many

Introduction

people believe that having an ambulance on site in case a boxer suffers serious injury is a standard practice, even though it is not. Requiring some form of health insurance for boxers would seem like a logical requirement, yet the range of the insurance coverage varies. Requiring qualified ring officials (judges, referees, etc.) to obtain some sort of certification is another example of a seemingly essential requirement that varies in practice. Likewise, due to the likelihood of lacerations during a given boxing match and the possible transmission of HIV-AIDS through blood contact, one would think that HIV testing should be an essential component for licensing of a boxer to help prevent the possible spread of the virus through blood contact during a boxing match, yet it is not. Finally, analyzing bodily fluids for the presence of drugs is another type of examination that varies tremendously among states. In recent years, drug testing in baseball has been of particular interest to the United States Congress; however, there is not a movement among the members of Congress to conduct a similar investigation into boxing.

The implications of the research compiled in this book are potentially far reaching. In terms of scholarly research, this project contributes to the American political literature by examining a specific policy area that presents challenges for the federalist system. Furthermore, the range of this study is nationwide, thus explaining the variance in all of the available cases. Boxing fans will be interested in this book's exploration of historical trends in the regulation of sport, and its detailed look at the regulations in boxing's foremost state: Nevada. In 2004, the United States Senate passed a bill that would establish a national boxing commission. This bill was introduced to the House of Representatives; however, it was not acted upon by the end of the session and died.[6] Senator John McCain and Representative Peter King of New York reintroduced this bill in the Senate and House in January 2005. In March, the bill passed the Committee on Commerce, Science and Transportation without amendment. Then, on May 9, 2005, the bill was passed by unanimous consent in the United States Senate without amendment. The Senate bill was referred to the House Committee on Education and the Workforce, and the Committee on Energy and Commerce. The latter committee approved the bill by a vote of 25-16 on June 29, 2005. Nevertheless, the full House voted against this bill. In 2007, Senator McCain and Representative King reintroduced this bill in their respective houses of Congress. As of the publication of this book, these bills were not acted upon.

INTRODUCTION

Scholarly Perspectives on State vs. Federal Policymaking

The literature written about state politics demonstrates the importance of sub-national government in the policymaking process. For example, political scientist David M. Hedge notes that after decades of federal dominance, a substantial responsibility for governing now lies within the American states.[7] Hedge identifies several changes that have taken place as a result of the resurgence of the states. He writes, "A variety of initiatives and reforms have increased citizen participation and input into state government; Blacks, Hispanics and women enjoy considerably greater representation at the state and local level; and higher levels of inter-party competition and a growing diversity of interest groups promise a better linkage between public opinion and public policy.... Governors now have more power than ever before and are more willing to use that power to effect innovative policy solutions ... [and there is a] greater use of the initiative and referendum."[8]

According to political scientist Virginia Gray, some of the political variables that account for different regulations among states include: political party control and inter-party competition, interest group strength, gubernatorial power, the political background of judges, professionalism of the legislature, public and elite opinion, other states' actions, national political forces and political culture.[9] In addition to the aforementioned political factors, Gray also writes that there are several socioeconomic factors that may also account for these differences, including: population size and composition, migration and urbanization, physical characteristics and natural resources, types of economic activities stemming from a state's physical endowments, wealth, and regional economic forces.

Political scientists Evan J. Ringquist and James C. Garand have found that "the American states provide an excellent comparative laboratory for developing and testing theories that account for policy differences across states, patterns of policy change over time, and the consequences of different policy choices.... In general, these policy changes are produced by three broad sets of forces: internal state political factors, external political factors, and policy specific factors."[10] Since the states can be considered laboratories for testing theories of policy differences, the three factors identified by Ringquist and Garand provide a useful framework to examine the differences in professional boxing regulations in the American states.

Specifically, *internal political factors* include: the level of state wealth and

Introduction

economic development, the tenor of political ideology, the presence and demands of organized interests, and the characteristics of state political parties and their control over the governorship and legislature.[11] *External political factors* include the environment in which each state operates, such as: changes in the national political environment, changes in national public policy, and policy choices made by neighboring states.[12] Finally, *policy specific factors* refer to characteristics specific to the policy in question, involving, for example: accumulated policy-relevant knowledge (the information that policy actors accumulate with regards to a specific issue), focusing events (such as accidents, uprisings, or other events that gain widespread media attention for a policy area), and issue redefinition (policy stories or symbols that provide political actors with general interpretations of complex policy issues).[13] Thus, Ringquist and Garand are in general concurrence with Gray in identifying the variables that account for the variation in policies across states.

Political scientist John Kingdon explains the importance of focusing events to motivate government officials to enhance existing policies or adopt new ones. He writes, "Problems are often not self-evident by the indicators. They need a little push to get the attention of people in and around government. That push is sometimes provided by a focusing event like a crisis or disaster that comes along to call attention to the problem, a powerful symbol that catches on, or the personal experience of a policy maker."[14]

Scholarly Perspectives on Regulating Sports

The scholarly literature on comparative state politics has identified several variables that help account for the differences in state legislation, but certain factors have particular importance in regulating sports. For example, political scientist Barrie Houlihan comments, "Explaining the variation in the patterns of administration is difficult but a number of significant factors can be identified, such as: wealth; tradition of voluntary organization; political, geographic and demographic characteristics; and salience of sport to the government and major political parties."[15]

Sports management scholar Laurence Chalip and political scientist Arthur Johnson further clarify that "to fully understand the extent to which government is involved in American sports, it is necessary to recognize that state and local governments are also intimately involved in sports policy."[16] The authors point out that although boxing qualifies as a major sport, it commands national attention only for certain championship fights. Chalip and Johnson argue that the occasional importance of boxing results in little federal regulation and control of the sport by the states.[17] Nevertheless, policies passed by state and federal governments have regulatory implications for American professional sports, even though sports and politics are often perceived to be independent of one another. Arthur Johnson and sociologist James Frey write: "Sport, especially in the United States of America, is an increasing area of litigation ... which has forced the state to devote increasing attention to the operation and internal machinations of both professional and amateur sports.... Government policy as implemented through legislation, court decisions, and bureaucratic rules and regulations is now an even more important variable in defining the nature and dynamics of American sport."[18]

Chalip and Johnson suggest that sports policies in the United States can be separated into three categories of public policy and law: antitrust law, labor law, and "other issues" such as tax policy, immigration laws, gambling, and copyright protection.[19] Thus, while there is not a formal department or mechanism within the federal government to regulate sports, independent pieces of legislation have had substantial effects on various sports. While the U.S. Congress has not taken an aggressive stance toward regulating American professional sports, many individual states have created various forms of state athletic commissions to provide the regulatory mechanism with varied success.[20] Houlihan explains that the restraint Congress has displayed toward regulating sports is logical: "Restraining federal expenditure and preventing federal expansion have often been the most rewarding electoral platform for aspiring candidates to Congress. It should therefore come as no surprise that federal government intervention in sport policy is rare.... The dominant perception of sport among the public and in Congress is that amateur sport is rarely, if ever, a proper focus for state action and that intervention directed at professional sport should be aimed at maximizing entrepreneurial freedom."[21]

According to John Wilson, over three hundred pieces of sports legislation have been introduced in the Congress since the 1950s.[22] However, very few of these bills became law. Houlihan summarizes U.S. federal involvement in sport as possessing the following characteristics: "first, an infrequent, but often unintended involvement in the policy arena; second, a lack of strategic commitment, third, a highly fragmented administrative pattern; and finally, a preference for pump-priming intervention over long-term administrative commitment."[23] The academic perspectives from the comparative state politics and public policy literature outlined in this chapter form the theo-

Introduction

retical basis for this book and guide the methodology and the selection of the variables involved in this study.

Methodology

The methods for this study involve a six-pronged approach: First, I present a historical analysis that highlights the major trends in professional boxing regulation over time. Second, I conduct primary research through surveys and interviews of boxing commissioners or designees. Third, I perform several common statistical analyses (frequency distributions, t-test means comparisons, chi square tests, and a multiple regression analysis) of data compiled through primary research that helps determine the possible causes of state variance of professional boxing regulations. Fourth, I carry out a case study analysis of Nevada, including interviews with state officials and a participant-observation of the Nevada Athletic Commission, to provide an in-depth look at the manner in which the regulatory practices gathered through survey research and statistical data analysis is carried out in practice. Fifth, I provide a glimpse into the regulations enacted by the newly-created Kansas Boxing Commission through an interview with boxing commissioner Aaron Davis. Sixth, I provide an examination of boxing regulations in Argentina, where a centralized national boxing commission may serve as an example of what to follow and not follow should a national organization to oversee boxing in the United States be formed. Finally, I conclude with an analysis of the possible adoption of a national boxing commission.

The historical antecedents of boxing regulations are essential to understanding the context in which professional boxing regulations vary in the United States today. Thus, the initial step in this analytical procedure is an examination of major trends of professional boxing regulations over time. An analysis of historical texts is used to accomplish this task.

A cautionary note: It is important to recognize at the outset of this text that the data for analysis was obtained mostly in 2005 for the year 2004. State laws and regulations change constantly throughout the United States, and it is practically impossible to capture all of the changes in a comprehensive study such as this. While there have been some changes since the data was collected for this study, the principles and general conclusions of the study remain unchanged. Thus, in 2004, 43 of 50 states had some type of regulatory agency that oversees boxing matches.[24] The states of Alabama, Alaska, Delaware,

Kansas, Minnesota, South Dakota, and Wyoming did not. However, the establishment of these boxing commissions varies widely: the California Athletic Commission was established in 1924 while Missouri did not establish one until 1983.[25] Since nearly all of the 50 states possess some sort of regulative body that oversees boxing, the question of organizational formation does not provide meaningful variance. However, the standards, compliance and enforcement of the regulations these bodies are supposed to uphold provides a gulf of variance that is examined in this study.

In terms of case selection, I analyzed all 43 states with entities that regulate boxing such as athletic commissions (in 2004) in an effort to obtain national data, and to apply my results to the entire nation-state. I consciously omitted territories of the United States such as Puerto Rico, the U.S. Virgin Islands and American Indian reservations because the analysis centers on issues specific to the relationship between federal and state government. Other geographic areas are important units for analysis for a further study that asks the appropriate questions and selects the proper variables to make those results more meaningful.

A survey of state athletic commission personnel was carried out. Data from the American Association of Professional Ringside Physicians annual report of state medical requirements for professional boxers was used in conjunction with survey data to develop an index that serves as the dependent variable in my analytical model. In addition to the survey results and AAPRP report, an analysis of the Lexis-Nexis database of state codes along with legislation published on state government Internet sites were used to determine current professional boxing regulations in each state. Furthermore, select interviews with officials in various states and a participant-observation of individuals responsible for the regulation of boxing in Nevada were conducted. Both a consent form and survey instrument approved by the University of Kansas Human Subjects Research Committee were sent and e-mailed to the respective chairmen of the state boxing commissions or their designees asking the following questions[26]:

Does the state that you represent:

1. Conduct pre-fight medical evaluations?
    If yes, what do these medical evaluations include?
2. Honor other states' suspensions of boxers?
    If yes, are the suspensions universally honored, or are exceptions allowed?

Introduction

3. Perform neurological testing of participants before each match?
    If yes, who is responsible for payment of the neurological tests?
4. Conduct post-fight medical evaluations?
    If yes, what is typically included in such evaluations?
5. Require standards for competitive match-ups, such as considering participants' records of wins and losses, caliber of opponents and numbers of past fights?
    Does the state athletic commission (or governing body of boxing in your state) have the ability to block a match that the commission views as non-competitive?
6. Ensure that emergency medical personnel and equipment are present during and after each match?
    If yes, who is responsible for payment of the medical personnel?
    Are ambulances required to be present at the location of the boxing match?
7. Require health insurance for boxers during each match?
8. Require registration (licenses) for boxers?
    If yes, what are the major criteria for approval?
9. Require certification and approval for ring officials?
    If yes, what are the major criteria for approval?
10. Require current HIV test results for licensing of boxers?
11. Require post-fight drug tests of participants?
    If yes, what types of drugs are tested for?

The following combination of data sources was used to identify the variance of boxing regulations in the United States:

a. Survey of State Athletic Commissioners and/or designees
b. AAPRP State Medical Requirements
c. State Code Data (From Lexis-Nexis Database, State Government Internet sites, State Athletic Commission Internet sites)
d. Interviews of selected commissioners and/or designees
e. Boxing literature (Published books, magazines, and newspapers)

The desire of state governments to provide information on the Internet enabled me to easily find the information outlined above.

The primary and secondary data was collected, compiled and prepared for analysis. Detailed information about the statistical terms and tests appears in Chapter 2. A Boxing Health and Safety Index (BHSI) was constructed and forms the dependent variable for each state, and is placed on a scale of 0 to 3 based on their fulfillment of specific health and safety testing requirements. Several statistical analyses were conducted. There are several independent variables that account for the variance between states on the BHSI. Consistent with the relevant comparative state politics and public policy literature, the following independent variables are hypothesized to influence the level of the health and safety index in each state:

- Number of boxing related deaths in a state (as compiled by the February 2004 issue of the *Journal of Combative Sport*, the most comprehensive resource available for this data.)
- The presence of certain types of gambling (as depicted in *The National Conference of State Legislatures* data)
- State wealth (median income, as compiled by the *2003 United States Census American Community Survey Summary*)
- Political culture (as designated by the *Elazar Scale*)

In addition to the data analysis described above, case study analyses of Nevada and Kansas, including in-depth interviews and a participant-observation, are conducted to illustrate how commissions place regulatory policy into practice. Finally, Argentina's centralized system of boxing regulations is analyzed for a comparative perspective.

1

A History of Boxing Regulations

The Genesis of Boxing (4000 B.C.)

The history of boxing regulations is as chaotic as the sport itself. There are numerous versions of boxing's origins. The task of outlining the regulatory history of the sport is complicated, as scholars of the sport do not universally agree upon dates, names and locations. The historical review that follows is an outline of the major regulatory developments of the sport based upon my discerning interpretation of the historical evidence to provide context for my analysis of present-day boxing regulations in the United States.

Some historians view the genesis of boxing as arising over six thousand years ago among the Sumerian people in southern Mesopotamia (present-day Iraq and Syria).[1] What is certain is that boxers are depicted on the tombs of Mery-Ra in the El-Minia Governorate (northern Egypt) and in the Mastaba tomb of Ptah Hotep in Saqqara (near Cairo) from the time of the pharaohs (3580 B.C.) in Ancient Egyptian civilization.[2]

Evidence of men fighting one another for prizes can be found in Book 23 of Homer's *Iliad*, produced in the 8th century B.C., depicting events from 1200–900 B.C. in Ancient Greece.[3] The Greeks introduced the sport, then called pankration, into the Ancient Olympics in 632 B.C.[4] A wine jar found in Etruria (present-day Italy) dating from 510–500 B.C. depicts two boxers being observed by an umpire and a boy holding a sponge and an oil flask.[5] The illustration of the umpire is significant, as it is evidence that the competition was organized and regulated.

A Greek cup depicting pankratiasts dating from 500–475 B.C. portrays this brutal version of the sport, which allowed punching, wrestling and kicking.[6] On the cup, one pair of boxers appear to be wearing hand-wraps while another illustration shows one boxer attempting to gouge out his opponents eyes while his adversary is biting his hand.

Despite the presence of other Ancient Greek artifacts dating from 440 B.C. to 366 B.C. that depict boxing at the Athenian Games, and terra cotta figurines of a boxing match and a lamp featuring a boxer working on a punching bag dating from the 2nd to 1st century B.C., some historians maintain that at some point in this period, contests among gladiators were banned and did not resurface until the early eighteenth century in western Europe.[7]

England was the site of boxing's resurgence in the early 1700s, as the aristocratic society had somehow determined that self-defense and sport were honorable activities. In 1723 King George I ordered a public boxing ring to be built in London's Hyde Park.[8] While still much more violent than present-day boxing, pugilism in eighteenth century England was a far cry from the barbaric version practiced in Ancient Mesopotamia, Greece, Egypt and Italy. While bouts in this time period were held without handwraps, bare-knuckles seem to have inflicted less damage than the leather himantes worn by the Greeks or the studded ox-hide caestus used by the Romans.[9] James Figg, who is commonly known as the "Father of Boxing," epitomized bare-knuckle boxing marked by skillful fighting instead of brute force. He was the first man considered to be the British heavyweight champion and established an academy to teach boxing. In 1743, Jack Broughton, one of Figg's students, developed the first set of rules to regulate the sport after killing a man in the ring.[10] These regulations are commonly referred to as Broughton's Rules.

Broughton's Rules (1743)

Broughton's Rules are significant since they represent the first attempt at boxing regulation since the days of the Ancient Olympics. These rules of the ring establish protocols for the fights themselves. The expression "to toe the line" has its origins in Rules I and IV, where prizefighters demonstrate their readiness to start a fight by meeting at the center of the ring. A far cry from stipulating the number of rounds a match was to last, under Broughton's Rules, competitors would fight until a fighter failed to come to the chalked line in the center of the stage (or ring), or until his second (called "chief second" today) would declare his fighter no longer able to continue. The purse for both fighters was also designated under these rules: the winner would leave with two-thirds of the money. Interestingly, these competitions were regulated by at least two umpires (or referees). In addition, if the two umpires found themselves in disagreement, a third would be called in to resolve a dispute.

Several rules, with slight modifications, continue to this day. For example, according to Broughton's Rules, if a fighter is knocked down, he has thirty seconds to rise and face his adversary (today it is a ten count, with the fighter who produced the knockdown going to a neutral corner). Also, the practice of the fighter's second being able to stop the fight has its roots here. Furthermore, the regulations prohibiting blows below the waistline or hitting a man while he's down also originate with Mr. Broughton's Rules. Perhaps the most celebrated champion under Broughton's Rules was Daniel Mendoza, a Jewish Englishman of Spanish heritage. He is credited with developing the art of defense.[11]

Toward the end of the Revolutionary War in 1778, British general Hugh Percy took a young African American, Bill Richmond, to England after seeing him engage in some barroom brawls. Richmond thus became the first American and first African American to engage in prizefighting on British soil. Another African American, Tom Molineux, followed his path to England in 1809 and boxed to much acclaim. Though he never won a championship, his two fights with British champion Tom Cribb were perhaps the most notable of the era.

The power of maritime travel enabled boxing to come to the Americas. By various accounts, the first official prizefight to take place in the United States came in 1816 between Jacob Hyer and Tom Beasley. Although men had tussled for money long before, this is considered official in the sense that the Broughton Rules were accepted by the fighters and a substantial amount of people were present to witness the action.[12] Hyer is thus known as the "Father of the American Ring" and commonly accepted as the first American to engage in a professional bout on U.S. soil. For much of the nineteenth century, prizefights were "usually staged in the back rooms of taverns, in stalls and out-of-the-way places where they could steer away from the police, since fights were prohibited by law."[13] Prizefighting in the United States was therefore forced into a self-regulated realm due to its illegality, yet it had a significant following. Notably, prizefighting was also outlawed in England during this period, and practitioners of the sport likewise had to find creative locations to practice their trade. Interestingly, boxing has yet to be legalized in England: it is permitted through a loophole in the law as an "exhibition of skill."[14] A second attempt to establish uniform prizefighting regulations came in 1838 after the ring death of "Brighton" Bill at the hands of Owen Swift.[15] These rules, established by the Pugilists' Protective Association, became known as the London Prize Ring Rules.

London Prize Ring Rules (1838)

While Broughton's Rules sufficed for the regulation of pugilism for nearly a century, the London Prize Ring Rules provide a more extensive set of rules that form the basis for the modern sport. Similar to Broughton's Rules, battles under the auspices of the London Prize Ring Rules were also observed by two umpires and a referee. The umpires were responsible for timing the bouts and ensuring that the rules were observed by the fighters and their corners. Any disputes among the umpires were to be resolved by a referee. However, there were several significant changes to the sport brought upon by the adoption of these rules.

One major rule change was the establishment of a standardized ring size of twenty-four feet. Two additional changes would enter the English-language lexicon. The concept of being "up to scratch" is based in the requirement that a fighter knocked down (or after the 30-second pause in between rounds) must step to the line etched in the center of the ring to show that he was ready to fight. The notion of something or someone being a "stand-up," or legitimate, entity comes from the requirement that a fighter who goes down without being hit (other than a slip) will have lost the contest.

Boxing purists may be surprised to find that water was not the only beverage consumed or allowed in matches fought under these rules. There is a specific reference to "other refreshments" that could be consumed by pugilists in Rule 20. Of course, while Gatorade did not exist in mid–nineteenth century England, from boxing's earliest days the idea of drinking substances other than water in between rounds was not only acceptable, it was officially sanctioned. Like the Broughton Rules, the London Prize Ring Rules also introduced measures that remain in effect for professional boxing to this day, such as outlawing butting, gouging, scratching, kicking, hitting a man while down, holding the ropes, and using resin, stones or hard objects in the hands, and biting. Mike Tyson, a boxing historian in his own right, should have taken note of the last rule. A system of penalties for violating these regulations appears in Rule 7. Any pugilist that goes down without being hit, leaves the ring or otherwise quits will be deemed the loser of the fight. It should be noted

1 • A History of Boxing Regulations

that these regulations even address the issue of gambling, as Rule 19 proclaims that all bets will be paid in cash at the conclusion of a fight.

Another remnant of the London Prize Ring Rules that modern observers of the sport can recognize is the designation of the corner. At the Great Western Forum in Inglewood, California, and elsewhere ring announcer Jimmy Lennon, Jr., would flip a red and blue colored disk to determine which corner the boxers would be designated as they entered the ring. Fighters were required to shake hands prior to waging battle, just as they are today.

Among the numerous changes to the London Prize Ring Rules, one can observe the victory trophy, which under

"Iron" Mike Tyson, shown here in a 1991 press conference, gained notoriety (and the nickname "Iron Bite") for his violation of one of boxing's earliest rules, "no biting," in his 1997 rematch with Evander Holyfield for the world heavyweight championship.

these rules was a colored handkerchief, while today the championship belt has become the most recognized trophy. Also, under these rules, fighters had just 30 seconds in between rounds, whereas today they have twice as long. One rule that has progressively been ignored over time is Rule 11, which stipulates that cornermen are to "refrain from all offensive and irritating expressions." Anyone who has watched a boxing match on television or has sat close enough to the ring at a fight knows that in practice, this rule is long gone.

Despite their illegality, prizefights continued to be held in the United States during the period leading to the U.S. Civil War, mostly in private clubs and barges. Historian Elliott Gorn writes, "The sport was completely illegal; the courts hounded boxers, and when fights did occur, they were roundly condemned in the press. Only a few dozen fights occurred before 1842, and then no matches at all were staged after a bout in Hastings, New York, in which one of the fighters died. All that changed forever in 1849."[16] However, Gorn may be overlooking some of the public bouts that took place between slaves, as documented by the 1835 to 1852 diaries of William Black, a free African American from Mississippi.[17] Nevertheless, the reference made to 1849 in Gorn's research refers to the first championship bout held on American soil between an Irish immigrant, James "Yankee" Sullivan, and Tom Hyer, son of Jacob, the "Father of the American Ring."

The Sullivan vs. Hyer bout was held in Still Pond Heights in Kent County, Maryland, on February 7, 1849. That Hyer was the victor after sixteen rounds is almost incidental when compared to the large-scale effects that the fight would have on the sport of boxing. According to Gorn, press coverage of this fight was unprecedented and in a significant change of perspective, journalists were now taking a stance that encouraged the legalization of prizefights.[18] The next major prizefighter to emerge in the United States was John Morrissey, a future U.S. congressman. Morrissey gained the American heavyweight championship and retired on the eve of the Civil War (1861 to 1865).

Marquis of Queensberry Rules (1865)

In the aftermath of the U.S. Civil War, the third major boxing reform was created. The Marquis of Queensberry Rules were written in 1865. It is unclear how much of the credit for writing the rules should go to John Sholto Douglas, Eighth Marquis of Queensberry, as many historians suggest that his Cambridge classmate John Graham Chambers is the actual author.[19] In any case, these rules are among the more celebrated in boxing as they introduce the use of gloves for prizefights. Significantly, the Marquis of Queensberry Rules were not designed for professionals, according to historian W. Russel Gray. "Devised in the mid–1860s," Gray writes, "the Queensberry Rules were intended for amateur competition and by 1872 were fully in effect in a tournament. Unlike prizefighters, the gloved Queensberry boxers did not compete for monetary stakes and side bets or the settling of grudges.... Instead they competed for trophies in three weight classes — light, middle and heavy.... Binding upon amateur competition at first, the Queensberry Rules in twenty years would govern prizefighting as well.... The Queensberry Rules gave prize fighting respectability, legality (or at least legal acquiescence), and the modern look of today's contests."[20]

With the introduction of the use of gloves and three-minute rounds with one minute of rest in between, the Queensberry Rules most resemble the sport of boxing as it is practiced today, with four notable exceptions. First, the present-day size of the ring is generally smaller, as acceptable sizes range from eighteen to twenty-four feet. Second, weight class determines the size of boxing gloves, from eight ounces (generally at 137 to 147 pounds and below) to ten ounces (over 137 to 147 pounds). Third, while the rules make reference to not allowing springs in a fighter's footwear, most contemporary boxers wear special boots that provide traction on the canvas mat. Finally, if a contemporary boxing match is stopped by an unavoidable interference it is generally ruled no-contest, at the referees' discretion, and it is up to the boxers and their management to determine if a rematch will be held.

Publisher Richard Kyle Fox deserves at least partial credit for increasing the acceptance of prizefighting in America. Beginning in the late 1870s, his publication, *The National Police Gazette,* was among the first American publications to establish a sports section.

Although prizefighting was illegal in all thirty U.S. states in 1880, Fox's publication created public interest in the sport with its regular coverage and promotion of matches.[21] During this period, John L. Sullivan, the Massachusetts-born son of Irish immigrants, had emerged as one of America's first great sporting heroes. Sullivan was known for his pompous boasts, claiming he could beat "any sonofabitch in the house." He won at least partial claim to the American heavyweight championship on February 7, 1882, with a knockout of Paddy Ryan under the London Prize Ring Rules. However, Fox refused to recognize Sullivan as champion as a result of his reluctance to meet boxer Jake Kilrain in the ring. Thus, Kilrain was proclaimed champion by virtue of his 1887 victory over British champion Jem Smith in the *Police Gazette,* until the matter was settled by Sullivan's knockout victory over Kilrain in 1889.

The first world championship to be decided by Marquis of Queensberry Rules came in the middleweight division, in an 1884 bout between Jack "The Nonpareil" Dempsey and George Fulljames. With a twenty-second round knockout victory, Dempsey, not to be confused with the legendary heavyweight champion who would rise to prominence in the 1920s, thus became boxing's first champion under Queensberry rules. However, the first professional heavyweight championship fight to be governed by these rules came on September 7, 1892, when John L. Sullivan and James J. Corbett fought at the Olympic Club in New Orleans, Louisiana.[22]

The Sullivan vs. Corbett fight ushered in a new age for boxing. Boxing historian and *The Ring Magazine* founding editor Nat Fleisher remarked, "The Queensberry era of boxing came triumphantly into its own with the successful staging of the battle of New Orleans.... One hour and twenty minutes after the start, the cool, smiling youth from California [Corbett] was crowned the new world champion in the first battle staged for that title under the Marquis of Queensberry Rules with gloves. It was the herald of a new day in boxing. The game was destined henceforth to rise to recognized respectability as a means of entertainment for all classes of both sexes."[23]

Although the Marquis of Queensberry Rules do not explicitly address weight divisions, weight limits for contestants have existed since at least the 1850s.[24] Just prior to the turn of the twentieth century, as the sport of prizefighting became more accepted in various nation-states, the National Sporting Club (NSC) was established in London, England, in 1891.[25] This was the first professional organization established for the regulation of boxing. The National Sporting Club of London created eight official weight categories in which boxers would compete, beginning in 1909.[26] As time went on and boxing's governing bodies came to realize that they could make more money sanctioning fights in more weight classes, the number of divisions has grown exponentially. At present, there are seventeen weight classes, ranging from 105 pounds or less through 200 pounds or more. Furthermore, with the increased size of humans in comparison to 100 years ago, there is even talk of creating a super heavyweight division for professional boxers.

While a gold and diamond belt was presented to John L. Sullivan in 1887, the National Sporting Club established the regular practice of awarding belts to champion boxers. The so-called Lonsdale belts were named after the president of the NSC, Lord Lonsdale, and awarded to British champions in each weight category. The practice of awarding belts to world champions was taken over by U.S.–based *The Ring Magazine* in the early 1920s and continues to this day.

Even though boxing emerged as a popular sport in the late nineteenth and early twentieth century United States, it was still largely an illegal activity. The loophole through which boxing was enabled to flourish during this period was through the establishment of elite private clubs in which to hold

1 • A History of Boxing Regulations

the bouts. The Sullivan vs. Corbett fight was held in a private club in New Orleans, but the event was followed as far away as New York, San Francisco, Boston, Washington and other major cities.[27] The economic aspects of this event would prove to be critical to the legalization of the sport, since it brought tourism dollars to the city, state and the clubs that held them. Nevertheless, opponents to the sport made their voices heard.

During the decade of the 1890s, a "Purity Crusade" sought to ban the sport throughout the United States, as those states that did not specifically prohibit prizefighting enacted them, and those that already had them on the books began to enforce them.[28] Even in Louisiana, a state that had reaped the economic benefits from hosting a major prizefight, state attorney general Milton J. Cunningham filed suit against the Olympic Club. While Cunningham's suit was unsuccessful, two years later Andy Bowen died following a knockout loss to George Lavigne resulting in public outcry against the sport.[29] In the immediate years following the Lavigne vs. Bowen tragedy, New Orleans would fade and eventually vanish as a mecca for boxing, and the sport's practitioners would be forced to ply their trade in New York and western states such as California and Nevada.

The case of Texas exemplifies the complexities of boxing regulation in the late 1880s through the mid–1890s. Historian Jeffrey Sammons explains, "An 1889 tax statute permitted prizefighting under certain licensing and taxing procedures, but in 1891 the legislature enacted an anti-prizefight statute that did not repeal the earlier statute and provided only weak penalties for violation. Attempts to significantly strengthen the newer law and to correct its defects failed. In 1895 a revised penal code was passed with the old prizefight statutes intact, as was a new civil statute with the 1889 prizefight provision ... the penal code became effective one day after the civil code, and prizefighting was therefore illegal."[30] The reluctance of Texas, Louisiana and neighboring Arkansas to legally allow boxing matches was in stark contrast to the Silver State of Nevada, which was already much less restrictive toward gambling and drinking alcohol. Nevada legalized boxing in 1897. Thus, the next major boxing event of the 1890s, Corbett's title defense against middleweight champion Bob Fitzsimmons, took place in a makeshift arena placed in Carson City, Nevada, on March 17, 1897. Fitzsimmons won the title with what became known as the solar plexus punch and would go on to win the world light heavyweight championship, making him the first boxer in history to win world titles in three different weight classes. "Gentleman Jim" would go on to star in Hollywood motion pictures.

Horton Law (1896) / Lewis Law (1900)

The State of New York, which within decades would become synonymous with boxing, made its first attempt to legalize boxing under the Horton Law in 1896. This law was ripe for corruption since the promotion of bouts was left unregulated and gamblers, corrupt officials and likewise corrupt managers took advantage of the flaws in the law.[31] The Horton Law was eventually repealed and replaced by the Lewis Law in 1900, a measure that allowed boxing matches to take place only between members of private clubs.

The well-known 1909 George Bellows painting "Both Members of This Club" is a depiction of the boxing matches that took place at such clubs.[32] Bellows' painting is commonly thought to depict then–lightweight champion Joe Gans (an African American) who fought at such clubs against white fighters. The social context of boxing at private clubs is eloquently illuminated by historian Peter Adams who writes that Bellows' painting "suggests that he had an understanding of how boxing in particular (and we can say sport in general) became a means by which marginal citizens could progress socially or economically by playing to an audience drawn from the dominant culture. The athletes knew that they functioned as 'members' only for a specified period of time and only if they played by the social rules as well as the rules of the game."[33]

An examination of Gans' professional record is illustrative of the importance private clubs had on the development of boxing at this time. For example, from 1891 through 1909, Gans fought in at least 155 official fights.[34] About a third of Gans' fights took place at private athletic clubs. Furthermore, it is striking that the clubs were located in disparate locations. The clubs where Gans fought included predictable major cities such as Baltimore, Boston, Brooklyn, Philadelphia, San Francisco, New York City, Chicago, Detroit and Denver. But his record also indicates he fought in a variety of private venues off the beaten path such as Tonopah, Nevada; New Britain, Connecticut; Athens, Pennsylvania; Providence, Rhode Island; and Trenton, New Jersey.

One of the most influential private boxing clubs to emerge in the late–1800s to early 1900s and hold regular boxing cards was the California Athletic Club in San Francisco.[35] Sammons emphasizes the importance of the western states in the development of boxing at the turn of the century, writing, "As eastern, Midwestern, and southern states turned against prizefighting, the newer, wilder, and somewhat lawless mining states of Nevada and California became havens for the sport, especially major championship fights, even though the activity was technically illegal."[36] The recorded boxing statistics provide mixed evidence for this shift. An examination of the number of fights held in selected states during the early 1900s indicates that the number of boxing matches that took place in New York and Pennsylvania is not much lower than in Nevada and California.[37] Nevertheless, San Francisco's hosting of Jim Jeffries' world heavyweight championship defense in 1901 turned California into the "undisputed boxing capital of the world."[38]

After Jeffries' retirement in 1905, Marvin Hart won the vacant heavyweight championship, and lost it in his first defense against Tommy Burns. This is significant because Burns became the first heavyweight champion to defend his world title against an African American challenger, Jack Johnson. On Boxing Day (December 26), 1908, Johnson took Burns' title with an astonishing fourteenth-round knockout in Sydney, Australia. Black and white Americans were initially unmoved by this happening, but Johnson's dominance of the division and especially his desire to cavort with white women raised the calls for a fight with Jeffries, the retired champion.[39] Thus, on July 4, 1910, Johnson and Jeffries fought before 16,000 people in Reno, Nevada.

Jeffries' cornermen stopped the bout after fifteen (of forty-five scheduled) rounds, sparking a nationwide racial unrest. Historian Randy Roberts writes, "Never before has a single event caused such widespread rioting. Not until the assassination of Martin Luther King, Jr., would another event elicit a similar reaction. The fight and its aftermath led reform groups to intensify their efforts to push for legislation that would abolish boxing."[40]

The governors of over fifteen states and most major cities throughout the United States banned the Johnson vs. Jeffries fight film.[41] Some historians suggest that Johnson is responsible for the decline in the popularity of the sport during the 1910s.

Frawley Law (1911)

Johnson's reign coincided with the 1911 Frawley Law that was passed in New York and created the first state athletic commission in the United States. Sammons writes, "The eastern movement toward state control resumed in New York in 1911, with the enactment of the Frawley Law. Under Chapter 779 of the Laws of 1911, the New York State Athletic Commission came into existence, and boxing or sparring matches, as opposed to prizefights, were

THE REGULATION OF BOXING

placed within the commission's purview."[42] One aspect of the Frawley Law, which was in effect until 1917, held fights that did not end in knockouts would be declared no-decision. The logic behind this law was that it would minimize the possibility of corruption in boxing outcomes. However, this aspect of the law became ineffective, as newspapers would declare unofficial outcomes of fights, hence the term newspaper decisions. People who wished to gamble on the outcomes of matches would agree to be bound by the decisions of specific reporters, and therefore the corruption that plagued boxing judges was transferred to the reporters covering the bouts.

Roberts argues, "The trauma of Johnson's eight years as champion led to a swifter decline in the popularity of boxing. It is true that during these years the search for a Great White Hope generated some interest. But when each Great White Hope turned into a Great White Joke, interest in boxing suffered drastically. When Johnson was forced to flee the country to escape prosecution for a violation of the Mann Act [which prohibited the transport of women across state lines for 'illegal sexual activity and related crimes'], the American public breathed a collective sigh of relief ... Americans wanted to forget the Johnson experience and boxing."[43]

Johnson was forced to defend his title in far away locations such as Paris, Buenos Aires and Havana. In a match filled with controversy, he lost the title to Jess Willard in 1915. Historian William M. Tuttle writes, "Jack Johnson, the 'Greatest Boxer of them All,' according to the local [Chicago] press, had suffered an unexpected defeat at the hands of the 'Great White Hope,' Jess Willard, the previous spring, and blacks that winter were increasingly suspicious that federal agents had arranged the outcome."[44] Roberts notes, "By 1916, the year Jack Dempsey traveled to New York, boxing was a thoroughly unpopular and disreputable sport."[45] Finding a site for the 1919 Willard vs. Dempsey fight illustrates the duality of legal thought on boxing. The sport had broad-based support among the military, which authorized boxing as a form of training, but had to deal with widespread opposition from the clergy and religious groups. Boxing was illegal in most states, and states that did allow it were not interested for a number of reasons. Thus, the fight landed in an outdoor stadium constructed in the unlikely location of Toledo, Ohio, on July 4, 1919. Roberts explains that "the importance of the year Dempsey won the crown cannot be minimized. It was a year of change — prohibition, women's suffrage, and the Treaty of Versailles. And it was a year of uncertainty — race riots and the red scare."[46]

Historians James Roberts and Alexander Skutt suggest that around this time boxing "began to shed its unsavory reputation when influential people like former President Theodore Roosevelt recommended controlled fisticuffs to promote health and fitness. This view, as well as a growing public acceptance of the sport as conducted on a professional level, led to its legalization in many states."[47] Although Roosevelt had repealed the Horton Law in 1900 when he was New York state governor, it is well known that he had a deep affinity for the sport. In his 1913 autobiography, Roosevelt wrote,

> With my father's hearty approval, I started to learn to box. I was a painfully slow and awkward pupil, and certainly worked two or three years before I made any perceptible improvement whatever. My first boxing-master was John Long, an ex–prize-fighter. I can see his rooms now, with colored pictures of the fights between Tom Hyer and Yankee Sullivan, and Heenan and Sayers, and other great events in the annals of the squared circle. On one occasion, to excite interest among his patrons, he held a series of "championship" matches for the different weights, the prizes being, at least in my own class, pewter mugs of a value, I should suppose, approximating fifty cents. Neither he nor I had any idea that I could do anything, but I was entered in the lightweight contest, in which it happened that I was pitted in succession against a couple of reedy striplings who were even worse than I was. Equally to their surprise and to my own, and to John Long's, I won, and the pewter mug became one of my most prized possessions.[48]

Walker Law (1920)

Boxing representatives from thirteen nation-states met in Paris in 1920 in a bold attempt to form a global regulatory body for the sport called the International Boxing Union. Meanwhile in the United States, New York once again legalized boxing. Celebrated author Roger Kahn explains the re-establishment of the New York State Athletic Commission: "In 1920 James J. Walker, a state senator from Greenwich Village, introduced a bill to make professional boxing legal in New York.... The state would license everyone significantly employed in boxing: promoters, managers, referees, judges, fighters. No mismatches, no crooked decisions, no tickets sold to fights that never took place. At least in theory.... A board of three state commissioners would supervise the sport and they could revoke licenses and, if necessary, call in district attorneys for criminal prosecution.... On April 26, this bill went to the desk of Governor Alfred E. Smith ... Smith signed it into law on May 25, 1920."[49] The Walker Law proved to be a critical turning point for boxing in the United States. It became a model for the legalization of the sport in other states, where similar legislation creating athletic commissions was passed. Furthermore, the new commissions lent structure and authority to the sport. Sammons notes, "As other states followed, the enormous burden of control fell upon newly empowered and expanded athletic commissions which would execute the laws, assure compliance with the legislative mandates, and oversee the sport."[50]

Such was the power of the Walker Law that it is still in effect to this day, albeit with amendments. Roberts and Skutt note, "Boxing came to be seen as a legitimate, major athletic pursuit, and when the first million-dollar gate was realized [in a 1921 bout between Dempsey and Georges Carpentier], promoters set up other high-profit matches. Boxing produced larger-than-life heroes like Jack Dempsey and Gene Tunney, acknowledged pillars of 'the Golden Age of Sport,' along with such stars as baseball's Babe Ruth and tennis player Bill Tilden."[51] The combination of boxing's legal status, the popularity of heavyweight champion Jack Dempsey and the acceptance of the sport by the media, all in the context of the carefree Roaring '20s, cemented the sport of boxing as a part of American culture that continues to this day.

The New York State Athletic Commission (NYSAC) quickly became quite powerful and in 1921, under the leadership of William A. Gavin, fifteen other states within the union formed an organization called the National Boxing Association (NBA) to proclaim champions and rank boxers. Thus, from the beginning of boxing's modern era the notion of split championships was present.

Professional boxing regulations would remain relatively stable in the coming years, with few major changes to the sport. One significant exception that gained notoriety from the infamous "Battle of the Long Count," the Jack Dempsey vs. Gene Tunney rematch in 1927, is the requirement that a challenger who knocks his opponent down must go to a neutral corner before the count is to begin. In the Dempsey vs. Tunney rematch, Dempsey forgot to follow this rule and referee Dave Berry refused to start the count for five seconds allowing Tunney time to beat the count and end up winning the fight by decision.

Other notable changes came in 1941 when the number of rounds for a championship fight was limited to fifteen, a rule that lasted until the 1980s when it was brought down to twelve; also the scoring system, which went from two judges and the referee awarding one point to a boxer for winning a round (and zero to the loser; the winner of the most rounds winning the fight) to three judges scoring on a "10 point must" system allowing for more differential scoring.

After the stock market crashed in the fall of 1929, the United States entered the Great Depression. Boxing journalists Stanley Weston and Steven Farhood characterize the period explaining, "During the times of economic depression, the common man needs to escape the hopelessness of everyday life. As a result, the entertainment industry generally flourishes. Boxing has always been part of the industry, but at the start of the '30s, the roll call of world champions suggested a fistic market not much healthier than the stock market."[52] However, during the latter part of this decade, legendary boxers such as Joe Louis and Henry Armstrong would become dominant champions. The event of the decade was the heavyweight championship fight between Joe Louis and Max Schmeling.

Germany's Schmeling, who had briefly held the heavyweight title from 1930 to 1932, knocked Louis out in the twelfth round of their first meeting in 1936. It was Louis' first professional loss, and the victory provided fuel for Nazi Germany's propaganda machine to demonstrate Aryan supremacy. Louis would go on to win the heavyweight title from "Cinderella Man" James J. Braddock the following year, thus setting up a rematch with Schmeling in 1938, just a couple of years before the U.S. became involved in World War II. Louis' dramatic first round knockout victory was a symbolic event for millions of people as he provided a devastating blow to the myth of Aryan supremacy. Historian Benjamin Rader explains the significance of the second Louis vs. Schmeling bout, as evidenced by the number of people who tuned in to hear the fight: "In 1938 he again fought Schmeling, this time in a fight fraught with international tension. Only two months before the fight Hitler had annexed Austria. Approximately two-thirds of the people in the United States heard the fight on the radio."[53] Americans of different races cheered Louis' victory, and many historians point to this event as an important step in the black struggle for equality. For example, boxing historian Bert Randolph Sugar writes, "Because most Americans viewed the contest as a battle between two political ideologies, Louis bore the colors of Americans of all colors. Franklin Roosevelt invited Louis to the White House and tenderly gripping his flexed muscle for conspiratorial news photographers said, 'Joe, we're depending on those muscles for America.'"[54]

The next major legislative act to affect boxing came in 1939, with the repeal of antiquated anti-fight film laws. According to Sammons, Senate hearings held in 1939 focused on four issues: "the common flouting of an unpopular law; the acceptability and popularity of boxing as reflected in its legalization by all states; the allegedly changed racial conditions, personified by Joe Louis; and the burgeoning television industry."[55] The following year, an unsuccessful bill sponsored by Representative Ambrose J. Kennedy was introduced to establish a national boxing commission. With the U.S. entry into World War II in December 1941, boxing and other leisure activities would take a back seat to the realities of war. Likewise in Europe, the International Boxing Union would cease to exist with the advent of World War II, but it was revived as the European Boxing Union in 1946 and has governed the sport on that continent for over sixty years.

The sport of boxing met the world of television on June 1, 1939, as experimental station W2XBS of New York telecast a heavyweight boxing match between Max Baer and Lou Nova.[56] The post–World War II era brought with it the television age, as the development of this technology hit its stride in 1946 with the broadcast of the Joe Louis vs. Billy Conn title rematch. Sammons writes, "The bout symbolized a return to normalcy, and the television and boxing industries were well aware that no other single event would so capture the nation's attention.... The Louis-Conn rematch marked a new era and led boxing and television analyst Jack Gould to conclude that prizefighting's greatest moments on television came during the medium's infancy."[57] Historian Benjamin Rader explains that for the sport of boxing, television was a double-edged sword: "In the late 1940s and early 1950s television lifted boxing into a new 'Golden Age' only to deliver it a blow from which it never fully recovered."[58]

Television technology at that time lent itself to boxing more than stadium sports such as baseball and football because a stationary camera could capture the images of a well lit ring in all its vivid detail and it fit the screen neatly. During this period there was little coverage of baseball, football or basketball since "the poor technical quality of the period favored small scale individual sports."[59] Networks and independent (local) broadcasters often televised fights, and soon the popularity of the sport garnered the attention of a major sponsor: the Gillette Company. Rader explains: "In the late 1940s, the passionate affair between television and professional boxing turned into orgy. Viewers in the bars of major cities and on their home screens (if they could afford sets) watched one or more fights nearly every night of the week. They could even see the best fighters perform: Rocky Graziano, Tony Zale, Sugar Ray Robinson, Jersey Joe Walcott and Ezzard Charles.... For many Americans, the Friday night Gillette fights became an institution."[60]

The vast quantity of televised boxing matches had many unexpected effects on the sport, and the saturation of boxing on TV began to decrease along with its television ratings. In 1952, 31 percent of all households watching television had their sets regularly tuned in to prime time fights; by 1959, that figure had fallen to 10.6 percent.[61] By the early 1960s, only the Gillette fights were broadcast on a regular basis.

1 • A History of Boxing Regulations

The early 1960s turned out to be a transitional period for boxing. The 1962 nationally televised tragedy of Benny Paret's death at the hands of Emile Griffith appears to be one of several factors in the decrease of boxing on TV at the time. The 2005 documentary *Ring of Fire: The Emile Griffith Story* depicts this tragedy and its aftermath in vivid detail.[62]

Other factors included the fall of the International Boxing Club (IBC) and televised Senate committee hearings on organized crime. The IBC emerged as the most prominent promoter of boxing events in the 1950s. Historian Rader writes, "By controlling the key arenas and through his connections with underworld figures, Jim Norris, the president of the IBC, drove independent promoters out of the fight game. Antitrust actions against the IBC, the convictions of Norris and mobsters associated with prizefighting [Frankie Carbo and Blinky Palermo] for income tax evasion, and the televised hearings by a Senate committee on organized crime (which included revelations about boxing) darkened the reputation of the sport that had always had difficulty establishing a positive image."[63] Senator Carey Estes Kefauver of Tennessee led the congressional committee hearings.

Ike Williams, shown here in 1991, was a popular world lightweight champion from 1945 to 1951.

Kefauver sought to create a national boxing commission under the U.S. Department of Justice. Although the state athletic commissions supported such a move, then-attorney general Robert Kennedy offered only lukewarm support for the measure and the bill failed in Congress in 1963, the year of Kefauver's death.[64] The following year, however, Congress and President Johnson at least addressed the issue of bribery in boxing by enacting a federal law that reads, "Whoever carries into effect, attempts to carry into effect, or conspires with any other person to carry into effect any scheme in commerce to influence, in any way, by bribery any sporting contest, with knowledge that the purpose of such scheme is to influence by bribery that contest, shall be fined under this title, or imprisoned not more than 5 years, or both."⁶⁵

The Rise of Professional Boxing Organizations (1962)

The decline in televised boxing along with the growing awareness of boxing's link to organized crime coincided with what would become a third major blow to boxing: the emergence of world governing bodies to regulate the sport. The National Boxing Association was replaced by the World Boxing Association (WBA), which was founded in Tacoma, Washington, in 1962. Historian Bob Mee explains, "The WBA had widespread support in the United States, with the exception of New York, which had always run in opposition to the old NBA anyway, and also drew good support from Latin America."⁶⁶ The WBA headquarters would soon move to Caracas, Venezuela. By the following year, a rival organization known as the World Boxing Council (WBC) formed with a base in Mexico City as represen-

Boxing trainer Gil Clancy and Emile Griffith appear in 1968 at Madison Square Garden in New York, a venue where Griffith fought over twenty-five times (courtesy Modesto M. Rodriguez).

tatives from eleven countries, mostly Latin American, converged on February 14, 1963. Mee notes: "Leading members [of the WBC] were the British Board of Boxing Control, the European Boxing Union, the British Commonwealth, and it also enjoyed a working agreement with the New York Commission."[67]

The cyclical trend of boxing's legal acceptance and rejection coinciding with the emergence of a dominant heavyweight champion continued in the 1960s. Just as John L. Sullivan, Jack Dempsey, and Joe Louis had done before him, Muhammad Ali emerged to pull boxing through the turbulence of the 1960s, while producing controversies of his own throughout the decade. Ali became heavyweight champion on February 25, 1964, with a surprising knockout victory over the feared Charles "Sonny" Liston.

Ali and Liston fought a rematch the following year, by a fight marred in controversy. On May 25, 1965, Ali knocked Liston out in the very first round with what became known as the "phantom punch" (though Ali referred to it as the "anchor punch"). The image of a rage-filled Ali standing over a crumpled Sonny Liston, mocking him to "get up" is one of the most widely seen photographs in sport. Sports outfitter Adidas even used this image for its 2004 "Impossible is Nothing," advertising campaign.[68] The questionable knockout victory was as much a result of Ali's lightning quick blow as it was the ineptitude of referee (and former heavyweight champion) Jersey Joe Walcott. When Liston went down, Ali refused to go to a neutral corner at first, and Liston eventually got up off the canvas. Walcott allowed the fight to resume, until being summoned by *The Ring Magazine*'s editor, Nat Fleischer, who informed him that Liston had been down for more than ten seconds. In an utterly confused state, Walcott abruptly stopped the action, lifting Ali's arm in victory. Accusations of the fight being fixed were rampant.

Two days following the Ali-Liston rematch, Congressman Oren Harris of Arkansas introduced a bill (H.R. 8635) to create a federal boxing commission, with the intent to clean up the sport from bribery and racketeering by issuing licenses to boxers and others involved in the business of boxing for fights that would be broadcast on network television.[69] Harris' idea was that by controlling those who would be licensed, criminal elements would be left out of the picture. Of course, the nature of the bill was based upon the notion that the fights could be broadcast across state lines; thus, it would be in the interest of the federal government to protect interstate commerce in this way. However, if a given fight was not broadcast, it would not be able to directly intervene, though it could theoretically provide the state commission with information to enable it to act on its own to stop a fight from taking place. And if a fight had been promoted by a television network was suddenly cancelled, it would undoubtedly cause problems for the network. The bill was passed in the House of Representatives by a vote of 346–4 in August 1965, but it failed to pass the Senate, and therefore was discarded.[70]

Ali emerged as a phenomenal champion, defending his title nine times before being forced into a boxing hiatus for his refusal to enter the United States armed services in 1967. Ali's refusal to report for induction resulted in his trial and conviction, which was affirmed by the Court of Appeals. It also resulted in the cancellation of his boxing licenses in the entire United States and the confiscation of his passport, keeping him from boxing abroad. Thus, while Ali appealed his conviction, he sustained himself by giving lectures at college campuses throughout the country and became a prominent anti-war figure. In 1970, Georgia, which lacked an athletic commission, authorized Ali to box, thus catapulting Ali back to the top of the boxing world for most of the 1970s. Ali's success in attaining a license to fight in Georgia after all the other boxing commissions rejected his applications came as a result of growing public discontent with the Vietnam War, changing racial norms in southern states and perhaps most importantly, Georgia state senator Leroy Johnson, an Ali friend, and Atlanta mayor Sam Massell, who cleared the path for Ali to be licensed in their state.[71] Then, the Supreme Court overturned Ali's conviction in June 1971 on the grounds that "since the Appeal Board gave no reason for the denial of a conscientious objector exemption to the petitioner, and it is impossible to determine on which of the three grounds offered in the justice department's letter that board relied, petitioner's conviction must be reversed."[72] While Ali and his counterparts Joe Frazier and George Foreman dominated the heavyweight division for much of the 1970s, boxing found itself involved in yet another major scandal.

In 1977, ABC Sports and Don King Productions organized a televised boxing tournament that was rife with inaccurate rankings, bribery, and extensive unethical behavior. While a federal grand jury investigation did not find enough evidence to warrant criminal proceedings, the publicity surrounding the scandal again contributed to the negative reputation of the sport. The United States Congress held hearings 1979 to consider legislation designed to create a Federal Boxing Board. A three-member commission would "register boxers and investigate matches to determine if bribery, racketeering, or other use of influence surrounded a fight. The board would be granted power to subpoena individuals having information about corruption in boxing matches.

1 • A History of Boxing Regulations

Two-time world heavyweight champion George Foreman is an anachronism. Not only was he a dominant heavyweight in the late 1960s and early 1970s, he also launched a wildly successful comeback twenty years later. Foreman is shown here with Evander Holyfield prior to their 1991 title bout.

The proposed legislation also provided a strong safety feature by establishing a 30-day suspension from fighting for any boxer who suffered a knockout or technical knockout."[73] Needless to say, this legislation didn't get anywhere. In the decade that followed, at least a half-dozen more bills to regulate boxing were introduced to the United States Congress. Each of the bills introduced in the 1980s, many of which were authored by then-congressman Bill Richardson, met the same inconsequential fate.

As U.S. legislation to improve boxing failed time after time, the world governing bodies known as the WBA and WBC would have a profound influence on the sport of boxing. In the 1960s and 1970s and the beginning of the 1980s, they were the only two universally recognized organizations governing the sport. Boxing historian Bob Mee explains that in 1983, the International Boxing Federation formed in the United States as "a split in the WBA led to disgruntled members, led by Bobbie Lee of New Jersey.... They survived because of their American platform. They claimed that the WBA was biased toward South and Central American nations, at the expense of the

THE REGULATION OF BOXING

Right: Promoter Don King, pictured here in 1992, has been investigated by the FBI and the IRS on several occasions, yet he remains one of the sport's most notorious figures.

Below: Former heavyweight champion Larry Holmes provided the International Boxing Federation with some semblance of legitimacy when he accepted the IBF title in 1983.

interests of the United States, which promoted the most championship fights."[74] The IBF gained widespread recognition and legitimacy only when then–heavyweight champion Larry Holmes embraced the organization and declined recognition by the WBA and WBC. Essentially, Holmes did not want to play by the rules, values and norms established by the WBA and WBC and decided that as the linear heavyweight champion, his status transcended that of the institutions.[75]

1 • A History of Boxing Regulations

Just as Holmes had provided the IBF with legitimacy, legendary champion Thomas Hearns did the same when he accepted the World Boxing Organization super middleweight title.

A fourth governing body for the sport emerged in the late 1980s, the World Boxing Organization (WBO) based in Puerto Rico. This organization was started by disgruntled members of the World Boxing Association. The first WBO sanctioned fight was held in 1988 between Thomas Hearns and James Kinchen for the super middleweight championship. Hearns' victory gave the WBO a measure of legitimacy and recognition, just as Larry Holmes had become the first standard bearer of the IBF five years earlier. Subsequent champions, such as Oscar De La Hoya (whose first world title was a WBO belt), Nigel Benn, "Prince" Naseem Hamed, and Marco Antonio Barrera, have solidified the legitimacy of the WBO in the eyes of many observers.

Boxing Scandals in the 1980s

The 1980s saw the sport enter into a period of disarray, primarily due to the proliferation of entities that claim to regulate the sport on a global level, and the failure of U.S. boxing-related legislation. Since 1983, at least six additional boxing organizations have arisen, creating rules and rankings for boxers and recognizing champions who are required to pay sanctioning fees for a particular organization's recognition. The organizations described are very similar in terms of their constitutions and bylaws. They establish the rules under which participants will compete, have licensing procedures for participants, create rankings of boxers in various weight divisions, recognize champions in each division, and charge sanctioning fees. They function independently from one another, although it is possible that a single individual may be recognized as champion or ranked by different institutions. They also have self-proclaimed jurisdiction over the same geographic space, which is the entire world.

The proliferation of world championships is a double-edged sword. Some argue that this proliferation is good for boxers, as they can earn more money if they engage in a fight promoted as a world championship. Furthermore, if a boxer fails to win a fight against one of his weight division's champions, he could then challenge one of the other titlists for a championship belt. Thus, there are more opportunities for a boxer to win a championship and make more money in the process. The counterargument holds that this proliferation of championships has led to far less name-recognition for boxers than in years past, diminishes the value of winning a world championship, and has led boxing into a gradual decline in popularity.

Media coverage of boxing in U.S. mainstream newspapers and maga-

1 • A History of Boxing Regulations

zines is unquestionably less than in years past. Fights are rarely televised on network television. Casual sports fans in the United States are hard pressed to name current world champions with any accuracy. Yet boxing has become a niche sport that enjoys a great deal of coverage in Internet media, cable and satellite television, and Spanish-language publications in the United States. There is a tremendous amount of televised boxing on cable and satellite television. Historic boxing matches are regularly televised on ESPN Classic and VS Channel. Live (or recent) fights are broadcast each week on ESPN2, Telefutura, TyC Sports, and Fox Sports. Furthermore, the sport is popular in Europe, Latin America, and Asia where boxing receives far more coverage in mainstream publications and on network television than in the U.S. Champions that hail from countries other than the United States are often household names in their respective countries.

As in previous decades, boxing was not immune to scandal in the 1980s. In addition to the problems arising from the proliferation of boxing organizations, many will recall some of the controversial fights of the decade. One of these was the 1980 rematch between "Sugar" Ray Leonard and Roberto Duran that ended with the tough Panamanian quitting in the ring by saying, "*No Mas.*" Another was the 1982 rematch between Aaron Pryor and Alexis Arguello, which was possibly the result of one of the more egregious violations. After the twelfth round of that highly competitive fight, Pryor's trainer asked one of his cornermen for a bottle "with the special mix." Although it was never proven if Pryor had indeed consumed a substance other than water, he came out with renewed energy and brutally knocked out Arguello in the fourteenth round, sending him to the hospital. When asked in December 2007 whether he thought that Pryor consumed a prohibited substance in that fight, Arguello replied, "I don't think so. I have asked [Pryor] myself."[76]

In 1982, Ray "Boom Boom" Mancini killed his opponent, Korean Duk-Koo Kim, in a nationally televised bout. The chilling memories of that dramatic event linger to this day. A series of articles and an ESPN Classic television special commemorated the 25th anniversary of this tragedy. Additionally, a Korean-made film entitled *Champion* provides a remarkable portrayal of this event from Kim's native country.[77] In the aftermath of the Mancini vs. Kim match, the World Boxing Council declared that its championship fights would be reduced in length from fifteen rounds to twelve and the Nevada Athletic Commission created a Medical Advisory Board.[78] This was a major change in the sport, since fifteen round championship fights had been the tradition for several decades. Within five years, however, the World

Boxing Association and International Boxing Federation would follow suit and boxing matches have not surpassed twelve rounds since 1987.

A Boxer's Perspective on Death in the Ring

In an ironic twist, less than one year after the WBC implemented the twelve round limit for championship fights, Francisco "Kiko" Bejines died after being knocked out *in the twelfth round* by Albert Davila in a fight for the vacant bantamweight title. Davila was interviewed exclusively for this book in December 2007. He recalls his fight with Bejines as a "bittersweet victory."

Davila says, "It was a bittersweet victory because I achieved the highest pinnacle in boxing, being a world champion, and yet I was never able to celebrate that victory because of the tragedy that happened. And it was sad, because it didn't have to go that way. It makes me angry that it ended in tragedy. To achieve the highest goal that you can obtain and have it end that way is sad. I never celebrated that

Oscar De La Hoya's first world championship was sanctioned by the WBO. De La Hoya is seen here hoisting the WBO belt after his 1994 victory over Jimmy Bredahl for the super featherweight title.

1 • A History of Boxing Regulations

Sugar Ray Leonard and Roberto "*Manos de Piedra*" (Hands of Stone) Duran were two of boxing's main protagonists in the 1980s (Duran photograph courtesy Modesto M. Rodriguez).

victory. Yet, I ask myself, why did that happen? No one is at fault. I was actually behind on the scorecards." The former champion recognizes that it is difficult to assign blame when a ring death occurs. He says, "Who do you blame? The commission? The promoters? The WBC? The judges? And another thing I heard, though I don't know if it's true, is that Kiko told his dad in the corner after the eleventh round that he couldn't go on, but his dad or management, which were some guys I worked with later on, replied just go out there and stay on your feet and you'll get the decision. If the fight went to the decision I would've lost. It's sad that these things happen, but that's the way it is." Davila's next fight was a ten round decision over Julio Rodriguez, just two months later. Davila recalls, "After the Bejines fight, my next fight was just to feel things out, and I won, but boxing is a risk we take in life."

Davila had his share of ring wars and championship fights, before and after the change in championship rounds. He says, "The championship rounds are tough. It was because of Mancini-Kim that they changed the rules." One of Davila's fifteen round fights was an attempt to wrest the title from Lupe

Ray "Boom Boom" Mancini was a media darling in the 1980s. His tragic victory over Korean challenger Duk-Koo Kim led to the reduction of rounds in championship fights from 15 to 12 (courtesy Modesto M. Rodriguez).

Pintor in 1980. Significantly, that was Pintor's first fight after his own tragic victory over Welshman Johnny Owen. Davila says, "I didn't think about [Owen's death at the hands of Pintor]. It's a risk we take every day in life. When we walk out that door, we don't know if we're going to walk back in. Every day I thank God for being alive, what He's given me, what He's done for me, but in that fight, I just wanted to win. My fight with Pintor was great. I felt I won it. I fought from bell to bell, and I never caught a second wind. I feel that I won the fight. It was close; he dominated the last three rounds, but I was ahead the first twelve." Davila lost a controversial 15-round majority decision. In a solemn moment, Davila asked whether I had seen the Pintor-Owen fight. He commented, "That guy [Owen] didn't belong in the ring with Pintor.... And then he died."

Davila, who became a boxing trainer after his fighting days were over, believes that state athletic commissions are doing fairly well to protect boxers. He says, "The commissions have their rules and regulations and they abide by them. A lot of times in big fights, they make exceptions and let some things go on, but as far as protecting fighters, I think that most commissions are very good. They look after the boxers and look out for their rules and regulations." Nevertheless, Davila laments that mismatches are still allowed. "The safety is there, but the problem is not the commission, it's the management and the training teams on both sides. If I have a good fighter, but I feel he's not prepared to go with a top fighter, why put him in there? You can ruin a career, you can ruin a person, and yes a commission could be stricter, but it's all about money. I don't want to badmouth any commissions, but some fights shouldn't happen."

1 • A History of Boxing Regulations

In spite of being involved in a ring death and being on the losing end of several questionable decisions during his career, Davila didn't leave the sport of boxing until one of the boxers he trained ended up with what he considers to be a raw deal. He says, "As a trainer, my last fight in the corner was when David Kamau fought Julio Cesar Chavez in 1995. I felt that David won the fight, but we didn't get the decision. Then I found out that the management of Kamau's team received more money than they said they were receiving. And we were given the money we wanted, but the only way Kamau could win was by knockout. But Chavez is a tough guy to knock out, and David wasn't a big knockout fighter. I thought to myself, I can't do this to a fighter. I can't betray him, so I got out." David Kamau lost a close 12-round decision to the legendary Julio Cesar Chavez in September 1995, and Davila decided on a career change.

Albert Davila won the WBC bantamweight title with a dramatic knockout of Kiko Bejines, who died as a result of the injuries he suffered in that bout. Davila is shown here in 1992, during his days as a boxing trainer (courtesy Modesto M. Rodriguez).

It should be noted that Davila has not ended up destitute and alone, like many former champions. He is healthy, despite having engaged in 66 professional fights, with a record of 55 wins, 10 losses and 1 draw. Davila says, "I feel good. Boxing is physically strenuous on your body, but I took care of myself in the ring, before and after fights, and I'm happy about the way things worked out. Even though I've seen other fighters that are pretty badly damaged, I feel I've been blessed because everything is fine, and I fought the best guys."

Davila works for a maintenance company and his wife works for a school district as a case worker for a Head Start program. All of his children are either in college or college graduates. He proudly explains, "My oldest son is a junior high teacher of U.S. history still going to school for a master's degree. My oldest daughter is working on a Ph.D. in sociology, my other daughter

David Kamau, pictured here in 1992 with trainer Davila in the background, lost a unanimous decision to Julio Cesar Chavez in 1995.

is a sophomore in college, an adopted son in junior college, and my twins are both in college; one is at Oberlin College, and one plays soccer at USC. Everyone has done well." The day after this interview was conducted, Davila's daughter Alyssa won the NCAA national women's soccer championship for the University of Southern California.

American Medical Association

In light of the Pintor vs. Owen, Pryor vs. Arguello, Mancini vs. Kim, and Davila vs. Bejines debacles in the early 1980s, it is not surprising that a 1984 American Medical Association (AMA) resolution called for the abolition of boxing. After the adoption of the resolution, AMA president Dr. Joseph Boyle said, "It has been increasingly evident from scientific investigation that there is both acute and long-term brain injury to people who are involved in boxing. Evaluation of that evidence indicates that people are seriously disabled even after short exposure to boxing. I believe that physicians all over the country should participate in a public dialogue which would ultimately lead to persuading legislators and the public that this is indeed a very dangerous sport and that it ought to be outlawed."[79] But of course, boxing has not been outlawed, and eventually some positive federal laws designed to help clean up the sport emerged.

In the early 1990s, a polemic decision in a nationally televised boxing match garnered the attention of congressmen. The split decision awarded to James Toney in his IBF middleweight championship title defense against David Tiberi outraged television viewers throughout the United States, including Republican William Roth, Jr., the senator from Tiberi's home state of Delaware. In the aftermath of the fight, which took place in 1992, Roth introduced legislation in the U.S. Senate to create a Professional Boxing Corporation (S. 2852). A similar bill was also introduced in the U.S. House of Representatives by Democratic congressman Bill Richardson of New Mexico (H.R. 5407). Neither of these bills was acted upon. In the following legislative session (the 103rd Congress), Roth and Richardson again introduced the legislation, which failed to become law once again. Almost simultaneously, Senator John McCain and Representative Robert Torricelli introduced legislation that focused on increasing the health and safety regulations for boxing. While these bills also failed to advance 1994, they would meet more success with their subsequent introduction in the 104th Congress.

Professional Boxing Safety Act (1996)

Senator John McCain introduced the legislation that would become the Professional Boxing Safety Act of 1996. This act is an example of a proactive federal law that seeks "(1) to improve and expand the system of safety precautions that protects the welfare of professional boxers; and (2) to assist State boxing commissions to provide proper oversight for the professional boxing industry in the United States."[80] With regards to health and safety, this federal law calls for the following:

- A boxing commission to regulate a match (states without commissions must have a commission from a neighboring state come in to regulate matches);
- a pre-fight physical exam;
- an ambulance or medical personnel with appropriate resuscitation equipment to be present at each match;
- a ringside physician;
- health insurance for each boxer;
- a license for each boxer.

The Professional Boxing Safety Act also requires boxing commissions to:

- Evaluate boxers' records;
- honor other states' medical, drug, and identity-based suspensions unless that suspension has been revoked;
- report the results of all matches to a boxer registry.

To eliminate possible conflicts of interest, the law specifically prohibits members of boxing commissions from receiving compensation from any person that sanctions, arranges or promotes professional boxing or those who have financial interests in boxers currently registered. There are specific measures detailed in the law for enforcement through the U.S. Attorney General's Office and criminal penalties for violators. Additional clauses are included for notification procedures for supervising boxing commissions and the law commissions studies to be conducted on boxer pensions and health and safety equipment and standards. The law also addresses boxing matches held on Indian reservations. The reservations are authorized to create their own regulatory bodies or ask their state commission to regulate fights on their territory. Should the tribal organizations choose to establish commissions of their

1 • A History of Boxing Regulations

James Toney, shown here when he was a middleweight, won a hotly contested decision over David Tiberi that resulted in renewed congressional attention to boxing.

own, they must adopt rules that are at least as stringent as the state commission where the reservation is located or the guidelines established by the Association of Boxing Commissions.

Muhammad Ali Boxing Reform Act (2000)

A second federal law that governs boxing in the United States was signed in May 2000. The Muhammad Ali Boxing Reform Act amends the Professional Boxing Safety Act of 1996. While most of the law deals with ensuring fairness in the economic aspects of boxing, it also seeks to assist state athletic commissions in providing adequate oversight of the sport and promotes honor and integrity in boxing competitions. Specific measures prohibit coercive contracts with promoters and broadcasters that may exploit boxers. The law also provides a process for the Association of Boxing Commissions to rate professional boxers, and for boxers to appeal their rankings in sanctioning bodies. Furthermore, the law requires full economic disclosure from sanctioning organizations and promoters to state boxing commissions and the boxers themselves. Such information must also be made available to state Attorney Generals upon request. The law also stipulates that there must be a firewall between promoters and managers. Detailed provisions for the enforcement of the act are also provided in the law.

The Muhammad Ali Boxing Reform Act makes very few specific references to health and safety. For example, it clarifies that the term "suspension" in the Professional Boxing Safety Act of 1996 includes "the revocation of a boxing license." It also changes the renewal period of boxer identification cards from two to four years, and urges boxing commissions to make a disclosure to boxers that includes "the health and safety risks associated with boxing, and, in particular, the risk and frequency of brain injury and the advisability that a boxer periodically undergo medical procedures designed to detect brain injury."[81]

While both the Professional Boxing Safety Act of 1996 and the Muhammad Ali Boxing Reform Act of 2000 make great strides in regulating the sport, neither act established a federal agency to provide oversight for these reforms. Thus, since 2000 Senator John McCain of Arizona has introduced legislation that would establish a national boxing commission. In 2004, Senate Bill 275 passed the Senate but was not acted upon prior to the end of the 108th Congress and died in the House of Representatives. Muhammad Ali testified in favor of this bill in September 2004. His testimony was read by his wife, Lonnie, as the effects of Parkinson's Syndrome have drastically impaired Ali's speech.

In January 2005, Senator McCain reintroduced the bill to the Senate (S. 148), while Representative Peter King of New York introduced the same legislation (H.R. 468), and Rep. Cliff Stearns introduced a similar version (H.R. 1065) to the House of Representatives in the 109th Congress. The United States Senate passed the bill without amendment by unanimous consent on May 9, 2005. However, it failed in the House of Representatives by a vote of 190–233.[82]

Professional Boxing Amendments Act of 2007

The current legislation, simultaneously introduced in the 110th Congress (2007–2008) by Sen. John McCain as S. 84 in the United States Senate and by Rep. Peter King as H.R. 4031 in the U.S. House of Representatives amends the Professional Boxing Safety Act of 1996 and would establish a United States Boxing Commission (USBC) within the U.S. Department of Commerce to administer the act. The purpose of the commission is to "protect the health, safety, and welfare of boxers and to ensure fairness in the sport of professional boxing." This would create major changes in the administration of boxing in the United States. This legislation would amend the Professional Boxing Safety Act of 1996 by:

1 • A History of Boxing Regulations

- Requiring tribal commissions to conform to minimal standards set by the state where it is located or the USBC guidelines;
- vesting the final authority to approve all professional boxing matches within the USBC;
- requiring testing for infectious diseases;
- setting standards for not allowing boxers with many consecutive losses to fight;
- requiring an ambulance AND emergency personnel with proper resuscitation equipment continuously on site;
- allowing tribal commissions to register boxers;
- requiring copies of boxing licenses at the USBC;
- requiring health and safety disclosures to be given to boxers;
- establishing procedures to review suspensions;

Since Muhammad Ali retired from boxing in 1981, he has been involved in numerous business ventures. In this 1991 image, Ali is promoting his self-named cologne at a department store while an adoring fan (the author's mother) places a kiss on his cheek.

- developing minimal guidelines for contractual requirements;
- developing guidelines for sanctioning bodies to rank boxers and for boxers to challenge their ratings;
- modifying the disclosures required by promoters, sanctioning bodies and broadcasters;
- requiring licensing of ring officials, including referees, judges;
- creating and maintaining a comprehensive medical registry;
- establishing conflict of interest provisions; and
- repealing studies required by the Professional Boxing Safety Act of 1996.

The legislation would create the USBC and stipulate the requirements for the three presidentially appointed commission members, the terms of their tenure in office, and their functions. The primary tasks of the commission would be to protect the health, safety and general interests of boxers and ensure uniformity, fairness and integrity in professional boxing. Specifically, the USBC would:

- Administer the Professional Boxing Amendments Act of 2007;
- promulgate uniform standards for boxing;
- oversee all boxing matches in the U.S.;
- improve health, safety and professional boxing standards;
- ensure the enforcement of this act through the office of the U.S. Attorney General and state attorney generals;
- assist state boxing commissions in meeting the minimum standards established by this act;
- coordinate the establishment and maintenance of minimum health and safety standards for boxing in the U.S.;
- establish publications and an Internet site;
- procure reasonable services and consultants; and
- take action to accomplish the provisions of this act.

The act would specifically prohibit the USBC from ranking boxers, promoting boxing events, and providing technical assistance to commissions that do not comply with requirements of the USBC.

In terms of licensing and registering boxers, the legislation lists the general requirements, applications, durations, and fees. The commission is to create or authorize a National Registry of Boxing Personnel to centralize the

Both "Kid" Akeem Anifowoshe (right) and Gerald McClellan (above) suffered blood clots in their early 1990s title challenges and were severely disabled. Anifowoshe died in 1994 (photograph of Anifowoshe courtesy Modesto M. Rodriguez).

data (records, medical information) on boxers and other boxing related personnel, such as promoters, managers, trainers and ring officials. Requirements for consultation with the Association of Boxing Commissions are stipulated, and the general process for suspending and revoking licenses and registrations is outlined.

Perhaps most importantly, the authority vested in the USBC to investigate violations and the subpoena power and ability to intervene in civil actions that a national commission would have is provided for in this act. Such authority would give the national commission, if it is established as U.S. law, the ability to actually enforce its own regulations. This would be an unprecedented step at the national level in the United States.

To assuage the potential concerns of state athletic commissions, the legislation provides a statement of non-interference in state athletic commission affairs, as long as they are not acting in a manner inconsistent to this act, and this legislation would not prohibit states from adopting more stringent requirements than those that would be called for by the national commission.

Appropriations must be granted for the USBC to carry out its duties, and it has the authority to collect fees for the activities and services it provides. The legislation also calls for various reports to ensure the appropriate administration of the commission. There is not any mention of funding for state athletic commissions to comply with the minimum standards and requirements that the U.S. Boxing Commission establishes. The only reference to this is in Sec. 203 (b) (6), which states that the USBC shall "review boxing commission regulations for professional boxing and provide assistance to such authorities in meeting minimum standards prescribed by the [U.S.] Commission under this title." This vaguely written clause does not define the type of assistance the USBC would provide. It is unclear if such assistance would come in the form of consultations or in the form of funds to carry out the necessary medical tests that a U.S. boxing commission would require.

As of early 2008, the House version of this legislation, H.R. 4031, was referred to the Committee on Education and Labor as well as the Committee on Energy and Commerce. The Senate version, S. 84, was placed on the Senate Legislative Calendar No. 65, under General Orders.

In the midst of attempts to legislate boxing at the federal level, several events that underscore the need for uniform health and safety regulations have occurred. In 1991, Nigerian super flyweight "Kid" Akeem Anifowoshe suffered a blood clot in his brain in a losing title fight against Robert Quiroga. Anifowoshe died three years later. In 1995, WBC and WBO middleweight champion Gerald McClellan barely survived after his brutal fight with Nigel Benn in London. This prompted the British Board of Boxing Control to require a paramedic team and ambulance standing by at every fight.[83] In a women's Golden Gloves (amateur) boxing competition held on April 4, 2005, in Colorado, Becky Zerlentes died from blows suffered in the ring, becoming the first woman to die in a regulated boxing competition. Just one week later in Texas, a featherweight named Leocadio Manon was abruptly removed from a boxing event after testing positive for HIV. If that bout had been scheduled in a state that does not require HIV tests instead of Texas, Manon's handlers, his opponent, the referee, and perhaps those sitting in close proximity to the ring would have been placed at a small but potential risk of contracting HIV.

1 • A History of Boxing Regulations

Tommy "The Duke" Morrison, pictured here in 1993 with promoter Bob Arum (left), tested positive for HIV in 1996 but now claims he does not have the virus.

The case of former WBO world heavyweight champion Tommy "The Duke" Morrison deserves special mention. In 1996, Morrison tested positive for HIV in Nevada.[84] He promptly retired and joined Magic Johnson as a celebrity spokesperson to raise awareness of HIV-AIDS. As the years passed, however, Morrison began to claim that he was misdiagnosed. An article published in the *New York Times* on July 22, 2007, says that the newspaper obtained copies of three documents that "purport to be tests of Morrison's blood" indicating that in one test, Morrison was negative for HIV antibodies, in another, HIV was not detected in his DNA, and in a third he tested positive for HIV, but he was negative for HIV in his RNA.[85] Based upon test results provided to the West Virginia Athletic Commission, a state that does not require HIV tests, Morrison was granted a license to box in February 2007. He defeated John Castle by a TKO in two rounds, and as of early 2008, fought only once more in Mexico, defeating Lawrence, Kansas, native Matt Weisharr in the third round.

Conclusion

Boxing regulations have had a long and intriguing history. From the origins of the sport in 4000 B.C. to the Professional Boxing Amendments Act of 2007, boxing has been regulated in an effort to make this inherently dangerous sport safe, or at least as safe as possible. While the roots of boxing lie in Ancient Egypt, it reemerged in a more modern form in England over 250 years ago. The modernization of the sport, through Broughton's Rules, the London Prize Ring Rules and especially the Marquis of Queensberry Rules has enabled the sport to survive to the present day. In the United States, boxing languished in illegal or semi-legal status for decades, until state governments began to legalize the sport in the late 1890s and early twentieth century. The state governments of New York and Nevada were at the forefront of boxing legalization and legitimization. The development of television and the increasingly powerful world governing bodies of the sport would play a dominant role in the sport's evolution in the latter half of the twentieth century. In the past two decades, emphasis has been placed upon strengthening the health and safety aspects of boxing regulations, and two significant federal laws have emerged to help clean up the sport in the United States. The pending Professional Boxing Amendments Act of 2007 is on the cusp of creating a federal boxing commission that will have the power to establish and enforce minimal health, safety and contractual standards for boxing in the United States.

2

DATA ANALYSIS

Introduction

The centerpiece of this text is a national analysis of professional boxing regulations in the United States as of 2004. The administration of a 2005 survey, heretofore referred to as the Boxing Health and Safety Survey (or BHS Survey), to existing state athletic commission chairpersons or their designees was utilized to establish how each state regulates the sport of boxing. An examination of an existing database of state medical requirements provided additional information. Since the BHS Surveys allowed for open-ended commentary, insight was gained as to the ways states implement their regulations.

There are many aspects to boxing regulations, however, this study focuses on health and safety issues. The specific issues of neurological testing, HIV testing and drug testing are emphasized. Once the data gathering and analysis processes were complete, a quantitative analysis was carried out. A dependent variable was created and data for several independent variables was gathered. The statistical results are revealing of the factors that may affect why states vary in their implementation of certain health and safety regulations.

First, I describe the instrument and the findings of the BHS Survey. Then I analyze the responses to each of the issues set forth in the survey. Next I explain the procedure for carrying out the statistical analysis, and finally I present the statistical results. Maps and charts depicting state boxing regulations are presented throughout the chapter.

The BHS Survey

The Internet facilitated the data-gathering aspects of this research. Through this medium, data on boxing regulations was compiled for all fifty states. State government, athletic commission Web sites, and the Lexis-Nexis State Code database served as the primary data sources, since they generally contain full-text state code and relevant regulatory documents. The Association of Boxing Commissions maintains an Internet site that includes information such as the names, addresses, Web pages and e-mail addresses of most state athletic commissions and their personnel. While this directory proved to be an excellent starting point for this process, much of the information on the page was outdated. Nevertheless, through electronic search engines the relevant documents outlining boxing legislation and regulations in addition to procedures, practices and other information about the regulation of the sport in each state were obtained.

As the information available on the Internet was compiled, a consent form and the BHS Survey were developed and mailed to the executive directors of the respective state athletic commissions or their designees.[1] The survey is modeled after information contained in the 2003 GAO Report on Professional Boxing and the Professional Boxing Safety Act of 1996.

The consent form, BHS Survey and a postage-paid return envelope were mailed to the forty-three (43) existing state athletic commissions in January 2005. Tim Lueckenhoff, the chairperson of the Association of Boxing Commissions (ABC), sent an electronic version of the cover letter and BHS Survey to the ABC e-mail listserv shortly thereafter. Subsequently in February and March 2005 the survey and cover letter were sent via e-mail to the individuals representing states that had not responded to the survey. BHS Surveys to New York and Florida were also sent via fax. Figure 1 indicates whether a state possessed a boxing commission in 2004. With the exception of Alaska, Alabama and Delaware in addition to four Midwestern states, the overwhelming majority of states possessed a boxing commission to oversee the sport within its borders. Two additional athletic commissions were created after this study was completed: Kansas and Minnesota. While the state of Kansas passed legislation to create a commission in April 2004, commissioners were not appointed until May 2005.

Through the efforts outlined previously, and numerous phone calls to state athletic commission executive directors, a total of thirty-eight completed BHS Surveys were returned. One additional state, Maryland, chose to send a letter and accompanying documents in lieu of the survey. Two different individuals from state athletic commissions in Michigan, Nevada and Wisconsin returned surveys. Furthermore, the state of Alaska, which dissolved its boxing commission in 2002, also returned a survey. The Washington, D.C., Athletic Commission also replied but is not included in the study because it is not a state. The boxing commissioner for the province of Quebec, Canada,

2 • Data Analysis

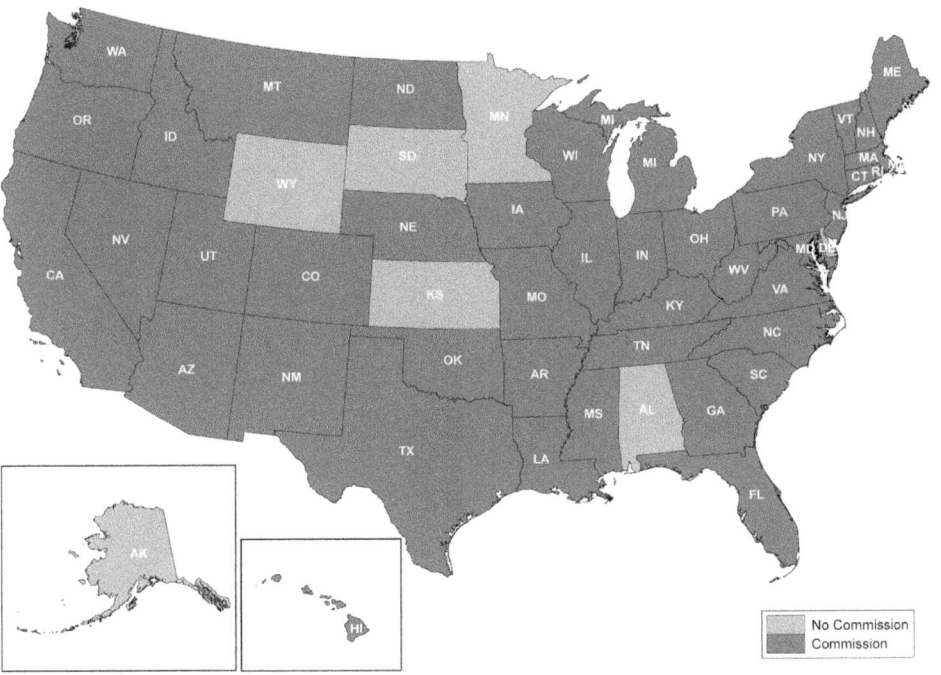

Figure 1: United States Boxing Commissions (2004) (Association of Boxing Commissions).

also returned a survey, but it was likewise not included in the study. And finally, one state returned a survey without identifying itself. Therefore, 32 of 43 (or 74 percent) existing state athletic commissions responded to the BHS Survey. More importantly, all of the 12 states that held the most boxing events in 2004 responded to the survey. The states that held the most boxing events in calendar year 2004 (in order of quantity, with the number of events listed in parentheses) are: California (126), Texas (60), Pennsylvania (52), Florida (48), Missouri (40), Michigan (27), New York (26), Ohio (25), Colorado (24), Illinois (24), Indiana (24), and West Virginia (23).[2]

In 2005, the Association of Boxing Commissions required each state athletic commission to report the results of all professional boxing events to Fight Fax, Inc., or www.boxrec.com, an Internet boxing archive. Since then, Fight Fax has emerged as the official source of boxers' records for the ABC. Boxrec.com remains a source of detailed boxing results from around the world that is continuously updated. While the data listed on boxers' records is not

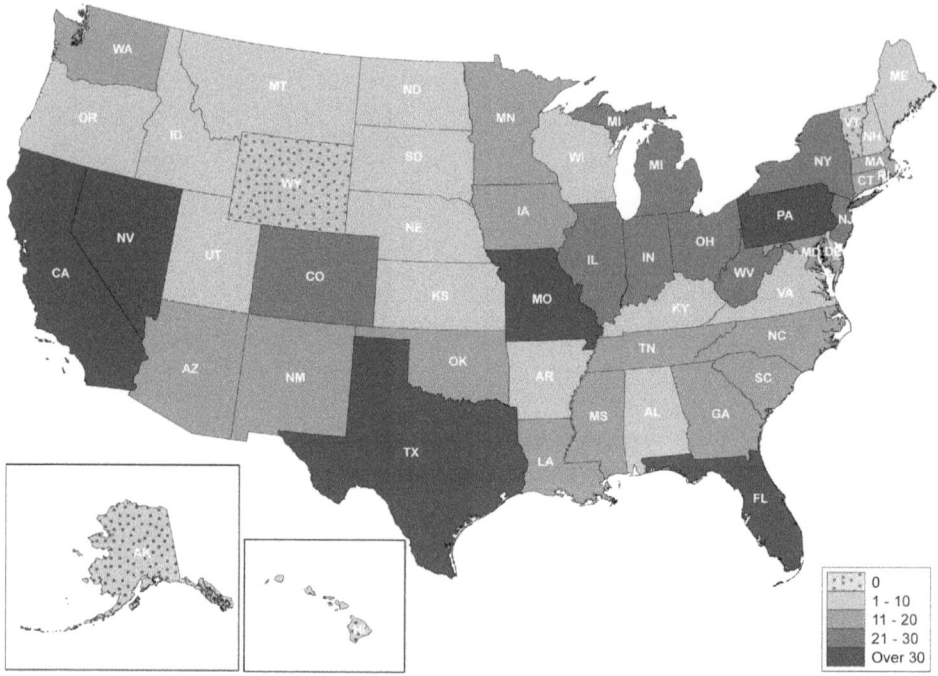

Figure 2: Boxing events held in the United States (2004) (www.boxrec.com).

100 percent accurate (and for that matter, no source that compiles worldwide results on a daily basis for events that have taken place for over 100 years can be 100 percent accurate), it is a very good resource to provide data that is pertinent to this study, such as the number of events held in various states. "Boxing events" are defined as a series of boxing matches that take place in the same venue on the same date. The number of boxing events by state held in 2004 is displayed in Figure 2.[3]

The most boxing events, by far, took place in California.[4] The Golden State accounts for 13 percent of all boxing events in the United States in 2004. Interestingly, a total of twenty-eight boxing events took place in the seven states that do not possess state athletic commissions. Some of these events took place under the jurisdiction of tribal commissions, while boxing commissions from neighboring states or the association of boxing commissions regulated other events. In some cases it is not clear if *any* commission actually monitored the events. The states of Alaska, Hawaii, Vermont and Wyoming did not host any boxing events in 2004, even though Hawaii and

Vermont had boxing commissions in place. The number of boxing events that took place was compiled using data from boxrec.com. Even if the data is not 100 percent accurate for each state, the general trends showing boxing activity in various U.S. states can be expected to be reasonably accurate.

Boxing fans may be surprised by the fact that neither Nevada nor New York hosts the most fights. While Nevada remains the host of many mega-boxing events, and New York remains a state closely associated with the sport's history, the popularity of boxing among the burgeoning Latino population in California and Texas is clearly associated with the number of events held in each state. Over one-third of the population in California and Texas is of Hispanic origin.[5] Seven of the top-twelve states that host boxing events are also in the top-twelve rankings of the Hispanic population in the United States.[6]

BHS Survey Results

As a result of the high response rate to the BHS Survey (74 percent) and the fact that the survey responses come from states that represent 84 percent of all boxing events held in 2004, the survey provides a revealing snapshot of boxing regulations in the United States. If one examines the data on a superficial level, it appears that states did quite well in terms of protecting the health and safety of professional boxers. For example, *all* of the states that replied to the survey indicate that they possess a boxing commission that:

- conducts pre-fight medical evaluations;
- requires standards for competitive match-ups;
- ensures emergency medical personnel and equipment are present during and after each match;
- requires health insurance for boxers during each match; and
- requires registration (licenses) for boxers.

Nearly all of the states that replied to the BHS Survey honor each other's suspensions in accordance with current federal law (two replied "don't know"). Most states conduct post-fight medical evaluations (25 of 32 or 78 percent), and require certification and approval for ring officials (25 of 32 or 78 percent). However, upon inspection of the open-ended answers for each of these items, a different picture emerges.

Pre-fight Medical Evaluations

While all states conduct pre-fight medical evaluations, the types of medical tests included in these examinations vary greatly. Many respondents listed all specific medical examinations they carry out, while others just listed a few or none at all. For more detailed information on the specific components of the pre-fight medical examination I consulted the American Association of Ringside Physicians data compilation of state medical requirements. In 2005, the AAPRP compiled data on the following 17 pre-fight and 3 at-fight state medical requirements for each state that has an athletic commission:[7]

Pre-fight Medical Requirements

- Complete physical exam
- EEG (brain wave test)
- CAT scan (brain x-ray)
- Neurological exam (by neurologist)
- Neuropsychological exam (neurological test)
- Negative HIV (AIDS test)
- Negative Hepatitis BsAg (Hepatitis B test)
- Negative Hepatitis Cab (Hepatitis C Test)
- EKG (heart test)
- Dilated eye exam (Eye test)
- CBC (blood count)
- PT/PTT (blood clotting test)
- MRI (brain x-ray)
- RPR (syphilis test)
- TB Test (tuberculosis)
- Gynecologic exam
- Other

Medical Requirements at Fight

- Mini-physical exam
- Urine drug screen
- Pregnancy test

Dr. Michael Schwartz, president of the AAPRP, authorized use of the medical information contained in the organization's Web site for this study. The AAPRP data compilation for 2004 reveals, for example, that Washington State appears to be the most thorough in its medical evaluations. The tests carried out by the Washington commission include an EEG (brain wave test), CT scan (brain x-ray), neurological exam (by a neurologist), neuropsychological exam (neurological test), HIV (AIDS test), Hepatitis B test, Hepatitis C test, EKG (heart test), dilated eye exam, MRI (brain x-ray), a mini-physical exam at the fight, a urine drug screen, and a pregnancy test for female boxers.[8] In contrast, the state of North Dakota, which did not specify on the survey the type of medical evaluations it carries out, did not indicate that it performed any of these tests in the AAPRP data collection except for a pregnancy test for female boxers and a urine drug screen. Notably, however, this state did not indicate that it tested for drugs on the BHS survey.

Another issue that exemplifies the range of replies is the timing of the pre-fight evaluations. For example, in Hawaii, a physical exam is required at the time of licensure, at the weigh-in, and one hour before the fight. In Michigan, "not more than 8 hours before a show, a physician should certify that each contestant is in proper physical condition to participate in the show."[9] Maryland is particularly thorough in its timing of medical exams. Maryland boxing commissioner Pat Panella replied, "The boxer must also complete a number of medical examinations within 30 days of initial licensure (some, within 30 days of the boxer's first bout that is scheduled to be held in Maryland) and within 30 days of license renewal.... An annual physical examination must be completed within 21 days of both initial licensure and license renewal.... In addition, the boxer must submit to the Commission negative tests for the HIV virus and Hepatitis B virus (Hepatitis B Surface Antigen test) within 30 days of initial licensure, within 30 days of license renewal, and as otherwise directed by the Commission."[10]

State Suspensions

According to the Professional Boxing Safety Act of 1996, "no boxer is permitted to box while under suspension from any boxing commission."[11] All of the states indicated that they honor other states' medical suspensions except for Connecticut and Montana, which indicated that they "don't know." Specifically, Connecticut's survey indicated, "There hasn't been a fight off the casinos in at least five years, so I can't answer this."[12] Montana did not give a reason for the answer. Larry Beddes of Idaho wrote, "They are to be honored by all states but, I have found instances where certain states may not have done so.... We honor them."[13] Many respondents indicated that this is federal law or that they receive the list of suspended fighters from Fight Fax, Inc., now the "certified boxing registry" of the Association of Boxing Commissions.[14]

Administrative or discipline-related suspensions are a different matter, however. In California and New York, for example, these suspensions are handled on a "case by case basis." Oregon indicates, "Exceptions considered for 'contractual' suspensions."[15] Tim Lueckenhoff, who in addition to serving as president of the ABC is also the boxing commissioner for the state of Missouri, writes, "Commission may allow boxers to fight who are on administrative suspension, but most states follow that suspension."[16] Marc Ratner, then-executive director of the Nevada State Athletic Commission, said, "We honor all [types of] suspensions."[17]

Post-Fight Medical Evaluations

Most states (78 percent) require some sort of post-fight medical evaluation. This can range from an as needed basis if a fighter is knocked out or suffers extensive damage in the ring, to the formal post-fight check that takes place in Virginia. Many states leave the decision to require a post-fight physical to the ringside physician. Commissioner Wally Jernigan of Nebraska writes, "This is determined by the attending ringside physician on an individual basis, we do not tell the physician how to do his job."[18] The post-fight check in Virginia consists of a document that is signed by the ringside physician and indicates the following information:

- Facial cuts/contusions
- Stitches required
- Any possible fractures
- Any evidence of neurological symptoms/concerns
- Is boxer stable
- Was boxer sent to the hospital
- The following tests are required prior to participating in boxing on any level

- Any other medical comments
- It is recommended that the above individual receive one of the following: No suspension; 30 Day medical suspension; 60 Day medical suspension; 90 Day medical suspension; Indefinite medical suspension until one of the above medical tests has been conducted and fighter cleared.

Oklahoma and Pennsylvania have similar post-fight physical exam documents, as does Texas, though the Lone Star State's is more general in nature. The Texas post-bout physical form, which is to be signed by a physician, simply records the following information in a small spreadsheet: Name of Promoter, Date, City, Name of Contestant, Win/Lose/Draw, Round, Time, Reason, Suspension/Rest, Comments/Recommendations. In addition to the items listed above, Florida utilizes the Glasgow Coma Score, in which the physician is asked to score a boxer on the response of his eyes, the clarity of his speech, and motor skills.

Standards for Competitive Match-ups

Although each state that replied to the BHS Survey answered "Yes" to this question, mismatches are commonplace. California is the only state that appears to have a systematic method of determining competitive match-ups. Former acting executive officer Dean Louhis wrote on his survey response, "Every fight is approved or not approved based on a rating of the proposed fighters. We rate fighters A through E. Fighters cannot be more than two rating classifications apart."[19]

When a person obtains a license to box in Maryland, Pat Panella writes, "Along with the application, the boxer must have a manager, trainer or other qualified person who is to certify to the commission that the applicant is physically competent as a boxer and possesses the skills of a trained boxer."[20]

The Nebraska Athletic Commission "reviews and approves all matches based on talent, record and skill level, and can disallow any match that we feel is not competitive or could be harmful to one of the contestants due to being out classed, we consider the health and safety of the contestants to be the guiding factor. It's better to stop a contest one punch too soon, than one punch too late."[21]

Commissioner Steven Allred of West Virginia explains, "Quite often bouts are **not** allowed by the Commission for various reasons, such as: fighter has been stopped in too many consecutive bouts, poor match-up, experience level is not equal to proposed opponent, etc. West Virginia is looking for competitive and entertaining bouts — not mismatched events! P.S. We *DO NOT* sell fights here."[22]

In Wisconsin, they block matches "only if we have direct or documented information regarding a boxer's lack of skill. If from another state, this information must be specific. We may contact the state where info originates to obtain more details," writes Commissioner Kim Prine.[23]

The emphatic responses by these athletic commission representatives prompted me to examine the results of boxing in their respective states in 2004 to see how many first round knockouts occurred, as a rough indicator of the mismatches that took place in those states.[24] In West Virginia, 23 of 124 bouts (18.5 percent) ended in first round KOs or TKOs in 2004. In Wisconsin only one of 14 fights (7 percent) was over in the initial round. For Nebraska only 3 of 27 bouts (11 percent) finished in the first round. In Maryland, first round stoppages occurred in just eight of 91 bouts (8.7 percent).

A troubling example of the consequences that mismatches can bring about is the Brian Viloria–Ruben Contreras flyweight bout held in California on May 28, 2005. This match-up, between undefeated North American Boxing Federation champion Viloria and Contreras, his thirty-two year old opponent with a 9-17-3 record, ended in tragedy when Contreras quit during the sixth round and suffered a seizure.[25] He was subsequently taken to the hospital where he underwent brain surgery to remove pressure from bleeding on the brain and remained in a medically induced coma. Contreras survived, but remains disabled as a result. Considering Contreras' advanced age for a boxer and his dismal record (he had lost five of his previous ten fights), how he was allowed to fight a twenty-four year old rising contender is puzzling. Significantly, the California State Athletic Commission announced that it would investigate the fight. In an article published on ESPN.com, then-interim executive director Dean Lohuis said, "We're just going to watch the tape and determine if all procedures were followed, try to determine if there was anything we could have done differently. We're not saying anything was improper. It's just our procedure when this kind of incident occurs."[26] The response from the California Athletic Commission is eerily reminiscent of the reaction from Missouri after the death of Randie Carver. A veteran fight observer claimed that Contreras had been brought in as an opponent and didn't have adequate time to prepare for the bout, or that he wanted to quit earlier in the fight, but was instructed to keep fighting. Such claims have not been substantiated, but clearly the veteran Contreras participated in a bout that he could not win, and nearly suffered the ultimate consequence for doing so.

Presence of an Ambulance or Emergency Medical Personnel and Equipment

Ensuring that a physician, and an ambulance or emergency medical personnel and equipment are present during and after each boxing match is a federal law, as mandated by the Professional Boxing Safety Act of 1996.[27] In general, the promoter pays the expenses for the presence of these minimal, commonsensical safety measures. Wisconsin has a mechanism in place whereby the promoter pays the state, then the state pays the medical doctor to "avoid a direct link between the two where [money] is concerned."[28]

Several commissions take advantage of a loophole in the federal law that waives its requirements, such as having an ambulance on site, if an alternative requirement "provides equivalent protection of the health and safety of boxers."[29] Some state athletic commissions have interpreted this to mean that if a boxing venue is located close to a hospital or if they have a "dedicated line to the ambulance," as Roxanne Peterson from Wisconsin writes, then the promoter does not have to have an ambulance on site.[30] In Maryland, "The location of a boxing contest may not be more than 15 minutes by ambulance from a hospital providing neurosurgical evaluation and treatment facilities, with a neurosurgeon on call. The medical facility of this regulation shall be notified by the State Athletic Commission 24 hours before a contest of the time and location of the contest, with a request for a neurosurgeon to be on call."[31] Conversely, Idaho state athletic deputy commissioner Larry Beddes writes, "It is very important to have an emergency service that is legally able to transport an individual without having to obtain a dispatch order to do so."[32]

This loophole in the legislation may be dangerous, as the example of Randie Carver mentioned in the Preface clearly shows. Fifteen minutes may be a tremendous amount of time to receive medical attention if your brain is bleeding from blunt force to the head (a subdural hematoma), or any other serious injury. While it is unclear how many boxers' lives could have been saved had an ambulance been present on site, the families of the fallen gladiators would surely argue that it would have been worth the cost to have an ambulance at the venue ready to transport a boxer to the hospital.

Health Insurance

Pursuant to federal law, all states that replied to the BHS Survey indicate that health insurance is required for "each boxer to provide medical coverage for any injuries sustained in the match."[33] However, as Tim Lueckenhoff of Missouri notes, "Federal law does not require a minimum [amount]. Most commissions set that minimum."[34] Several commissions that replied to the BHS Survey indicated the amount of insurance they require; the range is astonishing. For example, in Idaho, the amount of health insurance required is $2,500, while in Ohio it ranges from $2,500 to $5,000. In South Carolina, the minimal amount is $10,000, and in Michigan it is a whopping $50,000. Some states, such as Wisconsin, also require life insurance for boxers, even though it is not expressly mandated by federal law. Then there is the issue of liability insurance, which as Connie Beckman of Montana writes, the promoter "provides liability insurance for contestants, officials, and public."[35]

The alarming cost of health care in the United States, particularly for those without health insurance (including many boxers), necessitates the provision of health care coverage for competitors in boxing events. Fortunately, all of the states responding to the BHS Survey indicate compliance with this humane requirement. However, without minimal standards, promoters will be able continue conducting business by providing only $2,500 of coverage in some states. Anyone who has had the unfortunate experience of visiting the emergency room and seen the amounts charged for services provided at such visits realizes that $2,500 is an extremely small amount of coverage. Every boxer that enters the ring can be certain to receive blows to the head. While the vast majority of boxing matches end without serious injury the potential is omnipresent, and a more reasonable amount of coverage should be required by law.

Boxing Licenses

All states require professional boxers to be licensed in order to practice the sport, as mandated by federal law. Since the passage of the Professional Boxing Safety Act of 1996, licensed boxers in the United States possess a federal ID card that allows them to apply for professional boxing licenses in any state. This mechanism also allows for state athletic commissions to check if there are any medical or administrative (disciplinary) suspensions for a boxer in any other state by accessing the Internet site for Fight Fax, Inc.

In order to be a professionally licensed boxer in most states one only needs to demonstrate physical aptitude and capability to box. In Michigan, there is "no criteria, except at least 18 years old," according to the BHS Survey response.[36] Boxers making their professional debuts are often required to provide their amateur records to commission officials, as noted in the BHS Survey responses from Illinois and Hawaii. As mentioned earlier, if a boxer is placed on medical suspension, other states are required to honor such suspensions, while disciplinary suspensions may be honored at the commissions' discretion. For example, in Nevada, the commission honors both medical and disciplinary suspensions from other states.

A few states replied that they impose more stringent requirements for boxers to be licensed in their state. For example, the state of Indiana conducts "background checks" on boxers. Likewise, in New Jersey the commissioner conducts a review of boxers' files, including "medicals, criminal history, child support, talent and record," according to counsel Nicholas Lembo.[37] In Idaho, the state athletic commission advises boxers that they may conduct random drug tests. Finally, the state of West Virginia appears to have the most rigorous non-physical requirements for boxers. Steven Allred writes that a boxer "shall be of good moral character, is physically fit and mentally sound, has not been convicted of a felony or misdemeanor involving moral turpitude and is a minimum of 18 years of age (professional boxer only)."[38]

Certification and Approval for Ring Officials

While licensing of prizefighters is a federal requirement, licensing of ring officials is an entirely different matter. According to the Association of Boxing Commissions Regulatory Guidelines passed on July 21, 2004, "All licensees and officials involved in the actual conduct of an event shall be under the direct control of the supervising commission assigned to regulate the event.... All positions recognized by the supervising commission are required to be licensed."[39] The ABC offers training seminars for officials, and many survey responses indicate that having experience and passing the ABC seminar is their major criteria for approval. Others indicate that those who wish to serve as officials in professional bouts must have experience working with the amateur ranks. A few states have specific requirements for the amount of years an official has been involved in boxing. For example, in Montana, a referee must have five years of experience judging athletic events; judges must have three years of experience, and cornermen must "submit 3 references who can attest to ring experience."[40] However, according to the BHS Survey, only 75 percent of commissions require certification and approval for ring officials.[41] The reasons for this vary, but one troubling reason is expense: Idaho indicates that it does not require certification because the "commission can't afford the expense of certification."[42]

Therefore states with little resources allocated to athletic commission budgets are at a distinct disadvantage that may pose safety risks to the participants. Referees and physicians in particular must possess experience and training in boxing in order to properly carry out their duties. A referee with such knowledge would be better positioned to assess a boxer after a knockdown or when the boxer has received too much punishment and the fight should be stopped. Likewise, a ringside physician would benefit from recognizing whether a cut or swelling to a boxer's face should merit a stoppage of the fight, or if the boxer's eyes or body language indicate that he should not be allowed to continue.

Significant Differences

All of the states indicate on the BHS Survey and the AAPRP data compilation that they conduct pre-fight medical evaluations, require standards for competitive match-ups, ensure that emergency medical personnel and equipment are present during and after each match, require health insurance for boxers during each match; and require registration (licenses) for boxers. While there are degrees of differences among the implementation of those activities, they pass the parchment test, that is, the requirements are present in some form. Furthermore, nearly all states indicate that they honor each other's suspensions, conduct post-fight medical evaluations, and require certification and approval for ring officials. Again, differences in implementation methods exist, but an overwhelming number of states carry out those regulations. The most significant variance among states occurs in three key areas of boxing regulations: neurological testing, HIV testing and drug testing.

Neurological Testing and HIV Testing

Neurological testing is one of the three most contentious issues that state athletic commissions must deal with. *Only thirteen* of forty (32.5 percent)

2 • Data Analysis

In many states, fighters who are in their mid–30s or older are required to undergo neurological tests, such as Larry Holmes (left), who was 42 years old when he challenged Evander Holyfield for his heavyweight title in 1992.

states that replied to the survey or AAPRP State Medical Requirements listing require such tests in 2004. Of the eleven states that require neurological tests, there is disparity in the type, timing and administration of such tests. Several states, such as Pennsylvania, do not routinely require neurological exams, but may request them before allowing a boxer to fight in the state if, for example, a boxer has several consecutive losses or if a physician recommends one.

A small percentage of states require annual neurological exams. This is the case in California, and the boxer pays for the test. In Hawaii, a boxer also pays the costs of such an exam, but it is required only of boxers that are over 38 years of age, those who are knocked out and want to fight in that state again, or those who have "received a severe beating to the head."[43] Likewise, in Oregon, only boxers over the age of 36 are required to undergo such tests. In New Jersey, neurological exams are required, however, the promoter, boxer or manager pays for the test. The promoter pays in Oklahoma. The New York

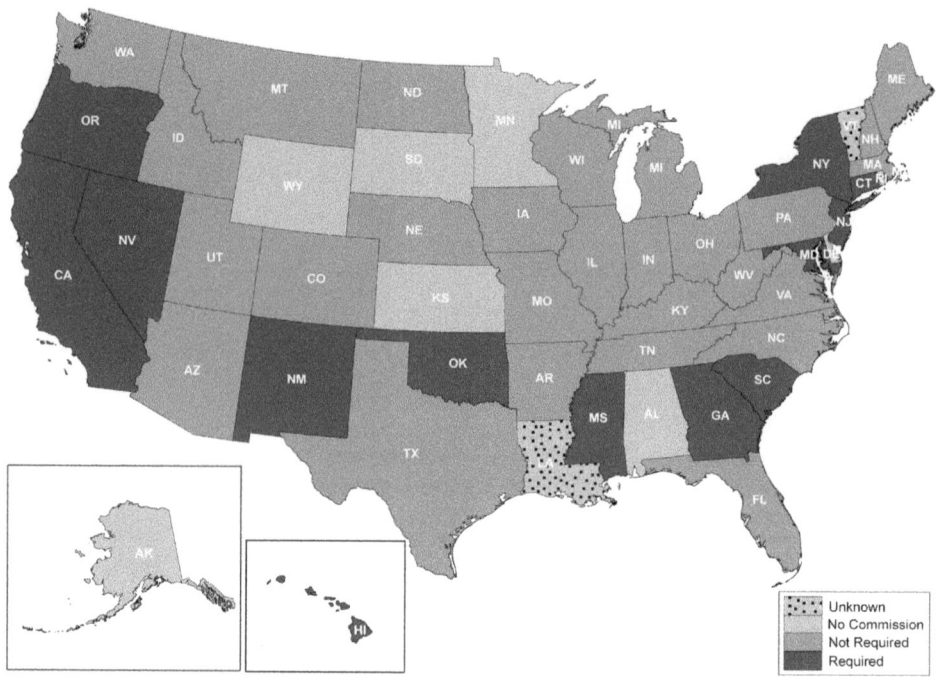

Figure 3: Neurological testing in 2004 (BHS Survey [2005] and AAPRP Medical Requirements Database [2005]).

State Athletic Commission requires boxers to pay $75 for an annual neurological exam, and during the pre-bout physical a neurological test is performed at no cost.

Figure 3 is a geographical indicator of the state athletic commissions that require neurological tests of boxers who wish to fight there for 2004. Again, *only thirteen* of forty states (32.5 percent) indicated that they routinely require such tests. Significantly, three major boxing states, Texas, Florida, and Pennsylvania, did not carry out such exams on a regular basis, placing a great number of boxers in potential jeopardy. Three states did not reply to either measure, and seven states do not possess boxing commissions. In the event there was a conflicting response from a commission, the reply indicated on the BHS Survey was used.

In terms of HIV testing, as of 2004 *only twenty-two* of forty (55 percent) respondent states required testing for the deadly disease.[44] The response of state athletic commission officials on this issue punctuates the inconsistency

2 • Data Analysis

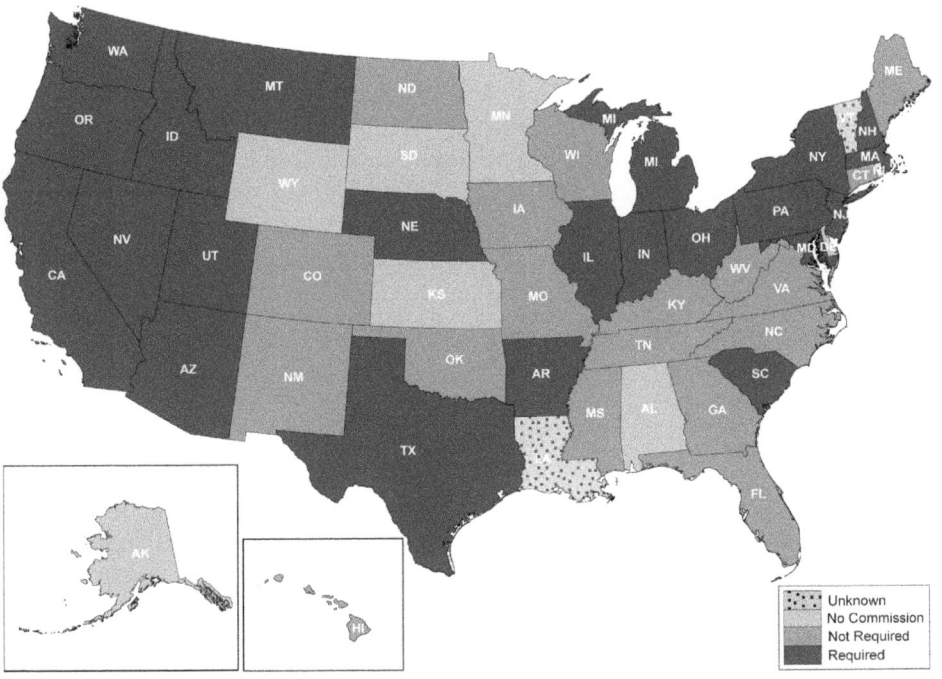

Figure 4: HIV testing in 2004 (BHS Survey [2005] and AAPRP Medical Requirements Database [2005]).

of health and safety regulations for boxers in the United States. While most states replied to this issue with "yes" or "no" answers, Illinois replied "Big Yes," and Colorado and Wisconsin indicated that they may require HIV tests on a "case by case basis," however, the respondents did not specify what would prompt them to ask someone to undertake an HIV test. In New Jersey, boxers must submit HIV test results and complete a "high-risk questionnaire."[45] Due to the incubation period of the disease, many states have set specific timeframes for the submission of a negative HIV test. This ranges from within 30 days of licensure or renewal in Maryland and Montana to within 180 days in Utah and once per year in Michigan. Figure 4 shows the disparity among the states on this critical issue in 2004.

An event that highlights the critical nature of HIV testing for boxers is the case of the scheduled junior featherweight bout between Leocadio Manon and Abner Mares referred to in Chapter 1. Manon, a 28-year-old boxer from the Dominican Republic, was scheduled to fight on an April 9, 2005, pay-per-view boxing event in Texas. Since Manon had fought mostly in his native country, where HIV testing is not required to license boxers, he would have to undergo the pre-fight physical in Texas in order to receive his license to box there. Manon tested positive for HIV the day before the scheduled bout, and a second test indicated the same result, thus resulting in his medical suspension.[46] Since Manon's scheduled bout with Mares was not for a world championship, his HIV-positive status would not have been detected in states that do not conduct such tests, and the bout would have taken place as scheduled.

Drug Testing

The issue of drug testing in sports, particularly for steroid use, has made recent headlines. As with the other items, an examination of open-ended answers on the BHS Survey is particularly revealing, since most of the states that require drug testing test only for certain drugs and do so on an infrequent basis.

The rules of the organizations that oversee boxing at the global level forbid drug use in championship bouts. For example, the rules of the World Boxing Association state, "The administration or use of drugs or stimulants, or physiologic substances in order to increase the performance of the boxer in an artificial and unfair manner, before or during the bout is forbidden. Any fighter who violates this rule shall be disqualified. Especially forbidden drugs are the stimulants, narcotics and their derivatives, psychotropic drugs, anabolic steroids, corticosteroids, diuretics, probenecid, and, furthermore, whatever other substance determined by the Medical Advising Committee of the World Boxing Association, which shall issue a list of forbidden substances."[47] Thus, championship bouts that take place in any U.S. state would require participants to undergo drug testing. However, the non-championship fights that make up the vast majority of boxing events would implement such testing procedures only if mandated by the state.

In the United States, *only twenty-six* of forty (65 percent) states that responded to the BHS Survey or the AAPRP Requirement Listing indicated that they fully or randomly test for drugs in non-championship bouts in 2004.[48] Several states conduct drug tests only on a "discretionary basis" if the commission suspects the use of drugs by a participant. Only one state, New Jersey, expressly indicated that it tests *all* boxers for "performance enhancers,

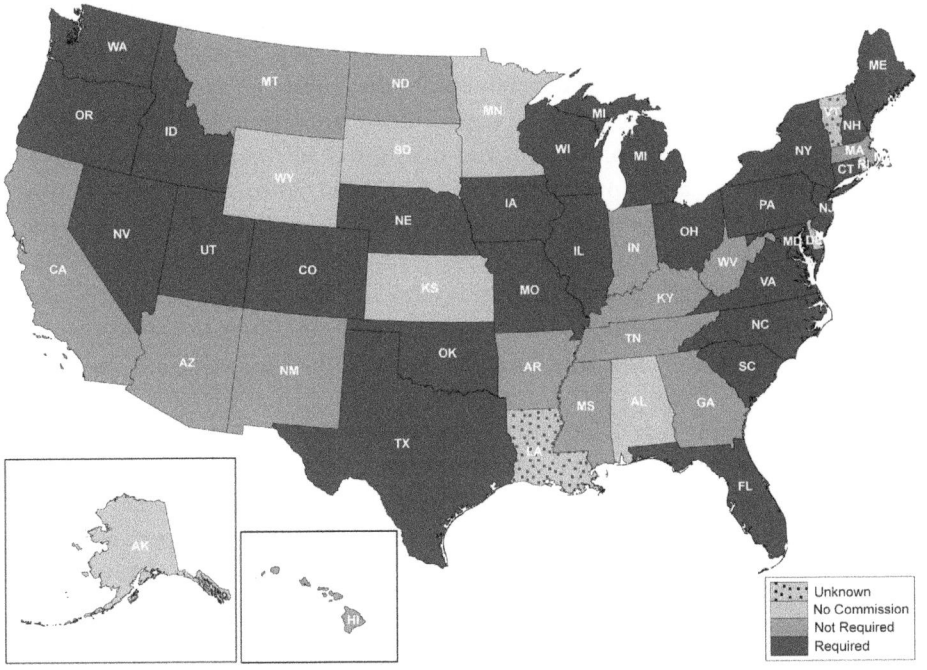

Figure 5: Drug testing in 2004 (BHS Survey (2005) and AAPRP Medical Requirements Database (2005)).

illegal drugs and painkillers."[49] Figure 5 indicates states that carried out full, random or discretionary drug testing in non-championship bouts in 2004.[50]

As Figure 5 indicates, states vary widely in their drug testing requirements. They also vary in the types of drugs that they test for. According to Dr. Margaret Goodman, former chairwoman of the Nevada State Athletic Commission Medical Advisory Board, the commission tests for "over 125 items including all anabolic steroids and masking agents." The survey response from Colorado indicates that drug tests screen for "cocaine, amphetamines, methamphetamines, Phencyclidine, Opiates, and Cannabinoids."[51] Thus, some states test for performance enhancing drugs, while others test for illicit drugs, or both. Another issue is whether the drug test is conducted before the bout or after.

Commissioner Pat Panella explains that it may be difficult for boxers to produce urine immediately after a bout due to dehydration suffered in the ring.[52] Thus, in Maryland, all boxers are required to provide urine samples prior to entering the ring to compete. Of course, pre-fight drug tests would not be able to account for any illegal substance given to a boxer during the course of a bout to enhance his performance. A long-standing rule in boxing is that a fighter must not receive any other substance than water during a boxing match, though Nevada began allowing electrolyte drinks in 2007. One state that has grappled with this question is Michigan, where pre-fight drug tests were carried out until February 19, 2005, when state legislation was passed and came into effect to make drug tests post-fight. Bradley Wright, then-chairman of the Michigan State Athletic Commission, said that the reason for this change is that "the preference of the boxing community is to make these tests post-fight and we wanted to get in line with the rest of the states. Boxers have one hour after the bout to produce urine for the drug test."[53]

An example that demonstrates the need for universal drug testing is the result of the April 30, 2005, World Boxing Association heavyweight championship fight between titleholder John Ruiz and challenger James Toney. Although the 12-round decision went to Toney, the urinalysis taken after the fight indicates that he tested positive for the steroid nandrolone. As a result of the positive test, the bout was officially ruled a no-contest and the title belt was given back to Ruiz. Additionally, Toney was fined $10,000 by the New York State Athletic Commission and suspended for 90 days.[54] If this bout had not been for a championship, or if it had been held in a state that does not carry out random or discretionary testing, the steroid would not have been detected, and the result would have stood.

Statistical Data Analysis

A statistical analysis of the data on health and safety boxing regulations in the United States for 2004 provides a revealing look at the factors that affected their implementation. This section is written with the intent of explaining the complex statistical analysis in a manner that is accessible to most readers. The data for the quantitative section of this study is primarily drawn from the BHS Survey. Again, the number of responses for the BHS Survey was thirty-two. However, in an effort to provide a more complete picture of boxing regulations in the United States, the data from the BHS Survey is augmented by data reported by eight additional state athletic commissions to the American Association of Professional Ringside Physicians (AAPRP), culminating in a total of 40 cases. Seven states that do not possess an athletic commission were removed from the analysis, as were three states that possess athletic commissions that did not respond to either the BHS Survey or the AAPRP State Medical Requirements listing. Thus, the number of cases (N) for this study includes all the possible cases for which reliable data exists: N=40. The lack of response from Louisiana, Vermont and Rhode Island is troubling, as they each have paid government appointees on their state athletic commissions. Coincidentally, in 2005, the head of the Louisiana State Boxing and Wrestling Commission, Anthony "Buddy" Embanato, was under investigation from the state inspector general for improper payments, shoddy record-keeping, intimidation of a promoter, and other possible violations of state law.[55] The Louisiana inspector general's report, approved by Governor Kathleen Babineaux Blanco in June 2007, found that the Louisiana commission committed fifteen violations, including those mentioned.[56] Yet as of early 2008, Embanato is still the chairman of the commission.

Dependent Variable

In statistical research, a dependent variable is simply the unit that the researcher would like to explain by analyzing it with respect to selected independent variables that may have an impact upon it. Since all 40 states indicate on the BHS Survey and the AAPRP State Medical Requirements listing that they carry out a majority of the health and safety regulations on the BHS Survey, the Boxing Health and Safety Index (BHSI) was created to capture the variance among states in the three areas of boxing regulations on which they most differ:

- neurological testing;
- HIV testing; and
- drug testing.

Therefore, in this study the dependent variable is the BHSI.

The states that reported their requirements on the three elements noted above to the BHS Survey or AAPRP were awarded one point for each regulation marked "required" and 0 points for regulations that are not required. Thus, scores for each state on the Boxing Health and Safety Index range from 0 to 3 (0 indicates that the state does not require HIV testing, neurological testing or drug testing; 1 indicates one of the three tests are required, and so on.) Although the tests are completely unrelated and may have varying degrees of impact on the health and safety of boxers, they are given equal weight in the BHSI.

Answers to the HIV testing question that were not marked "yes" or "no" on the BHS Survey, but contained an explanation such as "at random" or "at the discretion of the commission" were coded as "yes," because it indicated that a mechanism was in place to conduct such testing. Likewise, in terms of drug testing, some states that conduct random or discretionary testing indicated "no" on the BHS Survey responses. Such replies were recoded as "yes" to capture all states that have mechanisms in place to conduct drug tests if necessary. On the other hand, California indicated "yes" on this question, but it conducts drug tests only in championship bouts. In 2004, the state did not indicate random or discretionary tests in non-title bouts, thus the reply was recoded as "no," because participants in all championship bouts are required to be screened for drugs by the sanctioning world body, regardless of the state in which the match is held. Neurological exams were coded as "yes" only if

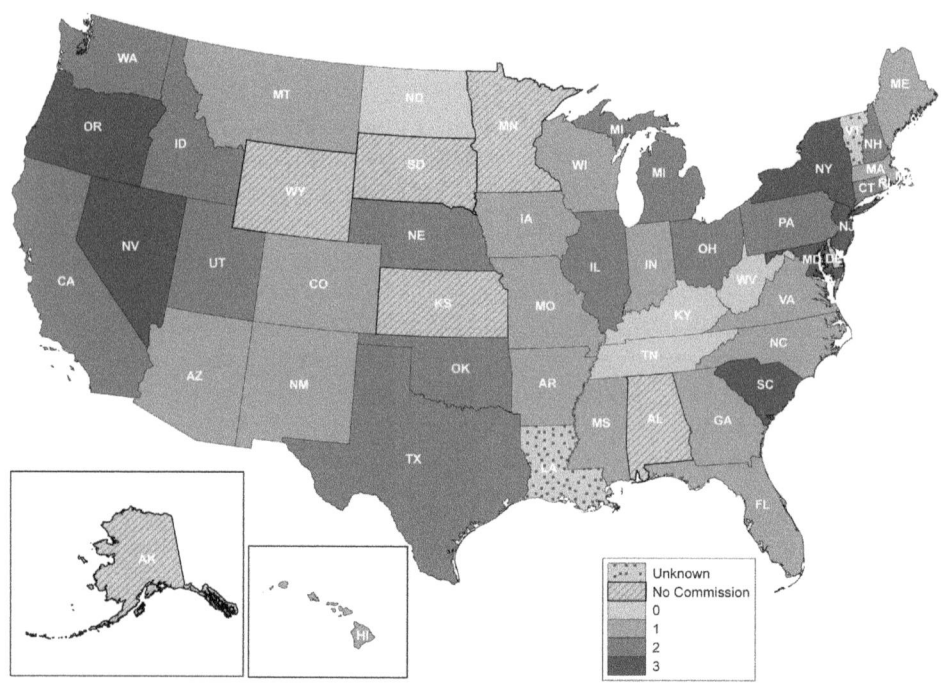

Figure 6: Boxing health and safety index (2004) (BHS Survey [2005] and AAPRP Medical Requirements Database [2005]).

they were systematically applied. Figure 6 indicates the state scores on the BHSI.

The data shown in Figure 6 is indicative of the disparity of state classifications according to the BHSI. Amazingly, there is a cluster of Eastern and upper Midwestern states (4 of 40 or 10 percent) that did not require any of the health and safety tests included in the index in 2004. These states held a combined 44 boxing events that year. Most states (17 of 40 or 42.5 percent) conduct only one of the three tests, while a few others (13 of 40, or 32.5 percent) are somewhat more progressive and have two of the three key tests. Only a handful of states (6 of 40 or 15 percent) earned the highest score on this index: Maryland, Nevada, New Jersey, New York, Oregon and South Carolina. Table 1 is a summary of state scores on the Boxing Health and Safety Index (the dependent variable in this study).

Table 1: Boxing Health and Safety Index Scores (2004)

State	BHSI Score 2004	State	BHSI Score 2004
Alabama	No Commission	Nevada	3
Alaska	No Commission	New Hampshire	2
Arizona	1	New Jersey	3
Arkansas	1	New Mexico	1
California	2	New York	3
Colorado	1	North Carolina	1
Connecticut	2	North Dakota	0
Deleware	No Commission	Ohio	2
Florida	1	Oklahoma	2
Georgia	1	Oregon	3
Hawaii	1	Pennsylvania	2
Idaho	2	Rhode Island	Did Not Respond to BHS Survey or AAPRP
Illinois	2		
Indiana	1	South Carolina	3
Iowa	1	South Dakota	No Commission
Kansas	No Commission	Tennessee	0
Kentucky	0	Texas	2
Louisiana	Did Not Respond to BHS Survey or AAPRP	Utah	2
		Vermont	Did Not Respond to BHS Survey or AAPRP
Maine	1		
Maryland	3	Virginia	1
Massachusetts	1	Washington	2
Michigan	2	West Virginia	0
Minnesota	No Commission	Wisconsin	1
Mississippi	1	Wyoming	No Commission
Missouri	1		
Montana	1	*Sources: BHS Survey (2005) and AAPRP Medical Requirements Database (2005)*	
Nebraska	2		

Independent Variables

The theoretical state politics literature described in the Introduction directly informs my selection of independent variables. In statistical research, independent variables are measures that affect the phenomenon captured in the dependent variable. In other words, using political theories as my guide, I have selected a set of measures (independent variables) that I believe will explain why states differ in their level of boxing health and safety regulations (the dependent variable). Political scientist Virginia Gray's work is perhaps the most influential for this study, as her research indicates that state wealth and political culture are two of the most important variables that account for the differences in regulations among states.[57] Likewise, political scientists Ringquist and Garand also find that state wealth, as an internal political factor, affects policy.[58] However, they also find that policy specific factors such as "policy-relevant knowledge," a "focusing event," or "issue redefinitions" are also important agents of regulatory change.[59] Political scientist John Kingdon's theory that focusing events provide the necessary push for policy makers to enact or enhance legislation is especially pertinent here. In the case of boxing, the dramatic aspects of a boxing related death can serve as a focusing event that may cause state politicians to re-evaluate the health and safety aspects of boxing regulations. Professors like Chalip and Johnson suggest that gambling plays an important role in sports policies in the United States and also explain how state athletic commissions have varied success in their implementation of regulations.[60]

The state politics literature therefore leads me to hypothesize that the following set of independent variables will predict the score on the BHSI: the number of boxing-related deaths in a state, historically; state wealth, as measured by median income; the presence of certain types of legal gambling; and the state political culture according to the Elazar Scale of Political Culture.

Boxing-Related Deaths

The February 2004 issue of the *Journal of Combative Sport* includes an article that contains the most comprehensive database available on boxing-related deaths. Joseph R. Svinth's article entitled "Death Under the Spotlight: The Manuel Velazquez Boxing Fatality Collection" includes data on the names, dates, match results, locations and sources of boxing-related deaths

2 • Data Analysis

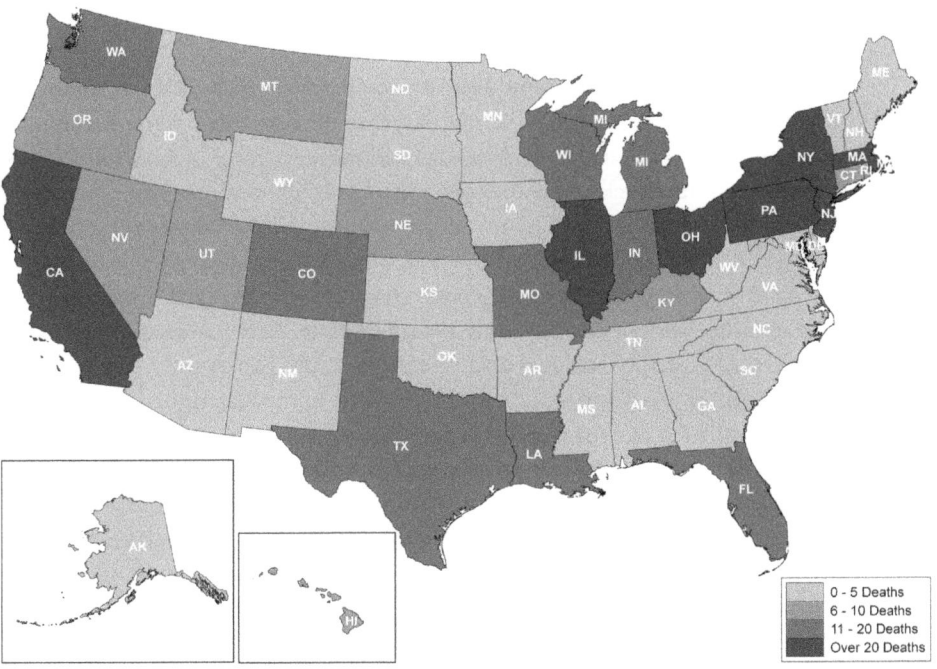

Figure 7: Boxing related deaths in the United States (1834–2004) (*Journal of Combative Sport* [February 2004]).

from throughout the world since 1741. The first boxing death occurred in London when George Stevenson died at the hands of Jack Broughton, thus prompting the establishment of Broughton's Rules (see Chapter 1). The first boxer to die in the ring on U.S. soil was Reuben (or Andy) Marsden in 1834.[61] Consistent with Kingdon's findings along with Ringquist and Garand's work, boxing-related deaths may serve as focusing events that can trigger policy change. It is hypothesized that states that have borne witness to such dramatic tragedies as ring deaths will be more likely to implement more stringent boxing regulations that those that do not. The measurement of this independent variable, documenting the number of boxing-related deaths in U.S. history depicted in Figure 7.

As Figure 7 indicates, most states have experienced few boxing-related deaths. However, states that have historically hosted an abundance of boxing events, such as California and New York, have likewise experienced more ring tragedies.

Gambling

Casinos and boxing have long been associated with each other. A majority of the most significant fights in the past few decades have taken place in the gambling mecca of Las Vegas, Nevada, and more recently in Atlantic City, New Jersey. Scholars such as Chalip and Johnson single out gambling as producing an effect on sports policy in the United States. The National Conference of State Legislatures compiles a list of gambling activities by state. Gambling is separated into five categories: charitable bingo, card rooms, casinos and gaming, Indian casinos, and sports betting. Each category of gambling is further classified as legal and operative; table games only (no slots); commercial bingo, keno, or pull tabs only; and compacts signed for non-casino gaming, such as pari-mutuel wagering and lotteries, however, casino games may be operating.[62] For purposes of this study, the measurement of this variable is coded on a scale from 0 to 3. Each state was appropriated 1 point for each type of gambling activity that was legal and operative. Charitable bingo and card rooms were not considered for this scale, as they are not relevant to boxing at all. It is theorized that states that allow casinos and gaming, casinos on Indian reservations, and sports betting would be more likely to host fights and therefore more likely to have measures in place to protect the boxers. Table 2 indicates the presence of specific gambling activities in each state in 2004 according to the National Conference of State Legislatures. This table shows that only the state of Nevada possesses all three types of gambling in a legal and operative standing. Furthermore, there are far more states with casinos on Native American territory than state territory. Finally, only four of the fifty states allow legal sports betting.

Table 2: Legal and Operative Gambling Activity in the United States (2004)

State	Casinos and Gaming	Indian Casinos	Sports Betting
Alabama			
Alaska			
Arizona		1	
Arkansas			
California		1	
Colorado	1	1	
Connecticut		1	
Delaware			

2 • Data Analysis

State	Casinos and Gaming	Indian Casinos	Sports Betting
Florida		1	
Georgia			
Hawaii			
Idaho			
Illinois	1		
Indiana	1		
Iowa	1	1	
Kansas		1	
Kentucky			
Louisiana	1	1	
Maine			
Maryland			
Massachusetts			
Michigan	1	1	
Minnesota		1	
Mississippi	1	1	
Missouri	1		
Montana		1	1
Nebraska			
Nevada	1	1	1
New Hampshire			
New Jersey	1		
New Mexico		1	
New York		1	
North Carolina		1	
North Dakota		1	1
Ohio			
Oklahoma			
Oregon		1	1
Pennsylvania			
Rhode Island			
South Carolina			
South Dakota	1	1	
Tennessee			
Texas			
Utah			
Vermont			
Virginia			
Washington			
West Virginia			
Wisconsin		1	
Wyoming			

Source: National Conference of State Legislatures, 2004.

State Wealth

As the research that political scientists have conducted on state politics overwhelmingly indicates, state wealth is an important factor that accounts

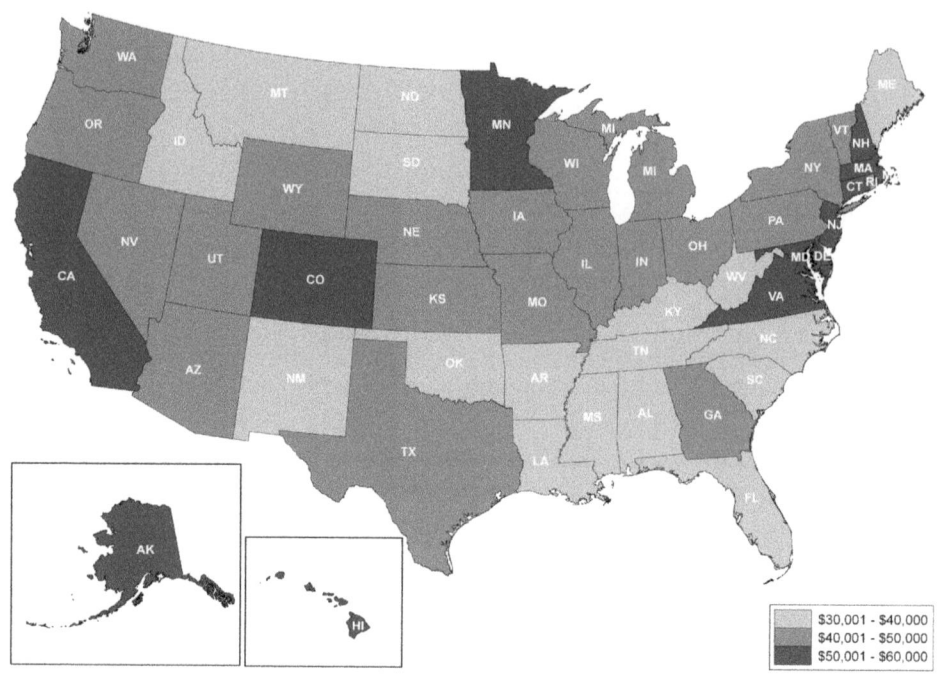

Figure 8: State wealth (U.S. Median Household Income [2003]) (U.S. Census 2003 American Community Survey Summary).

for the difference in policy regulations in the United States. Notable academics including Gray, Ringquist and Garand, and Houlihan all point to state wealth as an important variable. The median income in a given state as reported in the *U.S. Census 2003 American Community Survey Summary* is used as a proxy in this study to measure state wealth. This measure was selected to control for the disparities in state population or geographic size. Since states with higher median incomes tend to have more wealth overall, the informed hypothesis is that such states would be more likely to appropriate funding to state athletic commissions to enact measures that will help protect the health and safety of boxers. The figure below displays the disparity in median household income in 2003.

In 2003, most states tended to have a median household income between $35,000 and $45,000. Only three northeastern states had very high median household incomes (above $55,000).

Political Culture

Political scientist Daniel Elazar developed a scale in 1984 that categorizes states on the basis of their political culture. Political culture essentially reflects the values people share with respect to the government. For Elazar, there are three subcultures in the United States: *individualist* (states whose inhabitants favor a government that would not inhibit their material interests); *moralist* (states whose inhabitants favor a government that provides for the collective good); and *traditionalist* (states whose inhabitants favor an elitist style of government that preserves economic and social hierarchies).[63] Elazar then classifies each U.S. state according to these subcultures. In the current research, states classified as moralists are coded as "1"; individualists "2"; and traditionalists "3." According to Gray, political culture may account for differences in state regulations. The inclusion of this variable is to determine if there are any significant differences between the states' political culture and

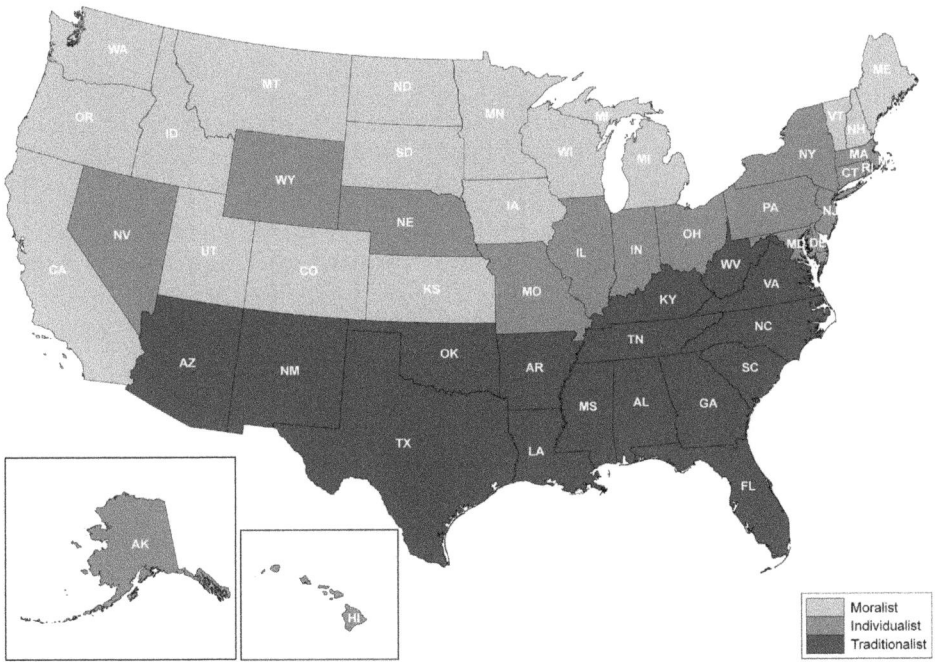

Figure 9: Political Culture in the United States (Elazar Scale) (Gray, Virginia and Russell Hanson). *Politics in the American States: A Comparative Analysis.*

the level of their boxing regulations. It is hypothesized that states that tend to be individualist or moralist would be most likely to conduct tests that help protect the health and safety of boxers. Boxing is an individual sport, in which participants can depend only upon themselves to make the difference between victory and defeat. This individualist mentality coincides with the political culture of individualist states. Also, since the moralist states provide for the collective good, of which health and safety can be considered a part, it is also predicted that states with that type of political culture would be more likely to score higher on the BHSI. Figure 9 shows the state classifications on Elazar's Index of Political Culture.

Figure 9 clearly indicates that Southern states are traditionalist, while upper Midwestern and Western states tend to be moralist. According to the Elazar Index, several northeastern states and a few other states such as Nevada possess an individualist political culture.

Table 3 shows a compilation of all of the variables analyzed in this study. States without athletic commissions in 2004 or those that did not reply to the BHS Survey or AAPRP Medical Data Compilation are excluded. The dependent variable (BHSI) reflects how many of the key health and safety tests (neurological, HIV, drugs) each state requires. The scale is 0 to 3, with each required test having a value of 1. The scores for each type of health and safety test by state in 2004 are also listed. The four independent variables for each state include historical experience with boxing-related deaths (the number of boxers who have died between 1834 and 2004); the presence of certain types of gambling (casinos, Indian casinos and sports betting) on a 0 to 3 scale, with each present type having a value of 1, state wealth (median household income in 2003); and political culture on a 1 to 3 scale (moralist=1, individualist=2, traditionalist=3).

Statistical Results

A series of statistical tests was conducted to analyze the data obtained by the BHS Survey and the AAPRP data compilation of State Medical Requirements. First, a common statistical test (t-test) was utilized to observe the differences among states that require or do not require the three key health and safety practices that compose the BHSI: neurological testing, HIV testing, and drug testing. A t-test is used to determine if the averages of two groups are statistically different from each other. Higher t scores indicate greater confidence that there is a significant difference between the means. In this study, the first group is formed by states that *require* a selected health and safety test, such as neurological tests. The second group is formed by those states that *do not require* neurological tests. That information is juxtaposed with the average measure (mean) of an independent variable (such as the average number of boxing-related deaths) for both groups of states to determine if there is a statistically significant difference between the two groups. The process of analysis was repeated for the other two health and safety tests germane to this study (HIV testing and drug testing), and the other independent variables (state wealth, gambling and political culture).

In addition to t-tests, another statistical test, Chi Square, was carried out to explain the differences in the percentages of categorical variables. Variables that are categorical cannot be ordered from high to low, or low to high (such as a state's designation on Elazar's political culture scale). While these tests were carried out for all of variables described previously in this chapter, the only data reported here are those tests that produced statistically significant results.

A third statistical test that was carried out in this study is a multiple regression analysis.[64] This is another common statistical test that is used to determine an equation that best represents the relationship between variables. In this study, the multiple regression analysis is used to examine the combined effects of (independent variables) boxing-related deaths, state wealth, the presence of specific types of gambling, and political culture on (the dependent variable) a state's score on the boxing health and safety index (BHSI).

The t-test statistical analysis is particularly revealing for states that carry out HIV tests as shown in Table 4. Eighteen of the states for which reliable data is available did not require HIV tests from boxers who wished to fight in their state in 2004. States that do not require HIV testing have experienced an average of only 5.61 boxing-related deaths. In contrast, the twenty-two states that require HIV test results from boxers have experienced an average of 19.04 deaths in the ring throughout history. In this instance, it is clear that states that have experienced more boxing-related deaths are those that tended to carry out HIV tests in 2004, as Table 4 indicates. Furthermore, the difference in the average number of boxing-related deaths in states that require or do not require HIV tests is significant at the .01 level. This means that we can be 99 percent certain, statistically speaking, that the relationship between a state's historical experience with boxing related deaths and the implementation of HIV testing is not random.

Table 3: Data Coding (2004)

State	Commission	Boxing Events	Neurological	HIV	Drug	BHSI	Boxing Deaths	State Wealth	Political Culture	Gambling
Alabama	No	4	N	N	N	N	4	35158	3	0
Alaska	No	0	N	N	N	N	0	52499	2	0
Arizona	Yes	20	0	1	0	1	5	40762	3	1
Arkansas	Yes	6	0	1	0	1	4	34246	3	0
California	Yes	126	1	1	0	2	71	50220	1	1
Colorado	Yes	24	0	0	1	1	11	50538	1	2
Connecticut	Yes	16	1	0	1	2	9	56803	2	1
Delaware	No	3	N	N	N	N	0	50583	2	0
Florida	Yes	48	0	0	1	1	12	39871	3	1
Georgia	Yes	18	1	0	0	1	1	42742	3	0
Hawaii	Yes	0	1	0	0	1	6	50787	2	0
Idaho	Yes	5	0	1	1	2	1	39492	1	0
Illinois	Yes	24	0	1	1	2	25	47977	2	1
Indiana	Yes	24	0	1	0	1	13	42067	2	1
Iowa	Yes	12	0	0	1	1	4	40526	1	2
Kansas	No	5	N	N	N	N	3	41075	1	1
Kentucky	Yes	4	0	0	0	0	8	34368	3	0
Louisiana	Yes	13	U	U	U	U	15	34141	3	2
Maine	Yes	5	0	0	1	1	5	39838	1	0
Maryland	Yes	17	1	1	1	3	5	57218	2	0
Massachusetts	Yes	13	0	1	0	1	26	53610	2	0
Michigan	Yes	27	0	1	1	2	18	44407	1	2
Minnesota	No	15	N	N	N	N	6	50100	1	1
Mississippi	Yes	13	1	0	0	1	1	32466	3	2
Missouri	Yes	40	0	0	1	1	11	40725	2	1

State	Commission								
Montana	Yes	1	0	1	0	1	35399	9	1	2
Nebraska	Yes	4	0	1	1	2	41406	6	2	0
Nevada	Yes	50	1	1	1	3	45395	8	2	3
New Hampshire	Yes	2	0	1	1	2	53910	0	1	0
New Jersey	Yes	21	1	1	1	3	58588	25	2	1
New Mexico	Yes	16	1	0	0	1	34805	5	3	1
New York	Yes	26	1	1	1	3	46195	73	2	1
North Carolina	Yes	16	0	0	0	1	38234	2	3	1
North Dakota	Yes	2	0	0	0	0	37554	3	1	2
Ohio	Yes	25	0	1	1	2	41350	37	2	0
Oklahoma	Yes	15	1	0	1	2	35129	1	3	0
Oregon	Yes	4	1	1	1	3	40319	7	1	2
Pennsylvania	Yes	52	0	1	1	2	41478	49	2	0
Rhode Island	Yes	1	U	U	U	U	48854	7	2	0
South Carolina	Yes	13	1	1	1	3	38467	4	3	0
South Dakota	No	1	N	N	N	N	38415	0	1	2
Tennessee	Yes	15	0	0	0	0	38247	5	3	0
Texas	Yes	60	0	1	1	2	40674	14	3	0
Utah	Yes	7	0	1	1	2	46873	7	1	0
Vermont	Yes	0	U	U	U	U	43697	1	1	0
Virginia	Yes	4	0	0	1	1	50805	1	3	0
Washington	Yes	19	0	1	1	2	46868	12	1	0
West Virginia	Yes	23	0	0	0	0	31008	5	3	0
Wisconsin	Yes	3	0	0	1	1	44084	11	1	1
Wyoming	No	0	N	N	N	N	43332	1	2	0

Sources: BHS Survey (2005); AAPRP Medical Requirements Database (2005); Journal of Combative Sport (February 2004); National Conference of State Legislatures, 2004; U.S. Census 2003 American Community Survey Summary; Virginia Gray and Russell L. Hanson, Politics in the American States: A Comparative Analysis. (N=No Commission, U=Unknown/No Response. For Neurological, HIV and Drug testing: 0=Not Required, 1=Required).

Table 4: HIV Testing and Boxing Related Deaths

HIV Testing	Boxing-Related Deaths	
	Mean	Frequency
Not Required	5.61	18
Required	19.04	22
Total	13	N=40
P ≤ 0.01	t = 2.66	

States that have higher levels of state wealth as measured by the median household income, are also more likely to conduct HIV testing, as shown in Table 5. There is a clear difference in the average of the median household income in states that do not require HIV tests from those that do. The statistics indicate that we can be 92 percent certain that there is a relationship between state wealth and the implementation of HIV testing for boxers. Those states with higher levels of wealth tend to implement HIV testing more than those with lower levels of wealth.

Table 5: HIV Testing and State Wealth

HIV Testing	State Wealth (Median Household Income, 2003)	
	Mean	Frequency
Not Required	41029.44	18
Required	44860.04	22
Total	43136.27	N=40
P ≤ 0.08	t = 1.75	

The political culture of a state, as determined by the Elazar Scale, significantly shows that states that are classified as individualist and moralist tend to conduct HIV testing of boxers whereas states classified as traditionalist do not, as indicated in Table 6. Of the twenty-two states that conduct HIV tests, eighteen are classified as moralist or individualist. Since political culture is a categorical variable, a Chi Square statistical test was conducted. The test indicates that we can be 91 percent confident that there is a relationship between the type of political culture a state has and whether it requires HIV tests for boxers.

Table 6: HIV Testing and Political Culture

HIV Testing	Political Culture			Total
	Moralist	Individualist	Traditionalist	
Not Required	5 (38.5%)	3 (23.1%)	10 (71.4%)	18 (45%)
Required	8 (61.5%)	10 (76.9%)	4 (28.6%)	22 (55%)
Total	13	13	14	N=40
P ≤ 0.09		chi²=6.7		

Of all the independent variables that may affect whether a state carries out drug testing of boxers, state wealth is the only one that emerges at a significant level as indicated in Table 7. The dynamic illustrated here is similar to what was found with HIV testing: the higher the median income, the more likely a state is to conduct drug testing. The average median income in states that conduct drug tests was $44,811, which is higher than the average in states that do not carry out such tests. This test indicates that we can be at least 95 percent certain that the relationship between drug testing and state wealth is not random.

Table 7: Drug Testing and State Wealth

Drug Testing	State Wealth (Median Household Income, 2003)	
	Mean	Frequency
Not Required	40343.60	14
Required	44811.88	26
Total	43136.27	N=40
P ≤ 0.05	t = 2.02	

A multiple regression analysis was carried out to determine the significance of all selected independent variables on the BHSI, which again is comprised of the combined state score of 0 to 3 on the basis of how many key health and safety tests are carried out in a given state. The results of the multiple regression analysis appear in Table 8. B, or Beta, is the estimated coefficient, or contribution of the independent variable to the dependent variable. SE, or Standard Error, is the level of certainty that the estimated coefficient is correct. Higher levels of SE indicate less certainty; lower levels indicate higher certainty. T is the Beta divided by the Standard Error. Larger T scores indicate more confidence in the data; lower T scores indicate lower confidence. R^2 is the percentage of variance on the dependent variable that is explained by the model. P, or probability, is the level of confidence we can attach to the estimated contribution of the independent variable to the dependent variable.

Table 8: Multiple Regression Analysis

BHSI	B	SE	T
Boxing-Related Deaths	.0128149	.0075529	1.65*
State Wealth	.0000498	.0000201	2.48**
Gambling	.1140916	.1604032	.71
Political Culture	.032674	.1753808	.19
Constant	-.9649545	1.083669	-.89

$R^2=.27$
N=40
*$P \leq 0.10$
**$P \leq 0.01$

The multiple regression analysis reveals that the two independent variables that are most likely to predict a state's score on the BHSI are the number of boxing-related deaths experienced in a state in addition to the level of state wealth as measured by the median income. These two variables, which are consistent with the state politics literature, are highly significant even while controlling for the effects of gambling and political culture. The results suggest that when considering the independent variables (boxing-related deaths, state wealth, gambling and political culture) together, boxing-related deaths and state wealth rise above the other variables in importance. In short, the multiple regression analysis reveals that experience with boxing-related deaths and state wealth are highly accurate predictors of the levels of boxing health and safety tests.

While frequency distributions (the number of observations that appear in a given sample) and commonly held beliefs suggest that issues such as a state's experience with boxing-related deaths or the level of state wealth are likely to dictate whether a state has higher standards of health and safety regulations for boxers, the advantage of the foregoing multiple regression analysis is that it conclusively proves that such beliefs are correct. However, the multiple regression analysis did not reveal gambling or political culture to be salient factors in the BHSI score when considered together with the other variables.

In terms of gambling, the results of the multiple regression analysis appears to contradict notions that states with a presence of certain types of gambling also have higher levels of boxing regulations. This is an instance where public perception, perhaps guided by the notoriety of boxing matches held in Las Vegas and Atlantic City, is not supported by statistical data. Likewise, the variable of political culture had a statistically significant relationship to HIV testing, but it was not significant for the requirement of neurological tests or drug testing. Therefore the significance of this variable diminished when used in conjunction with other independent variables to determine its impact on the BHSI. The model predicts 27 percent, or about one-fourth of the state variance on the BHSI. Therefore there are other factors that may affect a state's expected score on the BHSI.

Interview with Thomas Hauser

Thomas Hauser is one of the most prominent boxing authors of the last decade. He gained widespread recognition for his authorized biography of Muhammad Ali, and is the author of over 34 books. In 2005 he was honored by the Boxing Writers Association of America with the Nat Fleischer Award for career excellence in boxing journalism. He is currently the lead feature writer on SecondsOut.com, one of the most popular boxing Web pages on the Internet. Hauser has been one of boxing's leading voices for reform, and is an advocate for working to improve the health and safety aspects of the sport. He was interviewed exclusively for this study.[65]

Hauser believes there are two simple reasons why states differ on the BHSI. He says, "A lot of states just don't have the funds to conduct those tests. New York is very generous; it pays about 75 percent of the costs of the medical tests for boxers. New York pays for MRIs, the eye tests, the promoter pays for the physical and the blood tests, but that's a lesser charge, and New York is willing to do that. In Nevada, the fights are big enough that the promoter can afford to do that. But if you have a fight in, let's say, Utah, a small club fight, and there are eight fights on the card, meaning sixteen boxers, it's very hard to come up with the money to pay for all those tests." The lack of state-provided funding for HIV, neurological and drug tests is certainly plausible and supported by the statistical data on state wealth detailed in this chapter.

Hauser has a second theory, however, for why the lack of health and safety tests persist.

> A lot of states just don't care. They couldn't care less about the fighters, they accept medicals that they know are phony, and it doesn't seem to bother them. And a lot of them are afraid of scaring away fighters, I mean look what happened in Nevada. When Nevada said "no" to Mike Tyson, and wouldn't give him a license to fight Lennox Lewis, the fight went to [Tennessee]. Well, Nevada is the fight capital of the world, so Nevada could survive that. Other states are afraid that if they turn fighters down, they'll lose the big fights. There are now fighters who will not come to New York and fight because

THE REGULATION OF BOXING

Evander Holyfield, pictured here with trainer Lou Duva in 1992, was suspended in New York in 2004.

> New York put Evander Holyfield on [medical] suspension and tested James Toney [positive for steroids]. So if you're a fighter and you're taking steroids, you're not going to go to New York or Nevada where they test for them. You're going to go fight in [Tennessee] or in some other state where there are no tests for steroids. That is why you need a national standard, so people can't go and run and hide.

Hauser emphasizes his point by explaining the case of heavyweight contender Joe Mesi. He says,

> If Joe Mesi had fought in one of the great majority of states that don't have the same rules as Nevada [where his subdural hematomas were discovered], he'd be allowed to fight again. Very few states would have put him on permanent medical suspension. I'd carry it a bit further, if that story hadn't leaked, and I think I was the first one who broke it, nobody would have known. He would have gone on fighting. So you really need a national standard, in terms

of the other variations in medicals. I think it goes beyond that. There are still states that don't have ambulances at the fights. The training of the ring doctors differs radically state to state. Some states like New York have a serious program, other states look around for a guy who's willing to come out to the fights. And you have some states with the doctor sitting in the first row drinking a gin and tonic. It really has to be standardized. The HIV testing, I think, is not a significant issue. The MRIs, the steroids, and who will be allowed in the ring [are more important].

Hauser questions how the establishment of a federal boxing commission would affect states that do not have the funds to conduct tests. He says,

That depends on a wide range of issues. Would this be an unfunded mandate? Or would [the federal government] provide the funds for [testing]. If it is unfunded, then the states will probably pass the costs on to the promoters. And the promoters will just take it out of the boxers pay. But there's just so much you can take out from a four round preliminary fighter, so I suppose in some states there might be less boxing. But the answer is that if you can't conduct boxing in an atmosphere where the fighters are reasonably protected medically, then you shouldn't have boxing. That means certain medical tests, and having an ambulance and qualified doctors present.

Hauser's response echoes the concerns expressed by boxing commissioners Keith Kizer and Aaron Davis. While the proposed federal legislation to create a national boxing commission does not expressly call for states to institute HIV, neurological and drug testing, it does state that testing for infectious diseases is required. If a national commission determines that each state should be required by federal law to conduct the aforementioned tests, the funding source will be the most critical issue.

Hauser says that the main problem facing the Association of Boxing Commissions (ABC) is their lack of clout. "The ABC doesn't have the authority, and the manpower, and the willpower to do what has to be done right now in boxing," he says.

The classic ABC story I tell is [about] Tim Lueckenhoff, who is the president of the ABC. I wrote an article about it [in 2003] called "Professional Losers" in *A View From Ringside*. The day that article went online I got an e-mail from Tim Lueckenhoff politely saying that I had no idea what I was talking about, that these [journeymen] knew their way around the boxing ring, that they were there to pick up a paycheck, and he went to some of their fights and saw that they could protect themselves and that I should shove it, although he didn't put it in those terms. But it was a genially phrased letter, and literally two days after that, Bradley Rhone, who was one of the fighters I had written about in that article, was killed.

Although Hauser's statements are critical toward Lueckenhoff and the ABC, Hauser clarifies that "This is not a personal attack on Tim, and I don't want it to appear as such because I've always found Tim to be a pleasant enough person. But I don't think that the people in power at the ABC take these issues seriously enough. There's just no excuse for allowing a guy who's lost twenty-six fights in a row and been knocked out in 19 fights in a row to fight."

Hauser provides another example of a journeyman boxer that makes his way around the boxing circuit in states with less restrictive regulations. He says, "This guy, Robert Muhammad, who I've mentioned in a couple of articles, has had a subdural hematoma, and is now fighting again. He's been knocked out in something like seventeen of his last eighteen fights and he's allowed to fight in certain states, and that's nuts!"

Hauser expresses ambiguous thoughts about the American Association of Professional Ringside Physicians (AAPRP). He is uncertain whether the AAPRP should become the medical arm of any national boxing commission that is formed. He says, "That's what [AAPRP president Dr. Michael Schwartz] wants. I'm not sure that it's going to happen and I'm not sure that it should happen. There are things I like about what [Dr. Schwartz] is doing, and things I don't like about it. [Dr. Schwartz] is a good ringside physician. He created the AAPRP out of nothing, and I give him a lot of credit for the positives."

California's unique system of ranking fighters to allow fights to be made (described earlier in this chapter) is "nonsense" according to Hauser. He says, "All you need to know about California is the way they handled *The Contender*. Jesse Brinkley fought three days after he had five stitches in his eye. I mean, that's just repulsive. You don't let a guy get in the ring, I'm sorry if it screws up the TV show, that's tough! I mean he could have problems with that eye for the rest of his life. And of course the cut opened up in the fight on *The Contender* three days after it had been cut, and then the same eye opened up again when they had the live fights on TV."

In spite of his criticism of California's athletic commission, Hauser held hope for the executive director of the CAC appointed in 2005, Armando Garcia. Hauser says, "I've heard good things about him and maybe he'll start to turn things around like Ron Scott Stevens did in New York. But California's a joke. I mean, there are horror stories out there as to what they [have done]. There are medical scandals, there are issues where doctors were double-billing, they charged the promoters and they charged the insurance companies and it's just not right, the way they're regulating boxing in California. I can't write about every commission in the country." Hauser has strong reactions to mismatches in California, and points to the Viloria-Contreras fight highlighted earlier in this chapter as an example. He says, "The [California A-E Rating] System is nonsense. The fight shouldn't have been made."

Hauser is not hesitant to praise or criticize commissions for their protection, or lack thereof, of boxers. When the New York State Athletic Commission was undergoing a host of problems, Hauser was at the forefront of pointing out the issues that plagued that entity. Yet, he has also praised the commission for its improvements. He says,

> The NYSAC has turned around [between 2003 and 2005] largely because of the efforts of [Chairman] Ron Scott Stevens. We had this horrible situation, first with [former chairman and two-time heavyweight champion] Floyd Patterson [who was reportedly displaying the effects of Alzheimer's Disease while in office] and then with Mel Southard. Then Ray Kelly came in and he was certainly well-intentioned, he's an honorable man, he tried his best to do the job, but he didn't have the expertise to do it. He didn't know boxing, and his right hand man, Charlie DeRienzo, didn't know boxing either so, they made some progress by getting rid of the no-show jobs, and then Bernard Kerik came in, and Kerik was just a national embarrassment. He left two years ago [2003], about the time the state inspector general's report came out [explaining the deficiencies of the commission].

Hauser says that New York boxing commissioner Ron Scott Stevens has "done a very, very good job. He's well-grounded in boxing, he's been a writer or a promoter or a matchmaker, he knows the business, and he knows the sport and the whole climate of the commission has changed now. The people who weren't that good have been replaced with people who know the business and care. The whole attitude has changed, so now at the same time the commission is enforcing the law, it is working in conjunction with the whole fight community. It's becoming one of the better commissions in the country and it shows what one person can do if he has the authority to do it."

While Hauser has both criticized and praised the NYSAC, he has severely criticized Nevada for its selection of judges. He says, "Duane Ford, who I think is one of the most respected judges in the country, was a judge in De La Hoya — Mosley II and he was one of the two judges who voted in favor of Mosley. Bob Arum, the promoter, went berserk and subsequent to that, Arum has had 20 championship fights in Las Vegas. Duane Ford has only been assigned to two of them and those were two fights on the undercard of bigger fights where the outcome really was in doubt. Certainly one could come to the conclusion, if one were so inclined, that this was Arum's influence on the commission. In an article [entitled 'Nine Days in Nevada'] I write about other issues when the commission has been susceptible to outside influences."

Boxing insurance is another complex area; as Hauser explains, "If you're a promoter and you want to have a big fight in Texas, you might have to buy insurance from the guy who might referee the fight, whose father runs the commission or some agency in San Francisco." Hauser is making a reference to Texas referee Laurence Cole, whose father is Dickie Cole, the director of the Texas boxing commission. Laurence Cole and San Francisco based Joe Gagliardi run insurance companies that are major providers of boxer insurance.

Hauser is very direct about his perspectives on what needs to be done right now. He says, "I would have one federal commission regulating the sport with uniform standards in every respect: uniform medical standards, uniform conduct at the fights up and down the ladder. I would make the various state athletic commissions regional offices of the federal commission. It comes down to national solutions. In the NFL, the rules of the football games don't vary if the game is played at home for the New England Patriots or in Dallas with the Cowboys or in Indianapolis. You don't have thirty-two sets of rules and regulations. Boxing needs uniformity."

In addition to consistent national rules and regulations, Hauser is concerned with protecting boxers' economic interests. He says,

> I would have — and I think this is very important to making the business work properly — mandatory disclosure in a timely fashion — not the night of the fight when it's too late — but in a timely fashion, of all income streams to the promoter because all fighters and managers have to know that in order to negotiate properly. In every other major sport, the foundation stone of the unions' negotiation is the TV license fee. When NFL players sit down to negotiate with the owners they know what the owners are getting in TV rights — it's on the front page of every newspaper in the country. It's the same thing with baseball players and the NBA. Fighters, as a general rule, don't know how much the promoter is getting. So the promoter can tell them, "I'm getting two million dollars from Showtime." It could be a phony number but the fighters don't know any better.

The Professional Boxing Amendments Act of 2007 would require the United States Boxing Commission to establish minimal contractual guidelines.

Hauser also advocates for measures to protect boxers as members of the workforce. He says,

> I would also have a grievance system that would allow people to vindicate their rights without having to spend hundreds of thousands of dollars through civil court systems throughout the country. In baseball, football, basketball, every other major sport, you have a grievance proceeding, you have arbitration proceedings where these matters are settled. You don't read about Tiger Woods going to civil court having to sue to get his pay for winning a tournament

or a caddy going to court to get his money or all the other things that happen in different sports. There's a proceeding to get things done within the sport and boxing needs that so people can enforce their rights.

The Professional Boxing Amendments Act of 2007 would establish a grievance procedure.

Perhaps most distressing for Hauser is the lack of enforcement of current federal boxing laws. He says,

> Right now there's a law on the books that says that a sanctioning body that does not comply with the ratings requirements of the Muhammad Ali Boxing Reform Act, they're not entitled to a sanctioning fee. We all understand that each of the sanctioning bodies have phony ratings in some respect or another. The WBO had a guy in their rankings named Darrin Morris that died, and then kept rising in the rankings after that. Nobody's enforcing the law. Now, an individual fighter can't do that because he'll be ruined, but if the U.S. attorney's office went to court and said they want an injunction against the WBA collecting sanctioning fees, they'd have to clean up their ratings act. It's hard for a state attorney general in one state to do that because under the law only the U.S. attorney general or a state attorney general could do it, but if one state does, let's say the New York state attorney general does it, the WBA — and I don't want to pick on them, they could also pick on the WBC, the IBF and WBO — they won't sanction title fights in New York, but they will in some other state."

As far as Hauser is concerned, there are no model state athletic commissions. He says, "All of the commissions have one flaw or another. Nevada is a pretty good commission, largely because [former NAC executive director] Marc Ratner [was] a very skilled administrator, but Nevada is much too compliant in the face of pressure from outside influences. Also, Nevada, unlike other states, regulates boxing as a business, whereas other states regulate it as a sport. The economy of Utah isn't going to change if you get rid of boxing. The economy of New York isn't going to change if you get rid of boxing. [But] the economy of Nevada changes if you get rid of boxing because it is a key marketing tool of bringing people to the casinos for certain events."

Conclusion and Summary of the Statistical Analyses

Thomas Hauser's comments underscore the inconsistency of boxing regulations presented throughout this chapter, through the qualitative and quantitative results of the Boxing Health and Safety Survey (BHS Survey). For the benefit of readers without a background in statistics, a summary of the statistical results is presented here. Thirty-two of forty-three existing state athletic commissions responded to the BHS Survey. Data for eight of the remaining cases was obtained from data compiled by the American Association of Professional Ringside Physicians. All of the states that replied to the BHS Survey indicate that they conduct pre-fight medical evaluations, require standards for competitive match-ups, ensure that emergency medical personnel and equipment are present during and after each match, require health insurance for boxers during each match, and require registration (licenses) for boxers. Nearly all of the states honor each other's suspensions. Most states conduct post-fight medical evaluations and require certification and approval for ring officials. The most significant variance in state boxing regulations is in the area of testing, specifically neurological testing, HIV testing, and drug testing.

A quantitative analysis of professional boxing regulations was carried out. The BHSI (dependent variable) was created to capture the variance of states on the level of their testing regulations. Independent variables informed by the state politics literature were selected to determine their effects on the BHSI scores. These variables included boxing-related deaths, the presence of certain types of gambling, state wealth, and political culture. T-tests, chi-square analyses and a multiple regression analysis were conducted. The results of the statistical tests show that states that have higher levels of boxing-related deaths and state wealth tend to require HIV testing. Furthermore, states that have a moralist or individualist political culture tend to require HIV testing, while traditionalist states do not. As for drug testing, there is a significant difference in state wealth between states that conduct such tests and those that do not, as states with higher median incomes require drug testing. The multiple regression analysis reveals that boxing related deaths and state wealth affect the state score on the BHSI, even while controlling for the presence of gambling and political culture.

A Test of the Statistical Model

One can predict with confidence supported by data that states that have experienced higher levels of boxing-related deaths and higher levels of state wealth as measured by median household income, will have higher levels of health and safety standards for boxers. And conversely, those with lower levels of each can be expected to have lower levels of health and safety standards. This model can be tested by examining whether it predicts the BHSI score in the two states that formed commissions since 2005 (Kansas and Minnesota).

In Kansas, the measure of state wealth (median income in 2003) was 41,075 and the state had experienced only five boxing-related deaths in its history. The state scored 1 on the presence of certain types of gambling and 1 on political culture. Therefore the model would predict a low BHSI score of 1.29 for Kansas based upon its low number of boxing-related deaths and lower level of state wealth. On those two criteria, Kansas is similar to both Arizona (BHSI Score 1) and Iowa (BHSI Score 1).[66] In practical terms, this means that Kansas would be expected to require one of the tests that make up the BHSI.

In Minnesota, the measure of state wealth was 50,100 and the state had experienced six boxing-related deaths. Minnesota also scored 1 on gambling and 1 on political culture. The model would predict a medium BHSI score of 1.75 for Minnesota, since it has a low-level of boxing related deaths but a high level of state wealth.[67] Minnesota's experience with boxing-related deaths and state wealth are similar to both New Hampshire (BHSI Score 2) and Utah (BHSI Score 2). Thus, Minnesota would be expected to require two of the tests that comprise the BHSI.

The BHSI score for Kansas in 2007 is 1 as the Kansas commission carries out discretionary drug testing, according to boxing commissioner Aaron Davis. Kansas does not require HIV or neurological tests for boxers. In an interview with Minnesota boxing commissioner Scott Ledoux held on February 6, 2008, Ledoux stated that the commission requires HIV tests and has the discretionary authority to conduct drug testing. He said that the commission does not require neurological tests, though it can request such tests if a fighter has been knocked out or is an older boxer. However, the state statute that establishes the commission clearly states that the medical examination to license participants "must include" a neurological exam.[68] Ledoux's response indicates that the BHSI score for Minnesota in 2007 is coded as a 2, since he said the commission does not systematically carry out neurological tests. Therefore, the statistical model is accurate in predicting the BHSI score for both states, attesting to the utility of the analyses developed in this study.

3

CASE STUDY: BOXING IN NEVADA

Introduction

Whenever the topic of conversation is boxing, the states that usually come to mind are New York and Nevada. The legal roots of boxing in America can be found in these two states, as their respective governments legalized the sport just prior to the twentieth century (see Chapter 1). While significant boxing matches were held in both states during the early 1900s, the development of the sport in New York and Nevada took divergent paths over the next hundred years. Until the 1960s, New York landed the most of the significant fights that shaped boxing history. In the 1960s and 1970s Nevada, specifically Las Vegas, began to emerge as the most important site for boxing events. By the 1980s Nevada surpassed New York as boxing's central location.

While baby boomers and senior citizens may nostalgically recall the great fights held at Madison Square Garden in New York City, for younger Americans, Las Vegas has a greater association with the sport. Many of the most significant boxing matches of the past three decades have taken place in the Silver State. The images of classic fights such as Larry Holmes vs. Gerry Cooney, Marvin Hagler vs. Thomas Hearns, Julio Cesar Chavez vs. Meldrick Taylor, or Evander Holyfield vs. Mike Tyson all had the backdrop of the Las Vegas Strip.

This chapter is a case study analysis of boxing regulations in Nevada. First, the historical rise of Nevada as the preeminent state for the sport of boxing is examined. Emphasis will be given to the legalization of the sport and the creation of the state athletic commission. Then, the current structure of the state athletic commission along with state laws and regulations is analyzed to detail this state policy issue. The historical antecedents and current regulations are presented in this chapter to examine in detail the most prominent U.S. boxing commission. Interviews with former Nevada Athletic

3 • Case Study: Boxing in Nevada

"Terrible" Terry Norris fought in Nevada more than a dozen times. He's shown here in 1992 in the process of knocking out Meldrick Taylor as referee Mills Lane looks on (photograph by Modesto M. Rodriguez).

Commission (NAC) executive director Marc Ratner, former NAC Medical Advisory Board chairperson Dr. Margaret Goodman, current NAC executive director Keith Kizer, and world-renowned Nevada-based referee Joe Cortez were conducted to provide an in-depth look at boxing in the state. Since both Ratner and Goodman were the state athletic commission representatives that completed the Boxing Health and Safety Survey detailed in Chapter 2, they were given ample opportunity to elaborate on their state's boxing regulations for this book. Keith Kizer provides an in-depth update to Nevada's boxing regulations since he replaced Ratner, and Cortez provides insight based upon his extensive experience as a referee. Finally, a participant-observation of Goodman and other NAC personnel carrying out their duties at a boxing event was carried out in 2005. This approach complements the data analysis presented in Chapter 2 by providing revealing insight on how the laws and regulations designed to protect the health and safety of boxers in Nevada are put into practice.

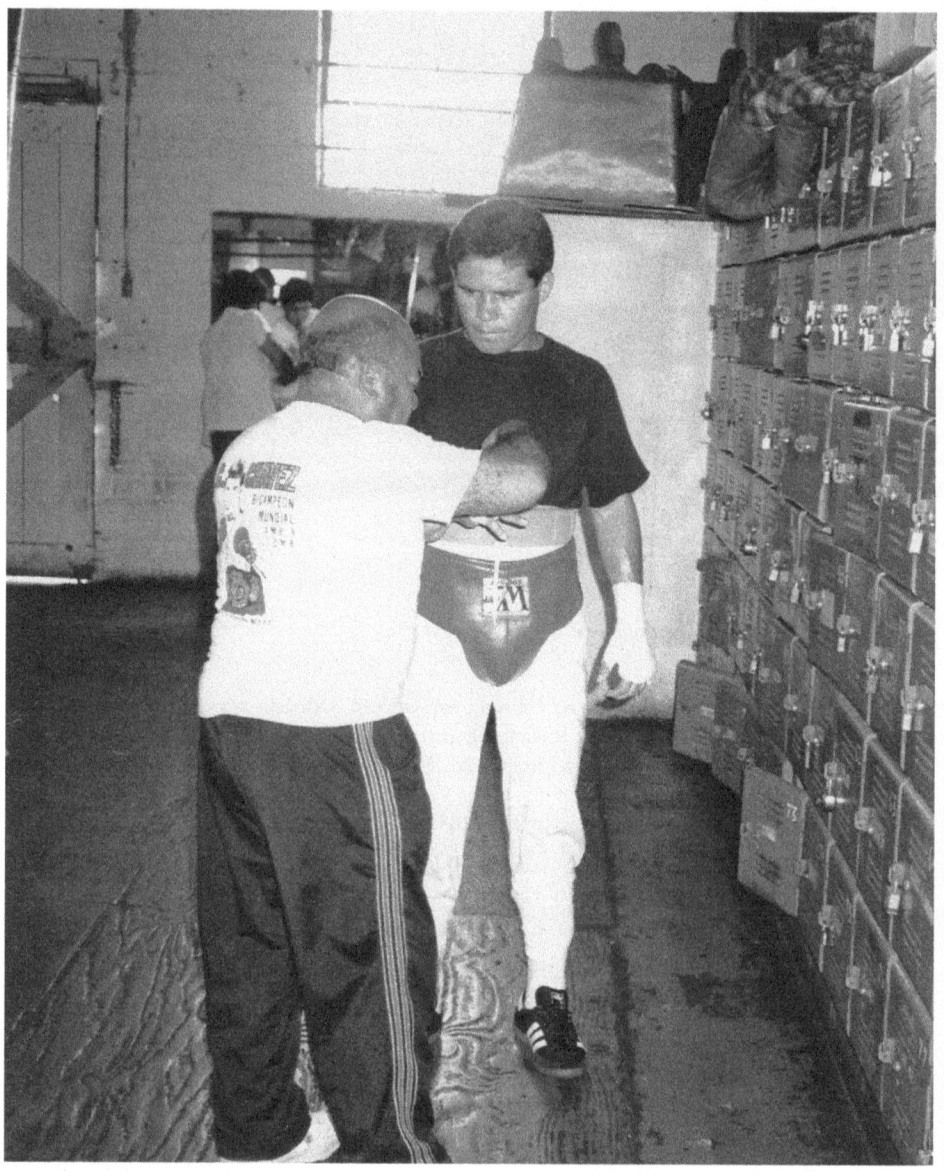

Julio Cesar Chavez, seen here getting his hands wrapped at the famed Azteca gymnasium in Los Angeles, participated in several Las Vegas mega-fights in the 1980s and 1990s.

3 • Case Study: Boxing in Nevada

Early Nevada Boxing History

The Nevada of the 1890s was a far cry from the glitz and glamour associated with the state, or at least Las Vegas, today. Historian David Thomson writes, "Late in the nineteenth century, Nevada was in a depressed condition.... There were some who feared that the state was slipping back into desert condition, and in the years from 1890 to 1900, the total population of the state *fell* from 47,355 to 42,335."[1] Historian James W. Hulse concurs, "In that long interval between 1880 and 1900, when Nevada's economy was in desperate straits, hope for a revival in the state's basic industry [mining] never died."[2] The precarious state of the Nevada economy in this period prompted its legislators to come up with creative ways to bring some much needed funds into the state coffers. According to Nevada state archivist Mella Rothwell Harmon, boxing became one of these means. She writes, "Nevada has always been willing to exploit ways of improving its economy. The chance came again in 1897.... During [the end of the nineteenth century] Nevada was also experiencing one of its cyclical economic downturns and was seeking ways to attract an infusion of capital. A golden opportunity presented itself, when there was a last-moment cancellation of a scheduled heavyweight championship fight to be held in San Francisco between titleholder Gentleman Jim Corbett and challenger Bob Fitzsimmons."[3]

Thus, the genesis of boxing in Nevada came in 1897 when the state legislature passed a bill that was signed into law by Governor Reinhol Sadler in order to host the heavyweight championship fight between Corbett and Fitzsimmons. An examination of the law's text, which states it is "an Act to restrict and license glove contests, or exhibitions between man and man, and to repeal all other Acts in conflict therewith. Approved January 29, 1897," is revealing of the brevity of time the legislators took to approve boxing in the state.[4] The single page law has just ten brief sections that address the following issues: the licensing requirements (any man over twenty-one years of age could box); the cost of a license to stage a boxing event ($1000, payable to the sheriff); the role of the county auditor to record the names of contestants; the requirement of a certification of sound health for participants; the prohibition of "intoxicating liquors" at the fights; the prohibition of boxing matches taking place on Sundays; the distribution of licensing funds to the state (nine-tenths would go to the state treasury, one-tenth to the county treasury); the authorization to charge fees for admission to boxing events; the establishment of a fine ($200–$1000) for staging a boxing event that is not in compliance with the act; and the immediate implementation of the act.[5]

Perhaps the most significant passage of this act, as it relates to the current research, is its health and safety provision. This section reads, "Sec. 4 The licensee shall ten hours before any proposed contest or exhibition under the provisions of this Act, file with the County Clerk where such contests or exhibition is to be held, a certificate in writing executed by two regular practicing physicians of this State, showing that the contestants named in the license are in sound physical health and condition."[6] Thus, from the outset of legalized boxing in Nevada, the need for a proper pre-fight physical examination from *two* licensed state physicians was a central component of its boxing regulations.

The 1897 Nevada boxing law paved the way for the Corbett vs. Fitzsimmons match that took place on St. Patrick's Day (March 17) in a makeshift ring in Carson City, Nevada. The match was significant for a number of reasons. First, the fight was the first championship bout to be filmed. According to a published report, the fight film grossed over $750,000 ($16.1 million in 2003 dollars).[7] Second, the fight ended in the fourteenth round with a solid left punch to the area just below Corbett's heart, thus creating what would come to be known as the solar plexus punch. Third, this was the first, and until recently the only, time that a middleweight champion would win the world heavyweight title. Archivist Harmon writes, "The event was a huge economic success, and it opened the door to future title fights in the state, filling the void created by the sport's controversial status elsewhere. Between 1897 and 1910, several prizefights held in various locations garnered national and international attention for Nevada."[8] Among the prominent fights held in Nevada during the period that Harmon refers to were Marvin Hart vs. Jack Root for the heavyweight title vacated by Jim Jeffries (1905), Joe Gans vs. Battling Nelson for the world lightweight title (1906), and Jack Johnson vs. Jim Jeffries for the world heavyweight championship (1910). (See Chapter 1 for the significance of these fights.) The emergence of world heavyweight champion Jack Dempsey took place in Nevada in the years following Johnson vs. Jeffries. Dempsey fought several times in Nevada towns such as Reno, Goldfield, Tonopah, and Ely early in his career.

An examination of fights held in Nevada between 1897 and the early 1930s reveals that Reno was the hotbed of boxing in the state at the time. Reno was the site of Hart vs. Root, Johnson vs. Jeffries and other significant bouts in the first half of the twentieth century. Famed boxing promoter George Lewis "Tex" Rickard backed many of Nevada's significant fights during that period. Historian Phillip Earl writes, "Coming to the state in 1904, Rickard opened the Northern Saloon in Goldfield, and soon became the community's leading citizen.... In September of 1906 he promoted the famed lightweight championship bout between Joe Gans and Oscar 'Battling' Nelson, one of the most memorable fistic events in history.... Rickard's crowning achievement in Nevada was the promotion of the historic 'fight of the century' between Jack Johnson and Jim Jeffries in Reno on July 4, 1910.... It was with Dempsey that Rickard staged the greatest boxing spectaculars and racked up the most awe-inspiring attendance figures and gate receipts in the history of the game."[9]

"Tex" Rickard is credited by some analysts with bringing legitimacy and acceptance to the sport of boxing. A shrewd businessman, Rickard had a knack for negotiation, entrepreneurship, and a keen ability to use the media to his advantage. Earl writes, "Rickard elevated boxing from the wretched, smoke-filled arenas into the realm of glittering, royal extravaganzas perfumed by the smell of money. Prior to Rickard's time, only tennis and polo had touched the pockets and fancy of the wealthy, but he was soon to change all that."[10] While Rickard's initial boxing mega-events took place in Nevada, he later moved his operations to New York in the 1920s. He leased famed boxing venue Madison Square Garden during this period and was integral in obtaining funding for a new Madison Square Garden.[11] Rickard's promotions broke all existing records for live gate-receipts, as highlighted by the Dempsey vs. Gene Tunney rematch in 1927 that drew a crowd of 104,943 and a gate of $2,658,660.[12] Rickard also helped establish *The Ring Magazine* along with publisher Nat Fleischer.[13] His untimely death in 1929 from appendicitis left a void in boxing that would not be filled until the likes of Don King and Bob Arum came around decades later. Earl notes that when Rickard died, "His body was brought to New York City to lie in state in a $15,000 bronze casket in the center of the arena which he had built."[14]

Establishment of the Nevada Athletic Commission

Although boxing was legalized in Nevada in 1897, the establishment of the Nevada Athletic Commission did not come about until 1941. That year, a bill was passed by the state legislature and signed into law by Governor E.P. Carville approving "an Act authorizing and regulating boxing and wrestling contests for prizes or purses, or where an admission is charged, and limiting such boxing contests to fifteen rounds; to create the Nevada athletic commission, empowered to license and regulate such contests and all participants therein; to prescribe conditions under which such licenses shall be issued and contests held, authorizing the said commission to appoint county inspectors; to prescribe a penalty for violations of this act, and other matters properly relating thereto."[15] This law has revealing components, several of which have been modified. However, the basic structure and functions of the commission continue to this day.

The 1941 boxing commission legislation called for five political appointees to serve on the commission at the pleasure of the governor. The first appointees were Wayne Hinckley, M.C. Tinch, Walter Collins, William Lewis, and W. Kellison. Interestingly, the members of the commission were not to be compensated for their work. The sole discretion over boxing regulations at the state level was vested in the commission. The commission was to issue licenses to participants, issue permits for events, collect fees, and carry out disciplinary oversight powers. This law also established the fifteen round limit for boxing matches.

Section 9 of the law is of particular interest to the current research, as it reads, "The commission shall have the authority to affiliate with any other state or national boxing commission or athletic authority."[16] This is significant for two reasons. First, because it indicates that as early as sixty years ago, there was discussion of establishing a national boxing commission, which of course has never happened in the United States. Second, it is important because it allows for a coalition of state athletic commissions, as would emerge in the 1990s with the Association of Boxing Commissions.

Las Vegas Becomes "Fight Town"

Las Vegas would not emerge as the preeminent Nevada boxing town until the latter half of the twentieth century. The first world championship fight to take place in the city was the 1960 welterweight fight in which Benny "Kid" Paret won a fifteen-round decision over Don Jordan at the new Las Vegas Convention Center. Author and journalist Tim Dahlberg writes that the convention center "would feature the likes of Liston, Muhammad Ali and others over the next few years, though it would be nearly two decades before the city began getting notice as the nation's new fight capital."[17] According to historian David Thomson, "the modern history of prizefighting in Nevada began in the early 1960s. For several decades previously, the center of the fight game had been in New York, at Madison Square Garden.... In March 1961,

3 • Case Study: Boxing in Nevada

Donovan "Razor" Ruddock drills Mike Tyson with a left to the body during their 1991 bout in an outdoor ring at the Mirage Hotel and Casino in Las Vegas (photograph by Modesto M. Rodriguez).

Sugar Ray Robinson fought Gene Fulmer [in Las Vegas], and in July 1963 Floyd Patterson lost his title to Sonny Liston."[18] The Patterson vs. Liston fight was the first heavyweight championship fight held in Las Vegas. Hulse argues that this was the first significant Las Vegas title fight.[19] Harmon writes, "Las Vegas hosted title fights in the 1930s, but the opening of the Las Vegas Convention Center in 1959 marked the beginning of big-time boxing in town. At the time, Las Vegas was usurping Reno's claim to the title 'Sin City,' and to enhance that image Las Vegas made a concerted effort to bring boxing matches to the convention center. Hotels and the Convention and Visitors Authority sponsored title bouts and other fights because they brought high rollers to town. By the 1980s Las Vegas had become so popular as a boxing venue that it outgrew the eight thousand-seat convention center, and several of the larger hotel/casinos began hosting fights."[20]

The first significant fight held at a hotel was the 1969 bout between

Sonny Liston and Leotis Martin, which was held in the new Las Vegas International Hotel (later the Las Vegas Hilton).[21] Dahlberg notes, "By the time the Las Vegas Hilton built a pavilion to hold the Muhammad Ali–Leon Spinks heavyweight title fight on February 15, 1978, the city was becoming a major player in the boxing world."[22] In the 1980s, hotels and casinos began to increase the size of their boxing venues. Dahlberg explains, "if Fight Town USA had a town hall, it was Caesars Palace, where huge arenas were built, and Ali–Larry Holmes in 1980 ushered in an era of mega-fights that still happen on a regular basis nearly a quarter of a century later.... Fight nights became events bigger than the biggest stars in the showrooms. Gamblers lured in by the prospect of a good fight dropped millions of dollars, and celebrities were always eager to be seen at ringside." Hulse also argues that by 1980 "Las Vegas became the favorite site in the nation for the staging of heavyweight matches."[23] The Larry Holmes vs. Gerry Cooney heavyweight championship bout, which was marred by racist overtones, attracted an attendance of nearly 30,000 fans in a temporary arena built in the Caesars Palace parking lot.[24]

Dahlberg explains the evolution of boxing venues in Las Vegas:

> The outdoor arenas erected first at Caesars and later at the Riviera, Dunes and Hilton eventually gave way to arenas built with big fights in mind.... Over the years, fights were held in parking lots, ballrooms, showrooms, temporary arenas, and even the UNLV basketball arena. They were staged in 110-degree heat, pouring rain and winds that sent grandstands rocking.... The MGM Grand can put 16,000 people in its arena, while Mandalay Bay's 12,000-seat building became home to fighters like Oscar De La Hoya and Lennox Lewis.... Almost every major Las Vegas hotel hosted a fight at one time or another, with some 40-odd fight sites coming and going over the years.[25]

In the 1990s and on into the early part of the twenty-first century, Las Vegas has remained the preeminent location for hosting major boxing matches. Evander Holyfield, Oscar De La Hoya, Roy Jones, Jr., and even George Foreman all had career performances in the city. While Atlantic City, New Jersey, has also had its share of significant fights featuring, for example, the 1989 Mike Tyson vs. Michael Spinks match, and more recently, several fights featuring Arturo Gatti, the majority of significant bouts still land in Las Vegas.

Structure of the Nevada Athletic Commission

The Nevada Athletic Commission (NAC) has regulated boxing and other professional sports such as wrestling and martial arts competitions since 1941.

3 • Case Study: Boxing in Nevada

Former middleweight champion Michael Nunn (left) and trainer Angelo Dundee appear at a 1992 post-fight press conference at the Mirage Hotel and Casino.

The NAC was established by and draws its legal authority from Nevada Revised Statutes (NRS) Chapter 467 (the current codified laws of the state of Nevada), and further clarified by Chapter 467 of the Nevada Administrative Code (NAC), the codified administrative regulations of the executive branch.[26]

The NAC consists of five part-time members who are appointed by the governor for three-year terms. When the BHS Survey was carried out in 2005, the members of the commission were Dr. Tony Alamo, John R. Bailey, Joe W. Brown, Dr. Flip Homansky and Raymond "Skip" Avansino Jr. The members select a chairperson annually; Avansino held this position at the time the Boxing Health and Safety Survey was conducted for this study. In addition, the commission selects a non-voting, full-time executive director to carry out the daily activities of the NAC; this position was held by Marc Ratner at the time of the BHS Survey. The executive director of the NAC is supported by a small office staff and can obtain legal counsel from the Nevada attorney general's office.

The Nevada Athletic Commission is unique in that it also possesses a

Roy Jones, Jr., pictured here in 1993, was a familiar face in Las Vegas rings.

Medical Advisory Board (MAB) established by the state legislature. The MAB also consists of five gubernatorial appointees who serve four-year terms. In 2005, the members of the MAB were Dr. Albert Campanna, Dr. Todd Chapman, Dr. Jeffrey Parker, and Dr. Anthony Pollard. The governor designates the chairperson of the Nevada Medical Advisory Board; Dr. Margaret Goodman held this position at the time of the BHS Survey. According to information posted on the NAC Internet site, "The board duties include preparing and submitting to the Commission appropriate standards for the physical and mental examination of contestants, advising the Commission as to the physical or mental fitness of a contestant and recommending physicians to be licensed as ringside physicians for the Commission. The Medical Advisory Board also prepares and submits recommendations for revisions in the law necessary to protect the health of contestants in Nevada. However, the board can only make recommendations to the Commission. The Commission must vote to adopt the recommendations of the board for the recommendations to go into effect."[27]

Nevada Boxing Regulations

At present, "Chapter 467 — Unarmed Combat" of the Nevada State Code regulates boxing in the state. The structure of the commission is defined as including an executive director, a chairman, commission members, inspectors, and a Medical Advisory Board. The code includes provisions for licensing and registration of all pertinent individuals involved in a boxing event, including boxers, promoters, seconds, referees, judges, and timekeepers. It requires boxers to possess professional identification cards as required by federal law, and outlines general requirements for contracts and other financial arrangements particularly between managers, promoters and boxers. In addition, the law sets forth requirements for the organization and promotion of boxing events, including issues relating to tickets, admissions, facilities, equipment and supplies. In terms of the regulation of the matches themselves, the administrative code details the rules and procedures relating to everything from the weigh-in procedure to the duties of the referee and ringside physician. Championship fights are to follow the Unified Championship Rules adopted by the Association of Boxing Commissions (NAC 467.009).

The law even includes requirements that address such issues as: the physical appearance of boxers ("each unarmed combatant must be clean and present a tidy appearance"— NAC 467.598), and the specific manner in which a referee should wipe the gloves of a fallen boxer ("with a damp towel or the referee's shirt"— NAC 467.735). Boxers who fail to pay child support need not apply to fight in Nevada, as there are provisions in the law to deny or suspend licenses for deadbeat dads (NRS 467.1015 and NRS 467.102). There are several grounds for disciplinary action and the suspension or revocation of boxer licenses that are not related to health and safety. Some of these grounds include engaging in illegal gambling, reflecting discredit to unarmed combat, being a reputed underworld character, and convictions on charges involving moral turpitude. Significantly, the law provides for the regulations pertaining to the often-controversial disciplinary proceedings. While it does not fit the scope of this research, it should be noted that this section of Nevada code also has provisions for the regulation of amateur boxing, martial arts, mixed martial arts and wrestling. Thus the chapter is entitled "unarmed combat" to encompass ring sports other than boxing.

The health and safety aspects of the Nevada State Athletic Commission laws and regulations are extensive. Provisions are in place to review licensing for boxers that are over 36 years of age or have three years of inactivity (NAC

467.017). In addition to a standard physical exam and ophthalmologic eye exam, boxers must provide results of the following exams: MRI and CAT Scan (performed within 5 years of the license application), HIV and hepatitis tests (taken within 30 days of the license application), and any other test or examination requested by the commission. Furthermore, the promoter of a boxing match must provide each boxer with at least $50,000 in insurance coverage for medical, surgical and hospital care for contestants injured in a match. There are also specific licensing requirements for ringside physicians, including the ability to perform CPR and a review of the applicant's past performance and abilities.

The issue of ambulances and emergency equipment being present at boxing matches held in Nevada is very specifically addressed in NAC 467.414. At least one ambulance and two advanced emergency medical technicians must be present at all times, from the moment the first fight begins until the last contestant has left the site. The personnel must be positioned at or near the ring. It is the promoter's responsibility to notify the ambulance service and the hospital, including the emergency room staff, nearest to the site of the matches of the event.

According the law, the emergency equipment required at each fight card includes blankets, a stretcher, a bottle of smelling salts, bandages, surgical tape, splints, a pair of scissors, a soft collar and a hard collar, an airway, sterile surgical gloves, and two small oxygen tanks with masks. Additionally, the chief second of a boxer must bring the following items: a clear plastic water bottle, a bucket containing ice, a commission-approved solution to stop bleeding, adhesive tape, gauze, scissors, and one extra mouthpiece. Ammonia is prohibited. The boxing gloves used by contestants must be either 8 or 10 ounces (depending on the weight of the contests), with an attached thumb.

Ringside physicians are required to perform a series of duties for each boxing event. For example, at the time of the weigh-in, they are to give each boxer a physical examination. During the fights to which they are assigned, they must be present at ringside, and cannot leave the site until the last contestant has departed. Of course, they must be prepared to assist if an emergency arises, and may be called upon to examine a boxer at any point during the match. After the fight is over, the ringside physician again examines the boxer in the dressing room.

The use of alcohol, stimulants, drugs and injections not approved by the commission is strictly prohibited in Nevada. The list of prohibited and accepted (though not recommended) substances is detailed in NAC 467.50.

Boxers are required to submit to a urinalysis or chemical test before or after a contest or if a commission representative directs him to do so. There is a disciplinary process in place if any prohibited substances are found.

The legislation that created the Medical Advisory Board is also found in Chapter 467 — Unarmed Combat. The law specifies that MAB members must be licensed physicians who have at least five years of experience practicing medicine. The duties of the MAB are as follows: "1. Prepare and submit to the Commission appropriate standards for the physical and mental examination of contestants. No standard is effective until the Commission approves it. 2. Recommend to the Commission for licensing, physicians who are qualified to examine contestants. 3. Advise the Commission as to the physical or mental fitness of the contestant, if it so requests. 4. Prepare and submit to the Legislature and the Commission reports containing and recommendations for revisions in the law which it deems necessary to protect the health of combatants in this state" (NRS 467.018).

Interview with Former NAC Executive Director Marc Ratner (June 2005)

Marc Ratner was the executive director of the Nevada Athletic Commission at the time the BHS Survey was conducted, and has been involved in the sport since his state emerged as a prime boxing venue over four decades ago.[28] Ratner resigned from the commission in May 2006 after more than twenty years of service, to become vice president of the Ultimate Fighting Championship (UFC). This interview was conducted in June 2005.

"I'm a lifelong boxing fan," Ratner says, "I started going to fights here in the early sixties, title fights, even back then, and club fights. I went to work for the commission as an inspector in the mid–'80s, became the chief inspector in about 1987 and became executive director in 1992." Ratner's tenure in this high profile position is impressive, considering that he does not have a contract and served "at the pleasure of the commission." His admiration of the sport and wealth of experience he brings to this position is significant. It is clear that Ratner loves boxing and wants to protect the boxers as much as possible.

While Ratner and a small staff are full-time state employees, the commission and Medical Advisory Board members do not hold regular office hours. Ratner explains, "The commission meetings are held about every three weeks as a telephonic meeting to approve officials and then three or four times a year we have a full in-person commission meeting." Since the commission members have careers outside of boxing, the quarterly frequency of these meetings seems to be appropriate.

The selection of ringside officials occasionally raises controversy. Ratner explained the process: "Judges and referees, if it is a non-title fight, let's say a club fight, it is my decision to determine who will be assigned to work a boxing match. If it is a championship fight, everything must be selected and approved by the commission. Doctors are rotated around. I work with the Medical Advisory Board chairman and we try to come up with a schedule, and once again, for championship fights the commission is involved." Many of the ring officials in Nevada are well-known to boxing fans and have carried out their professional duties for years. Thus, it makes sense that availability would be a primary factor in the officials' selection.

There are two types of rules that govern boxing in Nevada: statutes (state code) and regulations (adopted by the athletic commission). Ratner explicates the process to modify or adopt new rules: "[To change] statutes, you have to go before the state legislature. [To change] regulations you have to have hearings, you have to post for I think three days. Then the commissioners, not me, can vote on those. Statutes are laws; regulations are more policy. They're both in the books." The process of adopting or modifying boxing regulations in Nevada is typical of the process in other states that possess boxing commissions.

While Ratner welcomes the consistency of rules that may be provided by a national boxing commission, he is concerned that the federal legislation may cause some negative economic impacts in Nevada. He says,

> I'm very interested in [the pending federal legislation to create a national boxing commission]. I want to learn more about it. There are some states' rights issues that I'm concerned with. I think that the status quo is not working. I think that you need — there's an Association of Boxing Commissions that's based in Missouri with Tim Lueckenhoff as president — and I would think that the best thing that could happen is that the ABC have a federal backbone. Because you already have the states in a loosely combined effort to regulate the sport and a federal commission would be a complete level of bureaucracy and I think it would be interesting to see how it would work. But I don't want anything that would take away anything from the state. Let's say that they took a dollar from every ticket to fund this thing. That might be money that comes out of the state of Nevada more than any other state. I don't want the state of Nevada to be penalized.

The states' rights issue Ratner brings up is important. While the regulatory implications of the federal boxing legislation, should it be approved, will not have much effect on the health and safety measures already existing in Nevada, other issues may. It should be noted that the scenario of funding of the national commission with money from admission tickets is not explicitly stated in the federal legislation. However, as the data in Chapter 2 indicates, the pending legislation would have a profound effect on most states that do not have the level of health and safety standards currently in Nevada.

Ratner clearly believes that the disparity among health and safety standards for professional boxing across the United States is detrimental to the sport. "I have talked to Dr. [Michael] Schwartz several times. I think that [the American Association of Professional Ringside Physicians] is doing a very good job of organizing the ring physicians for the betterment of the sport. What the sport needs is one set of medical standards. A minimal set of medical standards that is the same in every state. And the same rules, so that you fight under the same rules in every state. We don't have that, and that's one of the things that the federal commission may be able to help us with." The Professional Boxing Amendments Act of 2007 is written in such a way that those appointed to the federal commission would have a great deal of flexibility in determining what the minimum national medical standards would be. There is no guarantee that Nevada's high standards will be implemented, however, it will at least force states that presently have a bare minimum of standards to improve.

When asked why he believes that many states do not conduct HIV testing, neurological testing or drug testing, Ratner replies, "There is no reason for states not to, but not every state has the level of fights that California or Texas or Florida or New York or New Jersey or Pennsylvania have. Those are the major states, but let's say that you only have one or two fights a year in South Dakota or South Carolina, maybe that's one of the problems." It should be noted that neurological testing is not conducted in Texas or Florida, while random or discretionary drug testing is not carried out in California or Texas (in non-title bouts). In contrast, South Carolina does require HIV and neurological testing. Thus, Ratner's comments are indicative of the misperception that states which host a high volume of fights are also those that have higher health and safety standards. Such standards for professional boxing can be improved with consistency, according to Ratner. He says, "I think nationally you need standards of some kind. You can go [further], but you need minimum standards where everybody's at least testing. And you need a central bank of these medical records so that if a guy fights here and then he goes to Louisiana that they can draw upon." The Professional Boxing Amendments Act of 2007 will create such a medical registry, if the bill is signed into law.

Nevada is serious about conducting medical tests designed to protect boxers. Ratner emphasizes,

> I've been in the business many, many years. We have more tests now than we've ever had, especially with these MRIs and after the fights with the CT-scans, we do find some irregularities and it's very, very important. The only reason you need a boxing commission is for the health and safety of the fighters. So that's our paramount reason for having one. We have a mandatory MRI when you fight here for the first time. And if you have anything subsequent to that, if you suffer a hard knockout we can ask for more tests. [As far as] HIV and hepatitis testing, we haven't found many HIV positives, just a handful. We've had some hepatitis throughout the years and we've found several steroid abusers also. We test for substance abuse, any performance enhancing drugs. For steroids, we do it at fight time, just before you go out. For the rest of the performance enhancing drugs we test afterwards, since you wouldn't want anyone to take something during the fight.

Ratner's comments reinforce Nevada's place at the forefront of state medical testing.

Interview with Dr. Margaret Goodman (June 2005)

Dr. Margaret Goodman was the chairperson of the Medical Advisory Board (MAB) of the Nevada Athletic Commission in 2005.[29] She is a neurologist by profession, and was appointed to the MAB by the Governor of Nevada. After more than a decade of work as a ringside physician, Dr. Goodman resigned her post as chief ringside physician in December 2005, though she remained on the MAB until her term expired in 2007. She is a frequent contributor to *The Ring Magazine* and ESPN.com. This interview took place in June 2005.

Goodman explains her background and role with the commission saying, "I believe that I became involved with the Nevada boxing commission in 1993 as a consultant in neurology, so when they had fighters that they thought needed an evaluation with a neurologist to determine the extent of injuries and possibly whether they should be allowed to continue to box, I consulted with them. I began working with the amateurs for about a year and a half and subsequent to that time, I was allowed to be put on as a ringside physician and I have been a ringside physician ever since. Approximately in 2000 or 2001, I was appointed by the governor to be chairman of the medical advisory board. The board is made up of five physicians of various specialties." Similar to the commission itself, the MAB meets "every few months or when there's issues," according to Goodman. "We've met to discuss expanding our testing; we changed our drug testing not too long ago and added more substances."

Goodman is very well respected by boxing experts. Boxing historian Thomas Hauser says, "Margaret Goodman knows her stuff well and she really cares about the fighters. I think she's the best ring doctor in the United States." For the past several years, Goodman has authored a section in each issue of *The Ring Magazine* entitled, "The Fight Doctor," where she provides educational commentary on many aspects of boxing health and safety.

The Nevada MAB was created in reaction to the nationally televised death of Duk-Koo Kim in his fight with Ray Mancini. Goodman explains, "It only had really been used on a periodic basis for such examples as when Evander Holyfield or Mike Tyson, when there have been issues that needed to be addressed. Once I became chairman of the Medical Advisory Board and as things changed with the members of the commission, they decided to use the Medical Advisory Board more and so we've been utilized in determination of medical fitness to box for some other fighters. Other instances that the advisory board [has been] used was primarily when Dr. Flip Homansky was the chief physician and consulted with the medical advisory board on issues such as hepatitis testing, HIV testing, steroid testing, and changes in our yearly medical requirements." Goodman says that Nevada was the first state to conduct HIV testing and steroid testing.

Ringside physicians play an essential role in the protection of professional boxers. Goodman explains the selection process for ringside physicians, "[In 2004, the commission] created a position of chief ringside physician and that really amounts to mostly a *work* position as opposed to being a *fight* position. We have thirteen different physicians and we rotate the fights depending on the commission and our executive director with some input from me. [Assignments to fights] are sometimes based on availability. That's one of the biggest things it's based on — which doctors are available for which fights. We've got doctors that have been ring doctors for as long as eighteen or nineteen years and some that have only been ring physicians for two years. So some of its based on experience and expertise and some of it is based on just when you're available to work." Her comments coincide with Ratner's remarks.

Goodman's duties at a boxing event are varied. "My main role at this point in that particular position is to review all of the medicals on all the fighters, make sure everybody's OK, and when there's issues as far as abnormal MRIs, blood tests, EKGs or eye exams, I'm the one that's set up to follow up on that and determine on a quick basis whether they will be cleared to fight. I [also] follow up on all the suspensions. My duties are different at every fight. I think that it just depends on which medical issues crop up. The [Medical Advisory Board] has a recommendation capacity only. Then the commission has to meet and approve [any recommendations]. There have not been any instances when the commission has disagreed with the Medical Advisory Board's opinion." The functions of the Medical Advisory Board as Goodman describes are a key element of Nevada's commitment to preserving high health and safety standards.

Goodman shares Ratner's opinion that all states should carry out the tests that form the BHS Index.

> Obviously, I believe that every boxer should undergo [HIV testing, neurological testing, and drug testing] at least yearly. What we have is on our general physical exam. You know the question has been raised in different states whether you need to have a neurological exam done by a neurologist or a neurosurgeon. We don't in certain instances on a routine basis, and we don't require a neurologist to do a neurological exam. A neurological exam is part of our general physical that we require on a yearly basis that is done by an outside physician that cannot be affiliated with the commission. On instances that we have higher risk fighters, and by higher risk, I mean fighters that come into what we call our "comprehensive category"—fighters that are thirty-six years of age and over, fighters that have fought more than 450 rounds and also fighters that have had poor records or poor performance. At that point I will make a determination for the commission as far as what testing needs to get done. And I will obtain outside opinions when needed, about whether or not we need to send them to a neurologist, if they need further MRI testing, or further lab work. So that's done on a case-by-case basis and I think that's what's really important because it should be individualized. Some fighters that are maybe the age of thirty-four or maybe thirty-seven that maybe don't have medical issues that maybe a fighter that's twenty-six that's had a lot of fights and ring age and requires a lot of testing.

Goodman explains the costs of medical testing for boxers: "MRI scans cost $425, I think the subtotals of the other tests could be $200 to $300 so the total would be just under $1000. But we only do the MRIs on a one-time basis and thereafter as needed. We don't do separate exams with a neurologist, so that's included in our physicals, the remaining lab work would be about two to three hundred more." In some states, the promoters absorb these costs, whereas in others, the boxers themselves have to cover the costs.

Goodman is particularly concerned about drug testing.

> [Drug testing] is important and should be carried out in every single card. We do them randomly, unless it's a championship fight. The problem with drug testing, specifically steroid testing, is that unfortunately most people

> know how to beat the system. So I think that there are more individuals that would test positive but they are very experienced or around people that are very experienced that can tell them when to stop the drugs so that they don't test positive. It's very easy to determine the house life of these drugs and there are people that get paid a tremendous amount of money that teach these guys when to take which particular drug, how to stack them for the most advantage, which ones come out of your system when, and so that's a sideline too of many individuals and a profession of others. We do our steroids test pre-fight mainly because we don't get enough urine if we do it post-fight. So [the boxers] get a pre-fight and a post-fight drug test. And we test for about 125–130 items.

Goodman comments are troubling in the sense that professional athletes can find ways to get around testing for performance enhancing drugs. However, at least the state is taking a proactive effort to deter boxers from taking such drugs by testing randomly in non-title bouts.

Goodman recognizes the multitude of issues involved with HIV testing. "HIV testing is difficult. We do that every calendar year; obviously there could be arguments that you should do it more often. The same is true for hepatitis B and C tests. It's just too difficult, and not thought to be cost effective for us to do it on a more regular basis, but many states don't do it at all." The incubation period of these infectious diseases does not completely guarantee that a yearly examination is sufficient. Several states require HIV testing on a more frequent basis than Nevada.

Goodman says she believes the disparity of state regulations of professional boxing has a lot to do with the lack of medical recommendations to the various state commissions and the complacent nature of many commissioners. "I think that number one, the way it is in most states is that the physicians don't have a great deal of input [in state boxing regulations]. And number two, the states themselves have certain regulations and either the executive director or whatever the position is they become complacent in feeling that they have to just abide by the regulations and not try to change the regulations. The bottom line is that the regulations, if they're insufficient, should be changed. And unfortunately, it's a state by state process and every state that has boxing should take that responsibility unless there's a time when we have a federal [law] that will tell the states what they have to do." These comments reflect a means for commissions throughout the United States to improve. By obtaining recommendations from licensed physicians, or by requiring at least one commissioner to be a physician, state athletic commissions could potentially improve their medical standards.

If a national boxing commission is created, Goodman does not believe it will have a significant impact on Nevada because of its already high level of health and safety standards for professional boxing.

> I don't think it is going to impact Nevada a great deal. If you look at what its designed to do in its current form, and I think it will get watered down to some degree if it passes, [Nevada] already abide[s] by all of the different things that they would require. The one thing that it would do is [enable us to know] that fighters [coming to our state] have been followed more carefully and will not slip through the cracks as easily. But when you see somebody that comes to your state that hasn't been followed for many years on all the testing that we put fighters through, when they come here it makes it a little difficult to determine what their actual history is. We can look at [their records from] Fight Fax and determine what their fight history has been, but it doesn't tell you everything. So I think it will also make a lot of medical information available to us that we wouldn't otherwise have. So their past medical history will be more known to us and in that sense it will make things a lot safer. The main thing that a federal [law] will do is give some kind of [enforcement] power to subpoena people that don't follow the rules. It will make it easier to know that other states will have to follow what certain states mandate.

The enforcement power Goodman refers to is an important aspect of the 2007 Professional Boxing Amendments Act. The bill authorizes the national commission to investigate, subpoena, and bring suit against any entity that violates provisions of the law.

Goodman says she believes that a federal commission would strengthen the Association of Boxing Commissions (ABC). "The Association of Boxing Commissions would become the main arm of the federal [commission]. In that sense, the ABC has its own medical committee, which I'm sure will be somewhat responsible for oversight as opposed to another organization. Because the databank holding the medical information and the medical people that the federal commission will use will probably be separate from all these other organizations to some degree. I think the ABC will have more [power] to be able to accomplish things. Right now, the ABC has no subpoena power and really has no power. I think we'll have to see if the bill passes and see who's running [the national commission] and end up stipulating who's going to be doing what." The Association of Boxing Commissions is explicitly mentioned in the 2007 Professional Boxing Amendments Act, in reference to contract agreements and challenges to ratings. But its role in conjunction with the United States Boxing Commission that would be created if the bill passes is not clear.

According to Goodman, having unified medical testing, and having a databank and having an overseeing body that has subpoena power to exert control can improve health and safety standards for boxers in the United States. "Because right now fighters shop from state to state, or promoters will take certain fights to certain states or managers will take fighters to certain states depending on their requirements in those states. I think that's a big issue and I think that would be wiped out and stopped once there's some federal legislation." Of course, this depends on which minimum standards are adopted and how aggressive the potential federal commission wants to push for requirements.

In addition to minimal standards for medical testing, conflicts of interest among ringside physicians are yet another issue that needs to be addressed in Goodman's view.

> One thing that we are really different in [from other states] is on conflicts of interest, especially conflicts of interest among ring physicians. There should no longer be any time in which a ring physician acts as a private physician for a fighter. That is a huge conflict that goes on in many, many states and contributes to all kinds of deleterious things as far as a fighter's career and safety and definitely needs to stop. And I think that is one thing that will definitely stop if federal legislation is passed. That is certainly something that is not allowed in our state, but most states still allow that, where a ring physician can make money and still be the private physician for a fighter and therefore have an inappropriate relationship with a fighter. Therefore if you're working a fight and making a determination of whether a fighter should fight again or continue their career you already have a private financial relationship with a fighter that makes you ineligible to come up with that kind of decision. And those doctors shouldn't work fights.

It is unclear, at least in the current form of the federal legislation, if this potential conflict of interest would be eliminated. There is a provision in the 2007 legislation prohibiting payment or other compensation to ring officials who officiate at the fights, but it is does not explicitly state whether the ringside doctor fits in the definition of ring official.

Participant-Observation of the Nevada Athletic Commission

Arrangements were made to conduct a participant-observation of Nevada Athletic Commission personnel at a professional boxing event.[30] NAC executive director Marc Ratner and Medical Advisory Board chairperson Dr. Margaret Goodman allowed unrestricted access to observe commission personnel carry out their duties to protect the health and safety of professional boxers at a boxing event that took place on June 24, 2005.

The Regulation of Boxing

The observed boxing event was held at The Orleans Hotel and Casino in Las Vegas, Nevada. The event could be described as an evening of club fights, a typical boxing event whose participants are not particularly well known but usually put on a good show for the fans. A total of six bouts were held, mostly between up and coming boxers and veteran opponents scheduled for four to six rounds. However, there were two main events held for championships: undefeated Uzbek Timur Ibragimov faced unheralded Brazilian Rogerio Lobo for something called the FECARBOX International Heavyweight title in a bout that was scheduled for 10 rounds. In addition, his undefeated Russian cousin and 2000 Olympic silver medalist, Sultan Ibragimov, fought Kansan Andy Sample for a manufactured championship called the World Boxing Organization Asian Pacific Heavyweight Title.[31] The geographic region referenced in the title of the championship led NAC Dr. Flip Homansky to quip that if Sample were to win, the Asia Pacific title would ironically go to Kansas.

The bouts were held in a casino ballroom where the ring, surrounded by chairs, was placed in the center. Paramedics and emergency medical technicians could be seen at one end of the ballroom. Goodman noted that two ambulances were on site and that boxing matches never start without their presence. She also emphasized the importance of having paramedics present as they have had years of training and were more capable of reacting to serious health problems than EMTs. Makeshift dressing rooms were located in an adjacent conference room where curtains separated the boxers to provide some semblance of privacy. About an hour prior to the first bout Goodman made her rounds to each of the dressing rooms to meet with the boxers as their hands were getting wrapped. NAC inspectors observed the hand-wrapping process to ensure that an acceptable amount of gauze was used and that nothing but the boxer's hands made their way into the gloves. As Goodman greeted each boxer, she ask simple questions such as, "When did you go to sleep last night? What did you eat for breakfast? When was your last meal?" She later explained that she wasn't asking the questions to find out the answers, but rather to hear them speak. She said, "You can't tell a lot medically, but you can talk with them and see how they are neurologically. I just want to get an idea where their head is at."

The weigh-ins for the event took place the previous afternoon. As each boxer presented himself for the official weigh-in, he also signed waivers and was given a physical check-up. She also met with the referees and discussed any potential issues that might trouble the boxers. Goodman said that a referee has never disagreed with her recommendation during a boxing match.

"Doctors don't get involved at the level of keeping someone off the card," Goodman said, but she had to do just that as one of the boxers was kept off the card due to abnormal blood and MRI tests. He would have to undergo further testing before being cleared to fight. By fight night, Goodman had already reviewed each boxer's medical and professional boxing records, and all were cleared to box.

At ringside, the commission members and affiliates took their seats along one side of the ring. This researcher sat between ringside physicians Dr. James Game and Dr. Goodman. Next to Goodman sat Barbara Barcenas, a full-time staff member of the commission whose primary role was to record each judge's scorecard in between rounds and distribute staff and participant paychecks. Barcenas appeared to be uninterested in the fights themselves, and she often looked away from the action in the ring. With respect to transparency, this is probably a positive attribute for the person who is responsible for accurately recording the scores of a match. Barcenas also held each participant's professional boxing license along with a disclosure form that indicated the addresses and phone numbers of area hospitals in the event that a boxer needed assistance after leaving the arena. Several judges, including long-time Nevada judge Duane Ford, were present, along with well-known referees such as Joe Cortez.

During the bouts, Goodman would record any cuts suffered by the boxers on an official log that had simple diagrams of a face on which the location of the cut was to be indicated. In the first bout of the evening, boxer Leroy Brooks suffered a cut and Goodman was summoned in the ring to inspect the wound. Within seconds of observing the eye with a penlight and wiping the cut with a 4-in. by 4-in. gauze, she made the determination that the boxer would not be able to continue. Interestingly, Goodman did not wear latex gloves as she observed Brooks, an optional practice in the state of Nevada. She explained, "If I'm going to wear gloves, then I may as well wear a mask and goggles since I tend to get more drops of blood on my face and around my mouth than on my hands. But sometimes if I have a big cut on my hands, I will use gloves." Brooks was given a 45-day suspension until he could fight again, and 30 of those days are to be without contact. This appeared to be the standard suspension for boxers who suffered cuts around the eye. Goodman noted that sometimes a boxer would also be required to see an ophthalmologist in order to be cleared to fight again.

After the bout was stopped and the boxers made their way back to the dressing room, they were met by Dr. James Game, whose responsibilities for the evening included conducting a cursory post-fight physical exam of each boxer. Dr. Game had an NAC post-fight checklist (written in English and Spanish) that asked the boxer if he had any of the following: headache, dizziness, nausea, memory loss, ringing in the ears, weakness, trouble with balance, changes in vision, pain, cuts, possible fractures, shortness of breath or chest pain or other. Each boxer signed off on the completed checklist, and in the case of a cut, Dr. Game recommended that the boxer go to the hospital for stitches, emphasizing that the cost for the procedure would be covered by the promoter (free of charge to the boxer). The doctor wrote an order for the necessary treatment. The boxer also received his check and boxing license at that time. With the boxers that appeared to be all right, the post-fight check took about a total of three minutes. Goodman said that on average, about one or two boxers from each boxing event are sent to the hospital. The boxer has the option to take an ambulance to the hospital or go there on his own accord.

Several brown paper bags with handwritten notations were present at ringside. These contained urine samples of the four participants in the championship bouts and the randomly selected boxers who were required to submit urine samples. There appeared to be a problem with one of the urine samples, which was apparently collected from the wrong individual, but the chief inspector of the NAC, Anthony Lato, Jr., realized the mistake in time to collect a pre-fight sample from the appropriate boxer. A staff person from the medical testing lab came to ringside to pick up all of the samples. Goodman said that the results would take about ten days to obtain.

In the co-main event that evening, boxer Rogerio Lobo was cut on the bridge of the nose, resulting in a 180-day suspension from Goodman pending an x-ray to determine if the nose was broken. During the post-fight check, Dr. Game told the boxer not to move the nose around or blow it. The boxer promptly cashed his check and left the hotel, but didn't complete the required post-fight drug test. Thus, Goodman changed the boxer's suspension from 180 days to indefinite and he would have to appear before the commission to have his license reinstated. Goodman noted that the costs of the drug tests were $45 for stimulants, $154 for steroids and $79 for a general drug screen, all of which would come out of the boxer's purse.

The six scheduled fights for the evening came and went without major incident. All of the bouts were entertaining for the fans, and for the record, both Timur and Sultan Ibragimov preserved their titles and undefeated records with quick knockouts. Perhaps the most comical event of the evening came during the post-fight check, when Timur Ibragimov was asked if he was experiencing any changes in vision, to which he replied, "Yes. I only see women. I haven't had a woman in two months." Goodman suggested that the humorous response was perhaps the best indicator that the boxer was neurologically sound. A few boxers had to get stitches, but no one was seriously injured. For the evening's work, Goodman was paid between $250 and $300. Although Goodman said at the time that she dedicated about twenty hours per week to boxing issues, the only income she received related to the sport was when she officially worked at a boxing event.

It is clear that the members of this commission are experienced professionals that have the boxer's health and safety foremost in their minds. While the pending federal legislation to create a national boxing commission will force most states to comply with a minimal set of health and safety standards, it will not likely affect the practices in Nevada, as they far exceed minimal standards and Nevada officials are continuously trying to devise ways to improve upon their already efficient system. Since the Nevada Athletic Commission is generally considered to possess the pinnacle of health and safety standards, the participant-observation was revealing of two dynamics. One is how little time doctors spend with boxers after a bout. The second is how easily a mistake can be made with urine drug tests.

The Aftermath of the Participant-Observation

On July 1, 2005, just one week after the participant-observation, boxer Martin Sanchez died after he suffered a knockout loss at the Orleans Hotel and Casino. According to published reports, Sanchez was examined by two ringside physicians, Dr. William Berliner in the ring immediately after the fight, and Dr. Jeff Davidson in the dressing room afterwards, who were "satisfied he was ok," but Sanchez was later rushed to the hospital after he was "seen walking strangely."[32] Perhaps there are lessons to be learned from the Sanchez case regarding the extent of the post-fight evaluations. A few months later, Levander Johnson died after suffering an eleventh round technical knockout against Jesus Chavez in an IBF lightweight title fight. Dr. Goodman examined Johnson in the ring prior to the start of the eleventh round and allowed the fight to continue.[33] After Johnson died, then–NAC executive director Marc Ratner called for the establishment of an Advisory Committee on Health and Safety to investigate those deaths and propose reforms.[34] Goodman resigned as the state's chief ringside doctor in late 2005, and Ratner handed in his resignation to accept a position in the UFC in March 2006. Several changes to Nevada's boxing regulations were enacted under the leadership of Ratner's replacement, NAC executive director Keith Kizer.

Advisory Committee on Boxer Health and Safety

On June 30, 2006, an advisory committee composed of Sig Rogich, Luther Mack, Assemblyman Harvey Munford, Dr. Jim Nave and Dr. Charles Ruggeroli (member-deceased) submitted a report to Nevada Athletic Commission chairman Raymond "Skip" Avansino, Jr., detailing key issues that needed attention. Through this report, the advisory committee recommended that the NAC adopt recommendations in three areas to improve the health and safety aspects of boxing regulations: medical issues and testing; equipment; and trainers and gyms.[35]

Medical Issues and Testing

The report identifies two key areas that the commission should address within the realm of medical issues and testing: Weight management and dehydration and health and well being of fighters before and after fights. The advisory committee suggested increasing weigh-in penalties (for fighters that weigh over the agreed upon limit), allowing the consumption of electrolyte drinks; increasing random drug and steroid testing before and after fights, requiring at least three ringside physicians at every event, hiring a part-time doctor as a consultant to the commission, requiring post-fight physical examinations of *all* contestants, requiring a post-fight CAT scan of each contestant, establishing a health and welfare fund for aging and retired contestants, and establishing a pension fund for retired boxers.

Equipment

There is a constant controversy over the size (weight) and composition (material) of boxing gloves. The lack of scientific evidence that conclusively shows the effects of certain types of gloves kept the advisory committee from making any concrete recommendations other than to carry out a scientific study to examine if there are any differences with respect to protecting the health and safety of boxers. The advisory committee noted, however, that "there have been a greater number of problems in the 135 to 147 weight range, so that weight range of fighters might be worthy of some additional focus."

Trainers and Gyms

The advisory committee noted in its report that the only requirement for boxing trainers was a short application and the payment of a $50 fee. Rather than attempt to implement a training course, the committee recommended establishing a test that trainers would have to pass, encompassing the issues of weight loss, dehydration, nutrition and general knowledge of Nevada's regulations. Recognizing the increase in Latino and Latin American boxers (and their Spanish-speaking trainers) they recommended this test be produced in both English and Spanish. The committee also suggested producing bilingual publications on training and nutrition. Another significant recommendation is for the commission to amend its regulations to administer significant repercussions to trainers that do not inform the commission of serious injury to a combatant during training, even if the fighter is training or fighting outside of Nevada. The committee also came close to recommending licenses for gymnasiums to provide jurisdiction over the gym owners, but variables such as foreign-based fighters and those who train in their homes caused the committee to exercise restraint on the matter.

Other Areas

The committee encouraged the commission to obtain funding for more medical research that could be used to justify changes in health and safety standards. Furthermore, the committee recommended dissolving the current Medical Advisory Board and replacing it with a board of doctors that would meet on a monthly basis to establish policies that help improve health and safety regulations.

Changes in Health and Safety Rules

In an official memorandum dated July 24, 2006, from NAC executive director Keith Kizer to "All Licensed Promoters and Matchmakers," Kizer explains five significant changes that were made effective by September 1, 2006.[36] These changes are based upon the report of the Advisory Committee on Boxer Health and Safety. First, at least three ringside physicians will be required to be present at each boxing event. This rule change results in an additional cost for promoters, as each ringside physician charges about $400 to $500 to work at a boxing event.[37] Second, all boxers will receive a postfight physical examination in the ring as soon as the fight ends, whether they win, lose or draw. While this change does not result in an additional cost to the promoter, it does call for television crews (as well as photographers and cornermen) to refrain from interfering with the combatants until the medical examination has been completed. Third, the commission makes clear that more testing for non-approved drugs, stimulants and steroids will be conducted. This change is made possible by the increased funding the commission received from the state. Fourth, a boxer may request to consume approved electrolyte drinks before, during and after fights, provided they are in clear, factory-sealed bottles of about 20 oz. in size. Finally, boxers weighing over 135 pounds will be required to wear 10 oz. gloves in competition.

Interview with Nevada Referee Joe Cortez

Joe Cortez, whose moniker "Fair, but Firm" is known in boxing circles the world over, is a former boxer himself. In the 1960s, Cortez became a six-time (amateur) Golden Gloves Champion in New York. He became a professional at the age of 18 and fought in Mexico and Puerto Rico, but he quit boxing in 1971. In the mid–1970s, he became a referee, initially working Golden Gloves fights, and later became a referee in professional boxing. Cortez reflects upon his early days as a referee saying, "In 1978 I ran in to the commissioner for New Jersey, Jersey Joe Walcott, the former heavyweight champion, and we were chatting a little bit and he told me: 'You know, Joe, you do a good job in New York, I would like to have you to become a referee for the state of New Jersey,' which I did. So in 1978 I became a professional referee in New Jersey. And in 1982 I refereed my first world title fight, which was [former WBA Junior welterweight champion] Aaron Pryor against Miguel Montilla."

Since then, Cortez has traveled across the world, serving as the third man in the ring in over 170 world championship fights. Since 1992, Cortez has been based in Nevada. He explains his move out west saying, "Nevada

3 • Case Study: Boxing in Nevada

Referee Joe Cortez oversees the first bout in the Azumah Nelson–Jeff Fenech trilogy, which began in 1991 (photograph by Modesto M. Rodriguez).

was looking for a new referee and I was approached by Chuck Minker who was the executive director at the time and he assigned me to work a couple of fights in Nevada as a referee and told me that if I was to move to Nevada, or if I was to consider moving there, he would give me those title mega fights, like [referees] Richard Steele and Mills Lane. So I accepted the deal, and in 1992 I officially became a referee in Nevada."

Cortez explains the referee selection process from the referee's perspective saying, "The executive director gets to know the officials, and he [makes his determination in consideration of] the style of the referee and his experience. The commission tries to use a rotation system, and while they don't hold up to it 100 percent of the time, they try to give everybody a fair shake."

Cortez says that the main concerns all referees have is the safety of the boxers first and the enforcement of the rules second. "In the past, we used to be more than referees, but that stopped when they cut championship fights down from 15 rounds to 12. We used to have three different jobs: enforcing the rules, watching out for the safety of the fighters, and scoring the fight. And when Duk-Koo Kim died of injuries received in the ring by 'Boom Boom' Mancini, they made some changes to improve the sport as far as safety was concerned. That's when they cut championship fights from 15 to 12, and they took away the scoring duties from the referee, using three judges instead of two plus the referee."

Prior to any fights that referees are assigned to work, Cortez says that they receive briefings as to any possible medical issues that boxers might have had in the past.

> We are briefed by ringside physicians and we also try to do a little background check on our own to see the records of the fighters, especially the main event fighters. We look for how they performed in their most recent fights. For preliminary fighters, the ringside doctors give us a brief history on them. Another tactic that I utilize while giving instructions to the fighter is asking them myself, "How did you do in your last fight?" And they tell me, "Well I won or I lost." If they lost, I ask: "How did you lose?" If they tell me, "Well I got knocked out," [then I ask] "How about the fight before that?" If they tell me, "I've lost," [I ask] "How did you lose that?" If they tell me "By knockout" again then I keep that in mind, keeping it in my memory bank. And then when they perform in the fight I look out for certain things. Since the red flag went up already in the dressing room, I am more prepared to considering stopping the contest a little early when I see that they are taking a lot of punishment.

Cortez has had the unfortunate experience of working a fight in which one of the contestants died.

> I refereed the fight between Robert Wangila and David Gonzalez back in 1994. Robert Wangila came in as a former Olympic champion, and a pretty decent contender [Wangila's record was 22–4 (16) at the time]. Wangila was winning the fight, but I saw that they were both taking a lot of punches to the head during the course of the bout. I called in the doctor to check out both fighters even though nobody got seriously hurt because I like to always be cautious. I believe that in the ninth round, Wangila got rocked a little bit by an uppercut and was holding on to Gonzalez as he fell to the canvas. I called it a no knockdown because it was a push but when he arose, I stayed close to the action because I knew that he was already a little hurt. He took a hard left and a hard right and I jumped in immediately and stopped the contest. The fans were booing me because I stopped the fight and they knew that Wangila was winning. As a matter of fact, two of the judges had him winning and the other had it even. And Wangila himself was a little upset that I stopped the contest. And when I was walking out of the ring that night, a fan came up to me and said, "Joe, you are my favorite referee, but tonight you did a lousy job. Why did you stop that fight?" I just looked at the guy. I don't like to get into confrontations with fans, so I decided to get

ready to go home. Everybody was still booing, walking out and then one of the officials came out of the dressing rooms and said: "Joe where is the doctor?" I said, "Well, I believe he left." So we paged him and got him [to come] back. We had to call an ambulance because the fighter, Robert Wangila, in the fight I had stopped moments before, was having seizures in the dressing room. Well, they rushed back to the arena and had to call the ambulance, which had already left the property. And so they rushed the kid to the hospital and then they found out that he had a massive blood clot in his brain. They performed surgery. I rushed to the hospital that night with my wife to see how his condition was, and the doctor told me that he didn't look too good. Two days later, he passed away.

Cortez punctuates his comments by adding,

I was just thinking about the fans that were booing me for stopping the contest, you know. People are quick to cast a judgment on the referee, when they are watching on television or they are one hundred feet away, and wonder, "why is he stopping the fight?" There are things that happen that only the referee, who is closer to the action, can make decisions about. He is a little bit more professional than anybody else. I think that [after Wangila died], the fans realized that I made the right call and they must have been saying to themselves, "Wow, we were booing that poor referee and he was really, in the end, right to stop the contest." There was a title fight lined up the same week, James Toney against Charles Williams on HBO, and they asked me, "Joe, are you OK to work the fight?" You know, because of what just happened to Robert Wangila. I said, "Absolutely, I feel [fine]," though I felt bad for what happened to Wangila and his family, but I was very confident in myself because I knew that I did the right thing [by stopping the Wangila-Gonzalez fight].

Cortez's sobering account of Wangila's demise points to two regulations that needed to be changed in an attempt to ensure the health and safety of the boxers. First, that the ambulance be present on site until the last boxer has been checked by a ringside physician and left the venue. Second, that a ringside physician must also be present at the venue until the last boxer has left. These procedures were implemented by Nevada in the aftermath of the Wangila fight. Had they been in place prior, a life may have been spared.

There comes a point for every boxing fan, when he is watching a great fight, and the referee calls over the ringside physician to check out a boxer. Such moments are often times met with boos from the live audience, as they can lead to an immediate stoppage. Cortez says that he always abides by the ringside physician's advice. "When the doctor tells me, 'stop the contest,' I automatically stop it. I don't hesitate, because I am not a doctor; he or she sees things that I cannot see. But it's a situation where the doctors have the full authority. We [referees] all respect the doctor's authority decision at that moment. We always consult with the ringside doctor during the contest, between rounds, we take his advice, and we listen. The ringside doctor will tell us if they think that the fighter has taken a little too much [punishment], or that if he takes more hard blows, we should consider stopping the fight. And we do just that."

Cortez singles out Dr. Margaret Goodman as one of the top ringside physicians in the sport. "I've enjoyed working with Dr. Goodman, a good ringside physician," he says. "She and I really had good communication. During the fight, I would look at her, she would look at me and we would understand each other. She would know when I wanted her in the ring, or she would look at me when she thought I should be ready to stop the fight. So, that is another point, that the doctor and the referee have good communication and know how to work with each other."

The most difficult call for Cortez is the decision to end a fight. He says, "Well, the most difficult call is stopping the contest, especially when a fighter is hurt. You know, we have to always watch really close, especially when a fighter is hurt and you have to start preparing to stop the contest. I like to always 'semi-call' in between rounds when I go to the corners, and show some concern for the fighter that is hurt. And I tell the corner man in front of the fighter himself, 'Listen, if your fighter doesn't show me something, I'm going to stop the contest' and it helps keep everyone on their toes because everyone knows that something is wrong and an action may be taken soon. That way, when you stop the fight, they know it was coming and that is good for boxing."

Cortez supports the creation of a national boxing commission, provided that the director of such a commission understands the sport. He says, "If they can bring some boxing people together and have a 'boxing czar,' who knows boxing, then I think it would improve the sport. But I don't want somebody who is politically appointed who has no idea about boxing. I don't see anything wrong with a national commission, provided that they put the right individual in there. If Congress were to pass something like that, it would have to require all states to follow the rules, implementing unified rules across the country. We would have to all be on the same page."

As a Nevada referee, Cortez attends or leads training seminars throughout the year. Some of these seminars are held in Nevada; however, he has been asked to train referees around the world for ABC certification. "We have a certification process that we have to take every two years," he says, "through the Association of Boxing Commissions."

Cortez, says that his moniker, "Fair But Firm," came from a television interview he was involved in, where they asked him, "Joe, what does it take to be a good referee?" He replied, "For one thing, you have to be fair with the fighter and, by the same token, you have to be firm." He explains that as he was watching the interview, he thought to himself, "Yeah, fair but firm. Hmm, maybe I can use that," and the phrase has stuck with him for the last five or six years. Cortez will usually repeat the phrase as he concludes his instructions to boxers in the ring.

Cortez views himself as being an elder statesman of the sport. "I've been a referee for thirty years now," he says, "so I bring a lot of knowledge into the sport and this is why I try to share my wisdom with my colleagues to enhance the sport. I've always told the officials that there is room for improvement." Cortez has a concrete suggestion for the improvement of health and safety for boxers. He says, "I think that trainers should be required to take a certification course, just as we do as referees, because sometimes you get trainers that come off the street and take these fighters' lives in their hands and they don't know what to look for themselves when a fighter is taking too much punishment, not only in the contest, but in the gym as well. In the gym, boxers are there five or six days a week sparring and they can take a lot of punishment there without proper supervision. Without these trainers really being trained themselves, it can be kind of hazardous for the fighters. So that is why I think that trainers should also be trained to know what to look for."

This simple suggestion begs the question as to why it is not implemented. Cortez replies, "It doesn't happen because nobody is there to enforce it. I've talked about these issues in the past. For example, when I mentioned raising the weight of gloves, increasing the ounces of gloves from eight to ten, which we implemented in Nevada for boxers over [137] pounds. I also requested that heavyweights increase their glove weight from ten ounces to twelve ounces. I recommended these [measures] two years ago, and they implemented that idea in Nevada last year. So I think that these are good safety measures, but the other thing I requested at that time was to have the trainers go through seminars and to create certifications for them so that we can improve the training techniques of trainers."

Another issue that Cortez believes would improve the health and safety aspects of boxing is educating trainers about the effects of rapid weight loss. He says, "There are a lot of fighters that blow up twenty, thirty, forty pounds in between fights, and then the trainers have them in a regimen to lose forty pounds of weight in six weeks. That can cause a lot of problems, such as dehydration for the fighters, and I'm not a doctor, but I think that can cause damage to anybody who loses that much weight so quick. That is why I think the trainers need to be trained to know what signs to look for as well. One of the other things that I also notice is that the trainers today, not all, but some, just tell their fighters to go out there throw a right hand, a left hook. How about defense? I don't hear, 'Show me a better defense, and don't get hit.' The name of the sport is 'hit, but don't get hit.' People love a crowd pleaser who's a banger that goes out there gets hit, gets cut, goes down, gets up, and goes down. That provides a lot of excitement for the fans, but for the fighter, that is not good, that is not healthy. We need trainers to train the fighters the proper way, with better techniques. More boxing, less slugging."

Interview with Nevada State Athletic Commission Executive Director Keith Kizer

The current executive director of the Nevada State Athletic Commission is Keith Kizer. He is a lifelong boxing fan and a lawyer, and was interviewed exclusively for this book in December 2007. He began working for the Nevada State Attorney General's office in October 1997 and soon began working with the athletic commission "as a backup deputy attorney, helping the senior attorney with some legal matters that appeared before the commission; nothing too extensive. Then, in May 1998, I moved up the ranks, became co-counsel and was heavily involved with them for the next few years and in 2001 actually became lead counsel. I carried out that job until the end of May 2006. Mark Ratner left the commission and I became the new executive director."

Since Kizer was appointed to the position of executive director there have been several changes to the NAC. On June 30, 2006, the Nevada Advisory Committee on Boxer Health and Safety released its report of recommendations to the NAC. Kizer says this advisory committee conducted "a lot of interviews and meetings, resulting in some very good ideas which I implemented when I took over, based upon their report." For example, Kizer says,

> We used to require two ringside doctors, and now we have a minimum of three. Anywhere from three to four ringside doctors are present at each event. Increasing the medical staff present helps [ensure safety]. In the past, after the fights, the doctors would always check the fighters in the dressing rooms and of course would attend to the ones that were seriously hurt, right then and there. But now both fighters get an immediate in-ring examination after

the fight. So now, even if a fighter knocks his opponent out within ten or twenty seconds into the fight, the victor would be also be checked, because odds are that even if you win in the first round by knockout, you may have been hit in the head once or twice yourself. So, it helps the fighters to know that the doctors are right there. They know that win, lose or draw, there is a doctor right there to attend to them as soon as the final bell rings.

Kizer explains that the commission has also "increased drug and steroid testing. We're testing more fighters than before for drugs and especially steroids. I think that steroids are the bigger deal of the two, but we are also still testing for drugs. We will also start doing 'out of competition' drug testing. In other words, a fighter may not have a fight lined up, he may not have a fight for a couple of months, but we can call him and [require him to] take an immediate drug test for steroids as opposed to just doing it at fight night." The promoter covers the cost of drug tests at the fight, but the commission would cover out of competition drug tests through funding received from the state legislature.

Another change, perhaps one of the more controversial, is permitting boxers to consume electrolyte drinks during a fight.

> In the past, only water was allowed. There are two reasons for this; first and foremost is safety. Boxing is not like being outside running a marathon, though occasionally there is an outdoor fight. The maximum time of a fight is thirty-six minutes, if it goes the twelve round distance. Most fights, of course, are much shorter than thirty six minutes. Nevertheless, there may be a long, grueling fight, there may be a fight outdoors, or a fight where a guy was a little dehydrated coming in, and it can't hurt to have these electrolyte drinks. This may not make the difference between life and death, but it may make a difference after the fight. The second reason for allowing electrolyte drinks is one of respect, or dignity. I mean, if baseball players, football players, golfers and bowlers can drink Gatorade during their event, why not boxers? Why aren't boxers treated at the same level as other athletes? I think that this will help a lot.

Kizer responds to obvious concerns over the security of the bottle contents saying, "We make sure [the drink] is in a factory sealed bottle that is clear, so we can make sure that no one is putting something that they shouldn't put in. And that the bottle is a size that is workable at the corner. We don't need it spilling around on the gloves."

In practical terms, it is impossible to conceive that electrolyte drinks will not spill on the canvas or on the boxers' gloves just as water does. Cornermen often have to wipe off the ring with a towel to remove excess water. There is no reason to believe that they will not have to do the same with electrolyte drinks, but the difference of course is that such drinks are sticky and could conceivably cause problems for boxers' foot traction on the ring. Should the electrolyte drinks spill on the gloves, they could very easily get into an opponent's eyes and cause further problems. Nevertheless, Kizer concedes that many boxers and trainers will not take advantage of the allowance of such drinks in the ring. He says, "It's very, very rare that a fighter would bring anything to the ring but water. I think that they are so used to drinking water they don't want any of these electrolyte drinks in there. But at least, again, it's their option. Baseball players don't have to drink Gatorade; they can drink water if they choose to."

A third change that the NAC implemented based upon the advisory committee recommendations is raising the weight of gloves worn by boxers 137 pounds and over from eight ounces to ten ounces. Kizer explains the rationale behind this saying, "All the boxers that have died in Nevada, which I think total eight deaths in [the past] sixty-four years, had been wearing eight ounce gloves [during their fatal fights]. Since September 1, 2007, we changed the cutoff from 147 to 137 so basically it affected two weight classes: junior welterweight and welterweight. They now wear ten ounces gloves." There have been eleven ring deaths in Nevada since 1934, but six of these have occurred since 1994.[38] Kizer also points out that the commission has hired a part-time research doctor to conduct all the pre-fight and post-fight medicals. He says, "He's also engaged in all these studies, mainly to review the myths and legends of boxing such as [the effects of] dehydration or losing weight, or regaining weight after the weigh in, drugs and steroids, equipment like the weight and composition of gloves. He will study the differences between gloves, such as Reyes gloves, which are a lot different than Everlast gloves, which are a lot different than Grant gloves, and so on."

Kizer also says that the state legislature has provided funding to produce a type of boxing health and safety manual. He says,

> If you go to Department of Motor Vehicles to get a driver's license, they will give you a twenty or thirty page booklet which gives you the basic rules of the road, tips for driving and safety and things like that. And reading the book is not going to make you [a great driver like race car legend] Mario Andretti, but it's going to give you the basic safety information. So we want to produce something like that. Maybe we will have a chapter on how to recognize and treat concussions. If boxers get hurt at the fight, we have ringside doctors and paramedics there, but a lot of these guys get hurt at the gym, so we need a chapter on that. Perhaps we will have a chapter on mouthpieces, describing the benefits of a good mouthpiece, or the detriments of a bad mouthpiece and how to tell the difference. And a chapter on dehydration, a chapter on weight cutting and regaining the weight after the weigh-in. Another chapter could be on drugs and the dangers of using steroids. Again, it doesn't have to be extensive or a book; this is more for boxers, trainers,

people like that, written for them to read and providing some basic health tips and understanding. Hopefully, we'll have it in PDF format on our Web site so that anyone can just go and download it for free.

Kizer says the commission meets every three to four weeks. The agendas for their meetings are posted at the athletic commission's Web page. The commission also has a process in place to approve upcoming fights by getting the medical reports on all the combatants. Kizer says,

> We make sure that they are OK, and then assign the officials to work those fights. We also set the times for the weigh-ins and set times for the fights. As it gets closer to the date of the events, we assign the judges and referees to their specific fights. And then, of course, we continuously work on side projects such as the health and safety book. But most of what we do is finding out who is fighting, and making sure they are licensable. Most specifically their medical records as well as their fight records are what I look at, making sure the match-ups are fair. There is always going to be a favorite, just like in football or baseball games, but we want to make sure that [the fighters are comparable in] skill and in experience.

Kizer maintains a four-person staff that makes sure all the medical information is received and completed, and determines which, if any, additional tests are required. The commission keeps the promoter informed, on a daily basis as the show gets closer and closer, about the information the commission has or needs for each boxer on a given fight card. As the executive director, Kizer generally decides upon the assignment of ring officials to specific fights. However, for special events or world championship fights, the assignments would be an item on the commission agenda, for the commission to approve.

While Nevada is at the forefront for medical testing, safety, and regulations many states do not conduct certain drug tests or any drug tests and in some cases neurological tests, or HIV tests. Kizer says he believes that the lack of such tests by other state athletic commissions is a result of the low volume of fights they host or the lack of funding from their state legislature. He says, "In some situations there may be a concern that the costs of the tests may be too much for the fighters or for the promoters. If the fighter has to pay the cost of the tests, that's money out of his pocket, and a lot of fighters don't get paid very well. If the promoter has to pay it, they just pass on the costs by paying the fighters less. Sooner or later the fighter pays for it and that is a concern. Our biggest concern is the physical health of the fighters but we're also concerned about their financial health. Some things like HIV testing, hepatitis testing, even MRIs, I think are at the point where they are a necessary cost, and hopefully other states will [raise their standards]."

Kizer says he does not believe that the creation of a national boxing commission will affect Nevada at all. He says,

> The U.S. senators that have been involved in creating that legislation have been very much in contact with us. Senator [John] McCain and Senator [Harry] Reid, for example, have come to our office for advice and information. They all said publicly that they look at us as a model. But we are a jurisdiction that is very limited. It stops at the Nevada border. So, the senators are looking at ways to try to hopefully make the rest of the United States commissions very akin to how we do things here in Nevada. We definitely appreciate that praise, although I think that there are a lot of states that do a great job as well as us, so by no means do we hold ourselves up as the only good commission, or the only commission that knows what they are doing, nor do we claim that we know all the answers, [because] we definitely don't. Fortunately, Nevada is pro-boxing, and there are a lot of venues that want to put up their money to have big fights or even the smaller fights for that matter. The hotel industry here especially has been very pro-boxing, very pro MMA, and they are willing to spend money to get fights to come here so it gives us the ability to, of course, be very active as a commission but not overly active, which is good too. This results in our judges, referees, doctors, staff, the commissioners, and the inspectors, to gain a lot of experience and exposure to the fight game. Not so many states have that luxury, and you can't blame them for that. They have other entertainment or sports events that take precedence. In Nevada, we don't have any pro football, or baseball, basketball, hockey or other major league teams. Boxing and MMA get a lot more exposure here than they would in some other states where they have so many professional teams that get a lot of the glamour, the press and the money. So, that puts us in a good position here and we definitely appreciate that.

Kizer's concern about a national commission is that it might be too redundant. He summarizes Nevada's position by stating,

> We want [the federal government's] help, we need their help, it's definitely welcomed, but we don't want any things that too superfluous, in other words: if it's just a matter of enacting the same licensing requirements, that doesn't help. However, the federal laws that already passed already have been very helpful. Both the Professional Boxing Safety Act of 1996 and the Muhammad Ali Boxing Reform Act of 2000 have been very helpful at setting some minimum standards on health and safety and dealing with issues involving sanctioning bodies and promoters. Even interactions among states has improved, so any kind of law, whether it becomes local, state or federal that helps improve the regulations of boxing is welcomed by this commission. Congress should be highly praised for the 1996 [Professional Boxing Safety] Act and the 2000 Ali Boxing Reform Act that amended it. I think every aspect of those laws have been a positive force for boxing. But again, my concern is that it is not superfluous or duplicative, because then is it is just going to cost promoters more money, which is going to be passed on to the fighters, and they are going to make less money.

Kizer claims he saw a report that indicates most of the costs of enacting new federal regulations should be borne by the promoters. He says, "If promoters have to pay an extra $10,000 for a fight card, odds are the total purses are going to be $10,000 less for the fighters, so that is a concern we have to have with all kinds of government regulations. Sooner or later, it gets passed on to the consumer or the boxers. This is a very important issue, and I think that Washington has been very cognizant of this, and perhaps that's why the bills that have been introduced to Congress subsequent to the Muhammad Ali Boxing Reform Act have not passed."

Kizer and the Nevada Athletic Commission are members of the Association of Boxing Commissions. He says,

> I've been very fortunate to be involved with them. I've been to a lot of their conventions over the last seven to ten years and I think it's a very helpful resource. I have made many contacts through the ABC since I became executive director [in mid–2006]. I've learned a lot going to the conventions and the contacts I made have helped me, for example, when we cross-train and exchange judges from different states. Talking with a lot of other executive directors has been a benefit to me. Sometimes I will call them up and say, "We haven't had someone from your state for a while. Who is your top judge? I heard about this judge; how good is he, or how good is she? You know, are they worthy to travel, or have they done good enough job that they'll represent your state well coming here to Las Vegas?" Or vice versa, I may get a call from an executive director from another state with that kind of question for me. It's helped with a lot of different issues: the glove issue, open scoring, other health and safety issues, drug testing, and rankings. A lot of different issues have been examined through this organization and I think it helps to have this type of association to discuss ideas and make presentations. I've always have good experience at those conventions and the group e-mails and things like that.

Kizer has spoken at the national conference for the American Association of Professional Ringside Physicians. However, he says, "Not being a doctor myself, I am not involved with that organization at all. However, any type of group that can get people [in the same profession] together talking, making presentations, and bouncing ideas off each other can only be a good thing." Kizer says that the Nevada Medical Advisory Board (MAB) meets on an annual basis separately from the commission meetings. "In the past, we had chief ringside doctors that would look at the medical reports that came in to make sure that everything is fine and everybody passed their tests and things like that. The MAB is more for the bigger issues, such as when we have a high profile case or we want an independent medical exam of the fighter." Kizer cites two examples of consultations with the MAB for high profile cases such as determining the licensing status of heavyweight contender Joe Mesi, who has reportedly suffered two subdural hematomas, and former world champion Marco Antonio Barrera, who has a metal plate in his head from a non-boxing related surgery. The MAB is also consulted for its expertise on issues such as drug testing procedures. Most medical issues are handled by ringside physicians or the commission, but as Kizer points out, the MAB is good to have for particular issues that may need to go through a more formalized process.

Kizer says he is content with the current state of health and safety regulations for boxers in his state. He says,

> We have the luxury of working in a state that is very pro-boxing and the legislature has been very responsive to us. The state legislature gave us money to pay for fighter post-fight CAT or MRI scans. The fighters that get hurt in the ring are going to be sent to the hospital to get a scan anyway, but this funding allows any fighter, win, lose, or draw, who doesn't get hurt in the ring, to get a free scan. This is a huge expenditure by the legislature. They basically increased our budget by 60 or so percent the last time around. So, it's nice to see them be so pro-fighter, as well, of course, giving us money for doctor-trainers, the training booklet, and for additional drug testing. Having a very responsive legislature and the business industry here being pro-boxing and bringing a lot of the big and small fights here has helped out a lot. We're always willing to listen to new ideas and recommendations, and we are willing to change things if they are needed. Boxing has been around over one hundred years, but probably every fourteen months or so, we are tweaking our regulations, making changes to try to make the sport a better sport to the extent we can. We see our role as being very limited. We are just the regulators, not the guys who get in there and fight. We are neither the promoters, nor the managers. We have an important role, but it should be a small role, to make sure it's a level playing field, that we have fair fights that are as safe as possible. Boxing will always be a dangerous activity, but [we want it to be] as safe as it can within the confines of the rules. And we want to make sure that the guys are fighting fairly, that they are legitimate fights, not fixed or things like that. Other than that, we leave it to the fighters. We get them in the ring, and let the best man or woman win, and go from there.

Kizer says that the annual budget for the state athletic commission is approximately $650,000 for FY2008. In terms of revenues, Kizer says,

> Last year [2007] was our best year ever. Our revenue has been going up every year since we approved MMA. Last year we made $4.834 million and the budget was $426,000. So before MMA we were probably averaging about $2 million to $3 million per year, and last year we almost made $5 million. This year we will gain about that same amount, if not more. We made about half a million dollars for the state on the Hatton-Mayweather fight by itself. That was just one fight of the sixty or so we had in the year, our second biggest

fight of the year, but still it helps. It is good to see the legislature give us another, roughly $200,000 for our budget that will basically be dedicated to the costs of a consulting physician, the post-fight scans, transportation for the fighters to the post fight scan centers, the informational booklet, the increase in drug testing, paying the inspectors, as well as out of competition drug testing.

Kizer concludes his thoughts on the current status of health and safety in boxing by saying,

> There are a lot of people involved in the sport of boxing, and it's a great sport. The most important person is the boxer, and we keep cognizant of that fact as much as anybody. But we try to deal with the managers, promoters, trainers, officials, inspectors, and the television networks that are involved on a respectful basis. For the most part, we achieve that goal. It helps set a very good framework to allow these athletes get fight the best fights that they can, in the safest possible atmosphere, and we have an understanding that this is not the easiest sport to compete in, by any means. The more interest that is out there, the better. That is why I am always happy when the media, fans or academics call me, because it can only be helpful to the fighter in the long run. Boxing is not, unfortunately, like major league baseball, where you have world class facilities, a great pension plan, and great surroundings. In boxing, once you get to the level of Oscar De La Hoya or Floyd Mayweather, things are great. But for most boxers, this is a tough [sport]. We try to ensure that the medical requirements are the same if you are a world champion, if you are making your pro debut, or your record is five and five. The medical requirements are the same, the doctors examine you and carry out the same pre-fight physical exam or post-fight exam. That consistency of care has been very beneficial to us over the years.

Conclusion

Nevada is at the forefront of the sport of boxing. It is a state rich in boxing history, being among the first to legalize the sport and hosting some of the sport's most significant events. Legislation was passed to legalize boxing in Nevada in 1897. The athletic commission created in 1941 has evolved into a prototype for other states to follow.

The state hosted several of the most important fights of the early part of the twentieth century, including Jim Corbett vs. Bob Fitzsimmons and Jack Johnson vs. Jim Jeffries. Jack Dempsey and promoter "Tex" Rickard launched their careers in Nevada, but the state would not achieve its status as boxing's capital until the latter half of the twentieth century. The Las Vegas Convention Center and several casinos started the trend of hosting major boxing events in the 1960s, and by 1980 the city became a fixture for major boxing events. In the 1990s especially, it has taken a proactive stance toward the improvement of health and safety standards for boxers, being the first to implement tests for HIV and steroids.

In-depth interviews with former NAC executive director Marc Ratner and former Medical Advisory Board chairperson Dr. Margaret Goodman and referee Joe Cortez reveal the importance the commission places on protecting boxers. The participant-observation provided tremendous insight into the activities carried out by the commission to comply with state statutes and regulations. Current executive director Keith Kizer has implemented several changes to the commissions ruled and regulations since he assumed office in mid–2006. And Las Vegas retains its reputation as "Fight Town, U.S.A."

4

CASE STUDY: BOXING IN KANSAS

Introduction

Kansas established its first athletic commission to regulate boxing in 1925. "Under the original 1925 law, boxing matches were allowed only when they were sponsored by a benevolent, patriotic, fraternal, or religious organization."[1] As a result of the few boxing matches held in the state, the revenue generated through boxing did not justify the expense of funding an athletic commission, and therefore the Kansas legislature decided to abolish the commission in 1980.[2] The driving force behind the reestablishment of an athletic commission in Kansas was State Representative Tom Burroughs, who introduced the bill (HB2713) to create the Kansas Professional Regulated Sports Act in 2004.

Representative Burroughs argued that Kansas has strong ties to the boxing industry, but because of the lack of a commission to regulate the sport, the state was limited in its ability to draw boxing events.[3] He also justified the necessity of a commission to protect and promote Kansas boxers, and argued that by hosting boxing events, the state could draw tourist dollars.[4] Burroughs' justifications are plausible, especially when one analyzes the number of boxing events held in Kansas and neighboring Missouri over the past decade. Between 1995 and 2004 (when the bill to create the Kansas Athletic Commission was signed into law by Governor Kathleen Sebelius, commissionless Kansas hosted a total of 36 boxing events (an average of 3 to 4 events per year), while next-door neighbor Missouri hosted 344 (34 to 35 events per year).[5] Missouri's boxing venues, especially those in or near the Kansas City, Columbia or St. Joseph areas, are easily accessible to residents of northeast Kansas.

Prior to the establishment of the Kansas Athletic Commission, up-and-coming Kansas-based boxers (and their fans) would mostly have to travel to

Missouri or other neighboring states to fight (or watch their local boxer compete), leaving their tourist dollars outside the Kansas state line. When one considers all of the expenses involved in going to participate or watch a boxing event, such as lodging, transportation, food, drinks, and tickets to the venue, those dollars can add up. And if a boxing event is held at one of the casinos, gambling revenue must also be taken into account.

Although the law to create the Kansas Athletic Commission was signed in April 2004, the commission was not appointed until mid-2005. In the first two full years of the commission's work, Kansas has hosted 22 boxing events (11 per year). In that same timeframe, Missouri hosted 68 events. An analysis of boxing events held in both states since 1995 shows that boxing in Kansas increased from an average of 3.4 events per year between 1995–2004 (without a commission) to 11 events per year between 2006–2007 (with a commission). The increase in Kansas boxing did not have any noticeable effects on Missouri, where the average number of boxing events per year remained virtually the same between 1995–2004 (34.4 events) and 2005–2007 (34.3).[6] This data suggests that there is a market for boxing in Kansas, and that both states benefit economically from the increase in boxing interest and events in both states. Furthermore, these statistics do not include the dozens of mixed martial arts (MMA), kickboxing and wrestling contests that were regulated by the Kansas Athletic Commission in the state during that time. For example, according to a report produced by Kansas boxing commissioner Aaron Davis, during Fiscal Year 2007, Kansas hosted 14 boxing events, 15 mixed martial arts events and 6 wrestling events. An official Kansas Athletic Commission brochure produced in early 2007 states that since August 2005, the commission has sanctioned more than 60 boxing, wrestling, mixed martial arts and kickboxing contests. The brochure also states that over 600 fight-sport related participants, including over 330 fighters, have been licensed by the commission. By the end of FY 2007, information provided by Davis indicated that over 1,000 individuals had been licensed by the commission.

The licensing of participants is a direct source of revenue for the commission. According to the Kansas Boxing Commission Web page, current licensing fees are as follows: promoter ($400); contestant ($40); referee ($50); judge ($50); matchmaker ($200); manager ($100). Seconds, announcers, timekeepers, and physicians are charged $20 for their respective licenses. Federal boxer ID cards cost $15, while permits to host professional boxing, kickboxing, and MMA events cost $25 per contest per day; wrestling event permits cost $150 per performance per day.[7] Before the Kansas Athletic Commission was re-established in 2004, the boxing commissions of neighboring states would gain licensing revenues to oversee boxing in Kansas.

Interview with Kansas Boxing Commissioner Aaron Davis

Aaron Davis became the first appointed commissioner of the newly re-established Kansas Athletic Commission in 2005. Having grown up in New Jersey, near the Philadelphia area, Davis has long been involved in athletics. As a high school student, he participated in basketball, football and track, but he practiced boxing in the summer. He earned a basketball scholarship to attend Wichita State University in Kansas, where coaches prohibited Davis from engaging in any boxing activity. Relegated to the status of a fan, Davis would attend boxing matches in Wichita and Kansas City whenever he could, and he maintained contact with people he knew in the boxing industry. In 2005, when he heard that Kansas was re-establishing an athletic commission, he put together his credentials and successfully applied for the position of Kansas boxing commissioner.

In an exclusive interview for this study, Davis spoke at length with the author about the inner workings of boxing in Kansas. This interview took place in December 2007. Davis says that the athletic commission returned to Kansas because there was a void. "We had a lot of fighters, but they had no place to display their fighting skills. A lot of fighters would go to other states or Indian reservations to compete and they felt that they couldn't get a fair shot because they couldn't fight at home. And even in the state of Kansas another state athletic commission would come in and govern the event. When Missouri or Colorado or other state commissions would come in, they would license the boxers, get the revenue, and receive all the proceeds and fees, while Kansas would be left with nothing. Then, Representative Tom Burroughs put together a bill, and now we have the new Kansas Athletic Commission."

The Kansas Athletic Commission, as it is officially known, is made up of five commissioners that correspond with the state statute that requires the commission to be composed of a physician, a post-secondary athletic director, and a chiropractor. The commissioners serve at the pleasure of the governor. Davis, who is the only full-time paid member of the commission explains,

The commission is made up by a very diverse crowd. None of the positions are paid, but we do pay for their mileage and they get a stipend for coming to [the state capitol] Topeka as they travel here from various cities in Kansas. They have been very supportive and knowledgeable. I also have two part-time administrative assistants that work with me and I receive assistance from one of the attorneys based in the Kansas Department of Commerce. There are also twelve inspectors that help me before and during the event, especially at the weigh-ins. They also help complete the day-to-day tasks of making sure our boxers are abiding by our rules and regulations. And of course there are referees, judges, timekeepers that are selected to monitor the events.

The commission is empowered by the Kansas Professional Regulated Sports Act to supervise all regulated sports and professional wrestling performances in the state. The state athletic commission can issue licenses, charge fees, and exercise subpoena power. The authority to establish rules and regulations necessary to carry out the oversight of professional sports is vested in the commission. All conditions of licensing, judging contests and handing down suspensions are to be carried out by the commission. Furthermore, the commission has the power to obtain injunctions or other orders to keep unlicensed or unregulated sports contests from taking place in the state. Grievance procedures are also determined by provisions within the sports act. Amateur sports are exempt from the commission's purview; they are to be regulated by "a nationally-recognized amateur sanctioning body approved by the athletic commission."[8]

The Kansas Athletic Commission meets on a quarterly basis, or if urgent issues arise they may meet as necessary. Davis compliments his commissioners and explains the role of inspectors saying, "All of the commissioners have been very helpful, proper and attended the meetings. I meet with the inspectors more frequently, for training purposes or to examine fighters' histories, and make sure that the fighters are training and ready to fight. The inspectors are my 'eyes and ears' throughout the state of Kansas who can confirm that boxers and mixed martial artists are training properly."

Funding the Commission

An Internet search of government documents throughout the United States reveals the difficulty of obtaining budgetary information for state athletic commissions. Some states are very forthcoming with providing electronic documents that show the funding levels for their respective boxing commissions, while other states' appropriations for boxing commissions are virtually impossible to find online. The reason for this is that many states channel funding for their boxing commissions through various departments (or subsets of those departments) within state government. In the case of Kansas, the athletic commission is housed in the Department of Commerce Legal Department. According to Davis, "Right now, our budget for Fiscal Year 2008 [July 1, 2007, through June 30, 2008] is $170,000, which is not a lot when it comes to commissions across the country. In the statute that re-established the commission, we were given three years to try to be self-sufficient. After Fiscal Year '07 ended [June 30, 2007], 20 percent of the revenue we receive from our fees is put back in the general fund with the Department of Commerce. When the commission was initially re-established, all of the money that we received in licenses and fees went to the commission, but now 20 percent goes back to the general fund, which makes it even more difficult to raise funds for the commission. We're doing OK, but we could be doing a lot better."

The range in funding for state athletic commissions varies widely. In Nevada, according to NAC executive director Keith Kizer, the commission receives $650,000 from the state, while in Minnesota, boxing's newest state athletic commission received a one-time appropriation of $50,000 for FY 2007, with the intention that the commission be self-funded after the first year.[9] The only employee of the Minnesota Boxing Commission is a part-time executive director, presently former heavyweight contender Scott Ledoux. Arkansas' situation used to be even bleaker: in FY 2005, the commission budget was only $34,178, supporting one part-time employee who was paid an annual salary of $15,000 per year.[10] It is no wonder that the state hosted only six boxing events in 2004. Other examples of state funding levels for boxing commissions obtained from state government Web pages include Ohio ($248,150 in FY 2006), and Florida ($428,732 in FY 2008).[11] Arkansas' budgetary situation has improved in recent years as the state government began to recognize the importance of boxing through the success of locally based world middleweight champion Jermain Taylor. In FY 2007 the Arkansas Athletic Commission budget was $170,838.[12]

The revenue gained by state athletic commissions is directly related to the types of boxing events they tend to host. Davis explains, "We sanction mostly small events, at armories, clubs, hotels, and sometimes the Kansas Expo Center. By November 2007, we had reached $135,000 in revenues since the inception of the commission in August 2005." For comparison, the Colorado Boxing Commission reported revenues of $158,984 for a two year period in FY '04 and FY '05 when Colorado hosted 37 boxing events.[13]

At present, the revenue gained by the state of Kansas through its hosting of boxing events is unclear. Davis does not have data from the Kansas Division of Travel and Tourism as to how much of an economic impact boxing events have on Kansas through the subsidiary costs of lodging, restaurants, car rentals and so on, though he notes, "We made a nice little splash for those types of businesses."

The increase in boxing events since the re-establishment of the Kansas Athletic Commission has been keeping Davis busy. He says, "Our local fighters want to fight in their backyard, and want to compete at the top level. These fights would not have happened without the fighters and local promoters, because the promoters won't put shows on if there aren't any bodies in the seats. On the local level, fighters need to go out and make a name for themselves so that people will want to come and watch them fight. And they've been doing a wonderful job marketing the sport, even though it is on a small scale." Davis recognizes that the level of boxing in his state is at the club-level and suggests that local boxers and promoters need to take active roles in the promotion of the sport. "We don't have reality shows like they do in Las Vegas. So our local guys need to go out and get sponsorships. The re-establishment of the commission has had something to do with the increase in boxing in the state, because people want to promote fights where they have sanctioned, safe events. But, I give kudos to the fighters and the promoters. They are doing things at the grassroots level to make this work."

While officials from Missouri have come to observe fights in Kansas and vice versa, the lines of jurisdiction are clear. Davis notes, "At first glance, we may seem to be similar states, but we're really not. There are more venues for boxing in Kansas City, Missouri, than there are in Kansas City, Kansas. Of course, they also have St. Louis, and we don't have those large or even medium size venues, or the casinos. Once the state [of Kansas] gets involved with the casinos, I see our business booming." Kansas expanded its gambling laws in 2007 to establish four state-owned, but privately-managed casinos by 2010.[14] Given the association of casinos and boxing events, Davis has cause to be enthusiastic.

Health and Safety

The state of Kansas has minimal health and safety requirements for boxers. At present, only physical examinations (including a pregnancy test for women) are required to be licensed. Davis says that in the next fiscal year, he would like to implement "all blood work, HIV tests, Hepatitis A, B, and C examinations and testing for steroids." Davis explains that a lack of funding is a problem for implementing these tests, but that funding is not the only problem. "We need to find a way to get the laboratories involved to offer the best rates for testing, and to educate the public as to why we are testing, and why we want to implement these specific tests." Davis says that Kansas has been "pretty diligent about not allowing people to fight with other state suspensions," in accordance with federal law. Kansas does not require HIV tests or neurological examinations to license boxers. It can, and does carry out "very discretionary" drug testing. Davis says that some boxers have refused to take drug tests and were taken off fight cards, while others have been tested for drug use and have been cleared to fight.

Perspective on a National Boxing Commission

Davis' thoughts on the prospect of a national boxing commission reflect his position as a boxing commissioner in a state that mostly hosts small boxing events. He says, "I think it's a great idea if [federal commissioners] understand that there are states that don't have the big fights. If they require us to implement the regulations currently in the states that have the million dollar fights, then Kansas, Missouri, Oklahoma and Colorado wouldn't have a leg to stand on. I hope that if the federal commission is developed, they take into consideration the small states and commissions because contrary to popular belief, most fights happen in smaller venues. You might have five mega-fights per year in the nation, but every week there are small club fights taking place in the Midwest. So I hope that there are people examining the real numbers, not just the big fights at the big commissions." Davis' comments point to the most fundamental question about a proposed federal commission: Who will fund the implementation of any new regulations (such as expensive medical tests) imposed by a federal commission?

As a result of the increasing popularity of mixed martial arts, Davis is also concerned as to whether a national boxing commission will also regulate that sport. Davis suggests that any national boxing commission *needs* to involve the regulation of MMA events. Davis claims, "If they leave out MMA, they will be missing out on a lot of fights that need to be regulated just as well as boxing. So, I am all for a national commission, if it's designed correctly and addresses some of the things that I talked about. If they don't, I think it wouldn't be good for all of the commissions." If a national commission requires states to conduct expensive medical tests, Davis says that states such as Kansas will "look to the promoters, or try to obtain additional state or federal funds for it if medical testing becomes a federal mandate."

The issue of regulating mixed martial arts is a difficult one for state athletic commissions, nearly all of which were originally established to regulate boxing or boxing and wrestling. According to information provided by the Association of Boxing Commissions, professional mixed martial arts is illegal in 13 states, legal-but-unregulated in 4 states, and of unknown status in two states.[15] Data provided by the Nevada Athletic Commission indicates that at the very highest levels, the gross sales generated by live audiences for boxing events are far greater than those for MMA. For example, in terms of gross sales, the top five boxing events each garnered between $13 million and $16.9 million, while the top five MMA events were in the range of $1.4 million to $2.6 million.[16] However, the top five boxing events took place in the late 1990s, while the top MMA events were held from 2002–2005.

The ABC and AAPRP

Davis has been a member of the Association of Boxing Commissions ever since he was appointed to his position as boxing commissioner. He is the chairman of the ABC Code of Conduct Committee and he is a part of the Mixed Martial Arts Rules and Regulations Committee. This committee is currently seeking a company to hold all MMA records such as Fight Fax, Inc., does for boxing. Davis says, "Right now, we don't have that same type of registry for mixed martial arts. We are looking for companies that could maintain our data, because we want to bring it up to the level of our boxing records for the safety of the fighters. We want to make sure that everyone's records are what they say they are."

As the chairman of the Code of Conduct committee for the ABC, Davis seeks to ensure that every commissioner in the ABC is beyond reproach. He says, "We want to be seen as a regulatory body, not a 'friend-of-friends party.' Boxing, excuse the pun, has had a black eye for many years because of judges' decisions, and referees' actions, and I think that if we want boxing to remain in the mainstream, we have to keep our noses clean throughout the whole sport." Davis suggests that there are rumors of boxing insiders being able to "get a certain referee or things like that" but he wants to make it a level playing field for all types of boxing events, as Davis puts it, "from the mega fights to the everyday local club fights." Davis says that the perceived lack of ethics or conduct has driven fans away from the sport. He emphasizes, "It's not that boxers are not athletic or that they don't have skills; rather, a lot of people think that boxing is like professional wrestling where there is a pre-determined outcome. I want to get that little shadow of a doubt out of boxing, and I'm going to start with Kansas."

Davis has also attended the national convention of the American Association of Professional Ringside Physicians, which he considers to be a "wonderful tool for any commission." He adds, "They have a lot of information for fighters. They have a wealth of information to make some key decisions. I learned a lot when I attended their convention and I hope other commissioners do the same. I think its important for ringside physicians to have an association to belong to so they can exchange information and obtain more training on head injuries that boxers can suffer in the ring." Davis says these organizations can improve by offering more localized training. "The ABC and AAPRP have training about once per quarter but they're only located in certain geographic regions. I would like to see training seminars take place in different regions, so that more referees, judges, and doctors can attend. I have made a commitment to my commission to get all Kansas judges and referees ABC certified within two years, and it's difficult when you only have three or four chances out of the year to get a person with a full-time job to go and pay their own way to places like Montreal or New York where these training seminars are held." Davis points out that the commission does not have funding to pay for the expenses of judges and referees to attend such seminars. "I believe some of the bigger commissions have funding to do that," Davis says, "but this is where Kansas and similar states are coming up short."

Relationship with Tribal Commissions

In the United States, American Indian reservations have the right to establish their own boxing commissions. As of 2007 there were eleven such commissions in existence with the state they are located in listed in parentheses:

- Mississippi Band of Choctaw Indian Boxing Commission (MS)
- Mashantucket Pequot Tribal Nation Athletic (CT)
- Miccosukee Athletic Commission (FL)
- Mille Lacs Band of Ojibwe (MN)
- Mohegan Tribal Department of Athletic Regulations (CT)
- Oneida Nation Athletic Commission (NY)

- Pascua Yaqui Tribe Boxing Commission (AZ)
- Peoria Tribe of Indians of Oklahoma (OK)
- San Juan Pueblo (NM)
- Siletz Tribal Athletic Commission (WA)
- Yakama Nation Athletic Commission (OR)

In Kansas, the Prairie Band Potawatomi Nation and the Sac and Fox Nation are considering forming their own athletic commissions, as they have casinos on their land and they are increasingly hosting boxing events. Davis says that the establishment of tribal commissions in Kansas "would be a good thing. They are looking to us, the ABC, and some of the existing tribal commissions for some of the fundamental information, and I've met with their representatives several times to provide input into some things they should be doing. In 2007 we sanctioned two fights at Prairie Band that were successful, and I think they want to continue to have boxing there with their own commission. For the events in 2007, they allowed the Kansas Athletic Commission to come in and regulate the fights on their property. But in the future, they want to regulate boxing on their own, and I think it's good for the growth of boxing. It just so happens they have a reservation within my state, but they can sanction events just as well as the Kansas Athletic Commission, once they get established."

Lack of Diversity Among State Athletic Commissioners

Aaron Davis, Joseph Mason (Colorado), and Armando Garcia (California) are the only three ethnic and racial minority directors of state athletic commissions in the United States, including the tribal commissions, according to Davis. Until recently, there had been four, but New Jersey commissioner Larry Hazzard was removed from office in 2007. Davis believes that this dynamic will change with time. He says, "It will take time for the 'old boy network' that they have to change. Usually those that are named commissioners are friends of friends of someone that's in power. I'm going to congratulate the State of Kansas for looking past friends and selecting the candidate with the most experience in athletics and marketing that also has a background in boxing, and I was selected from that pool. So I feel good about Kansas, but I don't know that every commissioner can say the same. I feel good, because I was hired and selected by Governor [Kathleen] Sebelius."

In spite of the lack of racial or ethnic diversity among the highest level of boxing regulators in the country, Davis says he does not think that the lack of diversity among commissioners affects the health and safety protections for boxers. He says, "I think that all the commissioners are very cautious of safety and I don't think the color or background of the fighter matters. No commissioner wants anyone to get seriously hurt, or worse, killed, on their watch, in their state. I don't think I could sleep at night knowing that a young guy got really hurt at an event where I'm supposed to be governing. I've met most of the state commissioners, I know most of them, and I don't think they have a harsh bone in their bodies. And since their personal and professional reputations are at stake, I really don't think that race is an issue, and I hope it's not an issue." Davis says that he has worked with a lot of promoters and managers, and he has not met any that are African American or Latino. "When I enter the building," Davis, a self-described 6'8" African American, says, "people are surprised, as if to say, 'what's he doing here? and they look at me like I'm crazy." Nevertheless, Davis maintains that he has "been treated fairly by other commissioners."

Conclusion

Kansas is making a proactive effort to attract more boxing to the state by re-establishing a state athletic commission. There has been a tremendous increase in Kansas boxing events since 2005. Commissioner Aaron Davis has raised the commission from the ashes by establishing the protocols those involved with boxing in the state must go through to participate in or host boxing events. Through its licensing process, the commission is gaining revenue for the state of Kansas that would have been obtained by neighboring commissions in the past. By virtue of hosting fights within the state, boxing events will attract an increasing amount of tourism dollars.

It is extremely difficult to start a new governmental regulatory body with relatively low levels of funding and staff. As with any state agency, improvements will come in time as long as there are knowledgeable and capable leaders in place. It is difficult to judge a commission that is just becoming re-established, but clearly there is much work to be done in terms of implementing health and safety regulations, especially with regards to requiring HIV and neurological tests for all boxers.

Davis is cognizant of the need to require more stringent health and safety regulations in Kansas. At present, only a physical exam is required. Although neurological and HIV tests are not required, the commission has the discretionary authority to test for drug use. The lack of these tests places boxers, their opponents, trainers, ringside officials and others at risk. It is absolutely necessary for the Kansas Boxing Commission to address these issues if the state wants to become an important host for Midwestern boxing events. Perhaps the commission will obtain more state funding to carry out such tests once the state-owned casinos are established.

5

AN ALTERNATIVE MODEL? BOXING IN ARGENTINA

Introduction

The aim of this study is to examine the variation of boxing regulations across the United States. However, the differences in states' boxing regulations, in the context of congressional efforts to create a United States Boxing Commission, leads me to seek an example of a centralized model of boxing regulations already in place. Such a model would have to be found in a country with a similar governmental structure as the United States, possessing three branches of government in a federalist system. In addition, this country would have to regularly host boxing events, possess a rich boxing history, and have a single national regulatory body to oversee boxing in addition to regional or local commissions that are subservient to it. Identifying such an example may provide an alternative model that the United States can look to in the event that federal legislation to create a national commission passes. One such model can be found in Argentina.

Governmental Structure

The Argentine Constitution is modeled after that of the United States.[1] It creates a federal republic, with power divided between a national government, provincial (state) governments, and municipal governments. It also establishes an autonomous federal district, *Buenos Aires Capital Federal*, which is similar in terms of its political autonomy to the District of Columbia. Three branches of government are constitutionally created: the legislative, executive and judicial. The *Congreso de la Nación* (National Congress) serves as the body of the legislative branch, with 257 members of the lower house (*Camara de Diputados*) serving four-year terms, while the 72 members of the Argentine

Senate (*Senado*) serve six-year terms. A (usually) duly elected president leads the executive branch, and can serve up to two consecutive four-year terms in office. An independent judiciary with a nine-member supreme court and various lower level courts are also established.

The twenty-three provincial governments in Argentina are structured in a manner similar to their counterparts in the United States, with elected governors and provincial legislators. Provinces are granted a similar level of autonomy as in the United States, and as in the U.S., provincial laws cannot supersede those of the national government. Provincial constitutions are also similar to those of U.S. states.[2]

Prominent Argentine Boxers

Argentina has made rich contributions to the history of world boxing, producing a few of the most outstanding champions and contenders that the sport has ever seen. Twenty-four Argentineans have won Olympic medals, placing the country eighth in the world on the all-time boxing Olympic medal winners ranking.[3] Thirty Argentines have won professional world championships from the four major sanctioning bodies (WBA, WBC, IBF and WBO), while four Argentine women have won world titles from one of the major women's boxing organizations, the WIBA, WBA or WBC.

Early in the twentieth century, Argentine heavyweight Luis Angel Firpo, "The Wild Bull of the Pampas," was immortalized by painter George Bellows in his championship fight with Jack Dempsey. In that historic fight, Firpo nearly won the heavyweight championship of the world by knocking Dempsey out of the ring. Dempsey was illegally assisted back into the ring by ringside reporters who were perhaps fearful of the title moving to South America. The popular American champion would go on to knock Firpo out in a fight that remains one of the most memorable in boxing history.

At mid-century, flyweight Pascual Pérez won a gold medal at the 1948 Olympics and would go on to become one of the most decorated flyweight champions in history. In the 1960s, heavyweight contender Oscar Bonavena was among the ten best heavyweights, narrowly losing to Joe Frazier and Muhammad Ali. The "Untouchable" Nicolino Locche was recently inducted into the International Boxing Hall of Fame (IBHOF) for his prowess in the junior welterweight division in the late 1960s and early 1970s.

Two Argentine world champions deserve special consideration: Carlos

5 • An Alternative Model?

Monzon and Victor Galindez. Carlos Monzon is widely regarded as one of the top middleweights in history; some consider him to have been the best. He was undefeated as champion, making a record 14 title defenses in the 1970s that was only recently surpassed by Bernard Hopkins in this era of splintered championships. Victor Galindez also holds the record for consecutive world title defenses in the light heavyweight division, matched only by the legendary Michael Spinks and Virgil Hill. Both Argentine fighters' lives would end in automobile accidents, Galindez when he dabbled in car racing; Monzon while driving on a weekend prison furlough. Despite the tragic ends to their lives, and in Monzon's case, a murder conviction for the death of his estranged wife, these boxers have entered into the IBHOF, boxing's hallowed ground, for their triumphs in the ring.

There have been scores of notable Argentine champions and contenders who may not have been at the level of Monzon and Galindez but briefly gained recognition as being among the best in their respective divisions. In the 1980s, flyweight champion Santos Laciar and middleweight contender Juan "The Hammer" Roldan

Luis Angel Firpo is buried in the famed Recoleta Cemetery in Buenos Aires, Argentina. A larger than life statue of Firpo stands over his tomb.

received many accolades. During the 1990s, three-time junior welterweight champion Juan Martin Coggi, junior middleweight champion Julio Cesar Vasquez and middleweight champion Jorge Castro all gained international notoriety. In the new millennium, world titlists Omar Narvaez, Jorge Barrios and Carlos Baldomir have found significant success in the ring.

A Brief History of Boxing in Argentina

According to journalist Jorge Roque Cermesoni, boxing began to be practiced in Argentina as early as 1895.[4] The first recorded professional bout in Argentina (and according to some sources, also the first bout held in South America) took place on October 9, 1903, between Irish immigrant Paddy McCarthy and Italian Abelardo Robassio.[5] Boxing schools, such as the Buenos Aires Boxing Club, were opened in the national capital, with McCarthy being one of the first professors of the sport in Argentina. One of McCarthy's pupils was the man considered to be the first sportsman of Argentina, Jorge Newberry, who in addition to being a boxer, also practiced soccer, rugby, and even baseball, a game he learned while studying in the United States.[6] Newberry was also a distinguished aviator, one of the first pilots in Latin America. Argentina's second largest airport is named after him.

Early in twentieth-century Argentina, boxing was considered an elite sport, mainly practiced by British immigrant men, and still had quasi-legal status. For example, while the sport was still technically illegal, the chief of police himself served as the timekeeper during the McCarthy-Robassio bout.[7] McCarthy and several British and American trainers would arrive in Argentina to train boxers in this period, and boxing matches were held in private clubs to bypass legal restrictions, just as they were in the United States. In 1910, the Buenos Aires Boxing

Nicolino Locche, seen here in his later years (1993), was known as "The Untouchable" during his championship reign (courtesy Modesto M. Rodriguez).

Club inaugurated championship fights in various weight classes.⁸

While on a world exhibition tour prompted by his U.S. exile, world heavyweight champion Jack Johnson fought in Argentina in 1914, winning by a three round knockout over American Jack Murray. Luis Angel Firpo made his professional debut against Australian Frank Hagney at the International Boxing Club in Buenos Aires in 1917, though many of his early fights took place in Chile, where a boxing federation had already been formed in 1912.⁹

The Creation of the Argentine Boxing Federation (FAB)

The *Federación Argentina de Boxeo* (FAB) was established on March 23, 1920, by a group of men representing various boxing clubs.¹⁰ Among the founders was Cesar

Santos Laciar was a prominent Argentine world champion in the 1980s.

Viale, secretary to the Buenos Aires chief of police, who authored several books on Argentine sports and is considered a pioneer in the development of sports in Argentina.¹¹ A splinter organization known as the Association of Argentine Boxing (AAB) arose in 1922. Boxers were affiliated to one organization or the other based upon the boxing club they belonged to. The Buenos Aires *intendente,* Dr. Joaquin Llambias, declared that if these two unions were to unite he would legalize professional boxing in the capital, and on November 13, 1923, the organizations merged under the banner of the FAB and boxing was legalized in Buenos Aires.¹² Other sources credit the Firpo-Dempsey fight held on September 14, 1923, with the legalization of boxing in Argentina.¹³ Not incidentally, this day is known as the National Day of the Boxer in Argentina.

Argentina's Madison Square Garden

Don Domingo Pace was among the very first boxing promoters in Argentina. He was the founder of the original Luna Park stadium in Buenos

Top: This unique 1990 photograph shows several boxing personalities. From left to right: former junior welterweight contender David Kamau, unknown trainer, promoter Tito Lecture, then-super bantamweight champion Pedro Decima, world renowned trainer Miguel Diaz, and the late "Kid" Akeem Anifowoshe, who died as a result of injuries suffered in the ring. *Bottom*: The famed Luna Park Stadium in Buenos Aires is Argentina's answer to Madison Square Garden.

5 • An Alternative Model?

Aires. Pace's son, Ismael, partnered with Argentine lightweight champion Jose Lecture back in 1924 to promote fights, and in 1932 they opened the new Luna Park stadium, a venue nicknamed the "Palace of Sports" that remains a fixture in Buenos Aires to this day. This stadium is a historical boxing locale that has similar mythical connotations to those associated with Madison Square Garden. In the 1950s, both Pace and Lecture died, and Lecture's nephew, Juan Carlos "Tito" Lecture, was left in charge. For 31 years, boxing was regularly held at Luna Park on Wednesdays and Saturdays, amassing an incredible total of 2,976 boxing events.[14]

The Luna Park ring was the site of most of the historic battles of Argentine pugilism. Some of boxing's greatest combatants, including Archie Moore, Sandy Saddler, Carlos Ortiz and Eder Jofre fought there. Over twenty-four world title fights and eighty-seven Argentine championships were disputed in the Luna Park ring.[15] To exemplify the importance of this boxing venue, the original Luna Park bell used to mark the rounds at countless fights is prominently displayed at the International Boxing Hall of Fame in Canastota, New York. Also, in February 2002, the Argentine secretariat of culture decreed the stadium a national historic monument.

Light heavyweight legend Archie Moore, pictured here in 1991, was among the elite boxers who fought in the Luna Park ring (courtesy Modesto M. Rodriguez).

However, between 1987 and 2002, Luna Park's doors were virtually closed to boxing, as Lecture had become disgruntled with the sport. After Lecture's death in 2002, boxing matches returned to the Luna Park under the auspices of new stadium manager Esteban Livera, Tito Lecture's nephew. Nevertheless, a return to biweekly boxing cards at the Luna Park is not in Livera's plans. Rather, his conceptualization is to host only major boxing events at the historic stadium, including world championship fights involving Argentine boxers.

In addition to the Luna Park stadium, Buenos Aires has another historic fight venue located at the FAB headquarters. In the late 1930s, the FAB constructed a permanent site for its operations, complete with a gymnasium and a small arena somewhat reminiscent to the Olympic Auditorium in Los Angeles. This installation also remains a fixture in Buenos Aires, and boxing matches continue to be regularly held there to this day. Other popular boxing venues include the gymnasiums of sports clubs such as *Ferro Carril Oeste*, which are roughly the size of large high school basketball gyms in the United States.

Perón's Influence

Juan Domingo Perón, Argentina's notorious president, was also a tremendous boxing fanatic and general sports aficionado. His first two terms as president, from 1946 to 1955, ushered in a unique era for Argentine

Juan Carlos "Tito" Lecture in his Luna Park Stadium office in 1990. Lecture was inducted into the International Boxing Hall of Fame for his work as a boxing promoter (courtesy Modesto M. Rodriguez).

boxing and other sports. As a democratically elected populist leader, Perón had the authority to channel government funds toward sporting projects, and Argentine sportsmen benefited greatly as a result. Yet his roots in boxing were formed long before he ascended to the presidency of the nation. Perón established one of the first boxing clubs in the interior of Argentina, "With money he gained in a fight which he lost against the 'malevolent Entrerian' Tapia, in the province of Entre Rios, he founded the Parana Boxing Club, a pugilistic pioneer in the interior of the country."[16] Perón was known for being a regular spectator at the fights held at the Luna Park, and in fact, that was the venue

5 • An Alternative Model?

The Argentine Boxing Federation has its own offices, gymnasium and arena in Buenos Aires.

where he would meet his second wife, Evita, at a fundraising event for the survivors of an earthquake in the San Juan Province.

The Peróns were publicly admired by the great sportsmen of their time, including popular boxers such as Pascual Pérez and Jose Maria Gatica, Olympians such as Delfo Cabrera and Formula 1 racing legend Juan Manuel Fangio. Scores of young children participated in the *Torneo Evita* youth soccer tournaments. In his third term as president, coming in 1973, Perón would establish the national *Ley de Deportes 20.655* to promote governmental support for the development of Argentine sports. The *Torneo Evita* was reestablished, and even a young Diego Maradona participated in one of these. Perón died in office in 1974, but the national sports law remains on the books to this day, with various regulatory amendments that have modified it over the past two decades.

Current Boxing Outlook

In Argentina there are approximately 7,000 amateur boxers, about 10 percent of whom will turn professional.[17] About 350 boxers train at the FAB gymnasium, while other important boxing gyms include the *Club Huracán* and *Club San Carlos*.[18] In addition to Buenos Aires, another center for boxing activity is the city and province of Córdoba, where many fight cards are held and many boxers train at the local *Gimnasio Corral de Palos*. Trainer Carlos Tello, who has guided the careers of several Argentine champions, explains, "In the interior of the country, live boxing is a big draw. In some instances, up to 1500 people attend boxing events. Occasionally, we have two simultaneous boxing events."[19] While many Argentine boxers from the interior of the country eventually migrate to Buenos Aires to practice their trade, some of Argentina's notable champions are originally from the provinces, such as Monzon and Baldomir (Santa Fe), Perez (Mendoza), and Narvaez and Laciar (Córdoba).

In a 2006 interview with ESPN Deportes, FAB president Osvaldo Bisbal indicated that boxing has been growing in Argentina over the past few years. In 2005, for example, "the statistics show that there is more boxing, more fights, more boxing cards, and more television coverage."[20] In 2005, there were 871 boxing matches spread across 417 fight cards, while in 2006 Argentina hosted 818 boxing matches in 374 boxing events.[21] According to the FAB's Web page, the most popular venues for fight cards, based upon the number of events held, were the *Polideportivo Municipal in Caseros* (Buenos Aires Province) and the FAB arena. These venues held an average of two boxing events per week over two years!

Despite the quantity of boxing activity in Argentina, one of the country's most prominent world champions, Juan Martin "El Latigo" Coggi, whose son is currently a rising prospect, laments the level of Argentine boxing. In an interview published in 2005, Coggi says, "The level of current boxers is far from that of Carlos Monzon or Nicolino Locche or others from the 1970s or 1980s."[22] Coggi also criticizes the FAB saying, "The FAB has centralized everything. That's why local gyms have been disappearing. That makes things complicated, because in the past there were hundreds of gyms in the *Capital Federal*, and now there's only three or four. The FAB is doing a lot of things wrong. It is not putting together the types of fights that it should, nor are the matchups even."[23] He also blames the media for boxing's demise: "The press doesn't report on this sport like they did before. In the eighties, there was a

5 • An Alternative Model?

Federación Argentina de Box

Box Profesional

Nº 0202   **RING - SIDE**

ESTADIO F. A. B.   -   C. BARROS 75

A ticket stub to fights hosted at the Argentine Boxing Federation's arena.

full page on boxing every day, and now only a small box on the bottom of the page is published."[24] Coggi's criticisms could easily apply to the United States, as local boxing gymnasiums are becoming relics of the past and the sport receives scant coverage from the traditional mainstream print media.

According to the official Web site of the Argentine government, "The regulations of the *Federación Argentina de Box* (FAB) are the only ones that must rule over all boxing matches, amateur and professional, feminine and masculine, that take place in the country, organized by entities or people, affiliated or federated by the FAB."[25] In addition, according to the Argentine Olympic Committee Web page, the FAB is the only official federation affiliated with that entity for amateur boxing. In fact, the FAB's medical director, Dr. Hugo Rodriguez Papini, is the Argentine Olympic Committee's pro-treasurer. Nevertheless, while there are some antiquated laws that were created to standardize professional and amateur boxing in Argentina, such as *Decreto Ley Nacional 282/63* and *Decreto Reglamentacion 2689* of April 1963, there is not a current national law in Argentina to back up the hierarchy of the FAB.

In April 2005, a *proyecto de ley* (bill) was introduced in the Argentine

Camara de Diputados de la La Nación (the lower house of the Argentine Congress) by legislator Irene M. Bosch de Sartori and others to legally establish the FAB as the *only* body that can legally govern amateur and professional boxing in the country. This bill was debated and tossed out in December 2006 for exhibiting an anti-republican corporatist nature, that if read a certain way would place more authority in the FAB than in the executive branch of government led at the time by President Nestor Kirchner.[26]

The reasons behind the introduction of this bill are unclear, as the FAB has been the *de facto* sole governing body of boxing in Argentina for several decades, and the FAB reportedly did not ask for any congressional sanction to be made on its behalf.[27] One possible reason for the introduction of the bill could be to keep a competing national governing body, the *Consejo Argentino de Boxeo Profesional* (CABP), the Argentine Professional Boxing Council, from gaining authority.

A Rival Commission

The CABP was established in 1999. It took an important step toward gaining legitimacy when it established an agreement with Fox Sports to televise its title fights in March 2006.[28] According to the CABP Web site, the organization was formed to raise the level of Argentine boxing to the levels of years gone by, through strict enforcement of their rules.[29]

The CABP is led by Eduardo Juan Palombo, an Argentine boxing judge. The organization issued an extensive set of standard regulations to oversee all aspects of boxing including licensing, medical examinations, conduct of ring officials, appeals processes, rankings, and penalties. They also claim to have the authority to sanction bouts for an "Argentine Championship," resulting in splintered titles at the national level just as they are internationally. With respect to health and safety requirements, the CABP requires neurological tests, among other medical examinations of all affiliated boxers. Drug testing is mandatory in all CABP sanctioned *championship* fights, and may be taken before or after the fight takes place, at the commission's discretion. However, the CABP does not require HIV testing of boxers.

On April 7, 2006, the FAB reportedly made an announcement through its Web page that "all those federated [licensed] through the FAB (boxers, trainers, judges, referees, and promoters) are absolutely prohibited from participating in boxing events that are not authorized by [the FAB]. Any transgression to this regulation will result in severe disciplinary sanctions, including the definitive cancellation of the violator's license."[30] The following week, three boxers and one trainer who participated in a boxing card sanctioned by the CABP were suspended by the FAB. The CABP responded to the suspension with a statement indicating that the CABP is a new federation that has regulated professional boxing in Argentina since 1999, as authorized by the *Inspección General de Justicia* [the Argentine Justice Department].[31] The CABP added that there is no relationship between their organization and the FAB, as each organization has its own rules and licensing procedures.

On another occasion when the CABP organized a fight card in Comodoro Rivadavia (Chubut Province), the FAB chose not to sanction or send officials to the event. This was despite the fact that the main event was a women's world championship fight between Claudia Lopez and Maria del Carmen Potenza. It is unclear if the fight was for the WIBA championship (an entity that the FAB is affiliated with) or that of the Universal Boxing Council (which is not recognized by the FAB), as they are both led by Luis Bello Diaz, who was representing one of these organizations at the fight. According to a published report, "The prior intimidations of the FAB to the organizer, the boxers and the municipal commission influenced and complicated the image of the event, undoubtedly diminishing the attendance, which had an important cost, considering the number of fights and everything implicated by a world championship fight."[32]

Perhaps as a result of these and other threats made by the FAB, very few title fights have been sanctioned by the CABP. A search of the boxrec.com database reveals only eight CABP title fights, four of which were in the super featherweight division. Thus, CABP championship fights pale in comparison to the hundreds of title bouts sanctioned by the FAB throughout its eighty-seven year history.

Expert Opinions

To gain further insight into the system of boxing regulations in Argentina, two Buenos Aires–based experts were interviewed exclusively for this book in January 2008: Osvaldo Bisbal, the FAB president, and Osvaldo Principi, the boxing analyst at TyC Sports (one of Argentina's main sports television networks). These interviews were conducted in Spanish and are translated by the author.

Since 1991, the FAB has been led by Osvaldo Bisbal, who served as an Olympic boxing referee and judge between 1984 and 1996. Bisbal joined the

FAB in 1977 and worked his way up the administration before serving as a judge and referee. He served in those capacities at the Olympic games held in Los Angeles, Seoul, Barcelona and Atlanta. He has also been a member of the World Boxing Council for over fifteen years.

Osvaldo Principi is a very well-known boxing broadcaster in Argentina. He has been involved in the sport for thirty-five years and currently provides the blow-by-blow commentary for boxing shown on TyC Sports. His broadcasts of Argentine boxing can be seen in the United States on TyC Sports International, a channel that is broadcast on satellite television provider DirecTV. Principi is also the author of *La vida es un ring*, a book that contains interviews of Argentine personalities, boxers, and other athletes about their passion for the sweet science. He is an expert on Argentine boxing, and a historian of the sport.

FAB Structure

The rules and regulations of the FAB are posted on the official Web page. The structure of the organization and its regulatory bylaws resemble those of U.S. state athletic commissions. Part I of the Argentine Boxing Regulations outlines the institution itself and explains the need for rules, licensing, disciplinary procedures and general considerations. Part II specifically applies to amateur male boxing regulations, including the qualifications required of the promoters, ring officials, trainers, and the boxers themselves. Part III addresses professional male boxing, also providing detailed regulations for promoters, ring officials, trainers, the boxers, the fights, medical examinations, anti-doping requirements, contracts, and the procedures for administering the Argentine championship bouts. Parts IV and V address amateur and professional female boxing, respectively, with the same categories as their male counterparts. Updates to the official regulations are posted on the FAB Web page.

Bisbal explains that the FAB was created by a group of private leaders and remains a semi-private entity that can be investigated only by the judicial branch of the government. The FAB has a 30-member *Consejo Directivo* (advisory board). Bisbal clarifies that the board is not *rentado*, or working for a salary, like the commissioners in the United States. However, he states, "If you were to visit our site any day of the week you would see at least ten board members here from 3:30 P.M. until 10:00 P.M. at night." The advisory board meets monthly, while the *Mesa Directiva* (executive board) including the president, secretary and treasurer meets weekly.

The FAB is affiliated with the WBA, WBC, IBF, WBO and the Women's

International Boxing Association (WIBA). It will recognize world championships sanctioned only by those entities. The World Boxing Association, through its executive vice-president, Gilberto Jesus Mendoza, has praised the FAB and Bisbal's leadership. In an interview that took place prior to the hosting of the WBA's KO Drugs event in Argentina, Mendoza said, "Considering our long friendship with Argentina, and knowing the seriousness and professionalism with which the *Federación Argentina de Box* (FAB) and its President, Osvaldo Bisbal, carry on boxing there, we're sure that this will be a magnificent event."[33]

While the FAB is the only legitimate national organization, in historical and practical terms, that governs boxing in Argentina, there are also provincial and municipal commissions that regulate boxing in their jurisdictions under the auspices of the FAB. Bisbal explains, "All of the organizations are independent. However, the difference between the Argentine and United States systems is that we only have one single set of regulations. That is, the provincial or city commission, or both, will oversee the implementation of the general rules, but those rules are dictated by the FAB. It is not possible for individuality or independence to exist in terms of the rules. The rules are made by convention, one set of regulations is stipulated by the federation, and all provincial or local organizations in Argentina are to respect the FAB's regulations."

As mentioned previously, in Argentina, provincial and municipal commissions exist, but they cannot implement rules that contradict or supersede those of the FAB. In Córdoba, one of Argentina's major provinces and centers of boxing activity, the provincial boxing commission depends upon the FAB, and the municipal commissions depend upon the provincial entities.[34] Thus, municipal commissions are restricted from entering into relationships with any entity other than the FAB, as mandated by local laws and regulations. In contrast, the municipality of General Villegas in the Buenos Aires province recently passed an ordinance allowing boxing events in its jurisdiction that are sanctioned by either the FAB, the CABP or other organizations.[35]

Principi explains the relationship between the commissions saying, "There are two national commissions, the *Consejo Argentino de Boxeo Profesional* and the *Federación Argentina de Boxeo*. Municipal commissions are *deglutivas* [swallowed] by the provincial commissions, which in turn do not have autonomy of making decisions contrary to the FAB. These are things that happen in the provincial territories."

Principi goes on to criticize the CABP, saying, "The CABP is a failure that has had fights on Fox Sports and presently on America Sports. They have not achieved a respectable level, though did achieve some level of legality, but their matches are ... not presentable. It's too bad, because the FAB is a *Casa Tomada* (a house taken over) where five or six people run everything and do not allow others to progress. In a submissive world such as boxing, everybody is obedient. In due time, the WBA or WBC will control the national boxing federations in South America, and those who run the federations today will go on to be members of the international organizations. Remember this, because that is how the leadership in boxing will end in South America. I don't think that the Argentine government is even aware of the creation of the CABP." When asked about the bill introduced in the Argentine Congress to declare the supremacy of the FAB, Principi replied, "There have been hundreds of attempts to reform boxing by municipalities, members of Congress and others, without any results. They tend to be mediums of self-promotion, more than anything."

Principis is critical of the FAB, saying,

> I would characterize the FAB as a historical institution that is going through its worst moments as a result of those that run it. The FAB doesn't answer to anyone, because the National Secretariat of Sports lacks character and understanding of what happens in national sports. In the future, I would like to see authentic boxing people have a voice and vote to elect those who govern the sport in Argentina. The biggest problem that we face is that there is neither an understanding nor love for what is being done to the sport. The FAB is an extremely bad producer of boxing that does not promote, nor civilize, boxing at all. The Argentine government should create a national boxing commissioner to oversee the FAB, with members from the government. Of course, this is something that will never happen.

According to Bisbal, the Argentine system of regulating boxing, with one set of national rules that provincial and municipal boxing commissions implement usually works well.

> Sometime we run into problems between the provincial and local commissions, but with our intervention, all the commissions historically have been able to come to an agreement because there is one single set of rules that they must follow. All they have to do is implement the rules. As long as the rules are followed, there cannot be any problems. A few times, commissions have assumed their right to be the exclusive entity to control boxing events, but this is at the provincial and local level, not in relation to the Argentine Boxing Federation. But again, through our intervention, normally, we have been able to resolve the issue. We have a good relationship with the provincial and local commissions. We think that if a situation arises in which three entities are vying for control of a fight, it is best that only one is in control.

Bisbal clearly implies that the entity that should be in control is the FAB.

Principi's harsh criticisms of the FAB lead me to question if Argentine boxers benefit from a single *de facto* national commission. For Principi, "The

5 • An Alternative Model?

interior [provincial] leaders are very weak. They do not have the character to be independent in their provincial territory. Their submission is suspicious in and of itself. It would be good to have one set of regulations, but not what we have today." The subservient nature of provincial and municipal commissions is troubling for Principi, however, if there is one national set of regulations that each commission must follow, there is very little room for independence. The alternative is, of course, to have a system in which national regulations do not exist and the provinces have the sole authority to regulate boxing in their respective jurisdictions.

Funding

The FAB does not receive funds from the Argentine government to carry out its regulation of professional boxing. However, Bisbal notes, "We normally receive about thirty to forty thousand dollars [per year] to support amateur boxing." So where does the FAB receive money to carry out its daily functions? Bisbal explains, "In Argentina, the biggest television station that controls televised boxing is TyC Sports. They deal with boxing promoters through the FAB to sponsor fights. We have eight years remaining on our contract with TyC Sports to televise boxing sanctioned by the FAB. The FAB provides promoters with television dates, the Federation receives funds from the television station and pays the promoters. Of course, the promoters do not receive 100 percent of the funds provided to the FAB from the television station." Thus, the primary funding source for the national regulatory body is a private television corporation that holds the exclusive rights to broadcast fights involving boxers licensed by the FAB.

Principi explains, "TyC Sports has a commercial relationship with the FAB, but I don't think that they invest even 50 percent of what they receive. TyC Sports is not interested in, nor does it participate in the quality of fights. If they are sold gold, they buy gold. If they're sold shit, then they buy shit…. And when there is shit, I say: this is shit. TyC Sports does not have a boxing office like ESPN or HBO does in the United States."

With regards to obvious potential conflicts of interest between the broadcasters, in this case TyC Sports, funding the activities of the regulatory body, the FAB, Principi says, "Everything is totally disorganized, because the inept promoters are part of the FAB. Boxing is reduced to being run by a minority group and it is very difficult to get in the group. The talented promoters do not get into the system, because it is a negative system."

Argentina's Responses to the BHS Survey

Bisbal responded to the BHS Survey in a phone interview held in January 2008. Bisbal's response to the same questions asked of U.S. state athletic commission representatives are complete and consistent with the FAB's posted regulations on their Web page.

Pre-Fight Physical Examinations and Neurological Exams

Bisbal explains, "There is a clinical medical evaluation for boxers. We require a blood and urine analysis, a chest x-ray, and a series of additional medical tests, including an electrocardiogram (EKG, to record the electrical activity of the heart over time), ophthalmological exam. Some exams must be completed every three months, others every six months, and some each year. In this country, you cannot box if you have suffered a detached retina. Boxers who wish to be licensed must present the results of an encephalographic exam (a radiographic examination of the brain) taken in the past year if the boxer is over 32 years of age. If the boxer is under 32 the Federation's Medical Council considers results of the boxer's record to determine if one is necessary. The Medical Council can also request a magnetic resonance imaging (MRI) or other examinations or evaluations that they deem necessary. The results of these exams must be stamped in the boxer's license. In addition to all of the tests required for licensing, a general physical evaluation is held at the weigh-in." The pre-fight medical requirements, if carried out as Bisbal states, are as stringent, or perhaps more stringent than those in the United States. Principi agrees with the exams that are in place saying, "The neurological exams and their renewal for boxers to keep their licenses is in the regulations. They should be done after each boxer's loss, and annually in normal cases. There is an official neurologist at the FAB, Dr. Noemi Tinetti."

Post-Fight Physicals

Post-fight physicals are not required by the FAB. Bisbal justifies this by emphasizing the battery of medical examinations that are required each trimester, semester, or annually. However, if the boxer loses before the scheduled number of rounds, he must conduct a neurological exam and is suspended for 30 days. He must also provide the new exam results to renew his license. If a boxer loses by three consecutive knockouts in one year, he is automatically suspended for six months.

HIV Testing

In spite of the extensive list of medical tests required to be licensed in Argentina, HIV testing is not required. In fact, it *cannot* be required as a result of Argentina's AIDS Law, established in 1990. This national law, *Ley 23.798*, and related privacy and labor laws are designed to protect HIV positive citizens from being discriminated against in the workplace.[36] Bisbal explains, "It is very complicated to require an HIV test from an Argentine citizen if he refuses to take one. To require an HIV test would have us enter into an imposition that perhaps many do not want to enter and we would enter into a legal problem. Nevertheless, it is our understanding, and the Medical Council of the FAB understands, that it will not take long for the imposition of HIV tests for boxers to be approved. But according to the current law, it is not permitted in Argentina." Some U.S. state commissions have used similar privacy law arguments to justify their lack of HIV testing.

The Argentine Boxing Federation does not have much difficulty in implementing regulations, as long as they are not prohibited by law, as in the example of mandatory HIV testing. Bisbal notes, "If we haven't implemented a rule, it's not because we haven't been able to. The only impediment we face, which sometimes keeps us from implementing rules that we would like, is the consideration over whether a rule is feasible and whether we will be able to enforce it. Yet each year we make some modifications to our rules." Principi adds, "The Argentine AIDS Law does not allow for mandatory HIV testing, as the right of refusal to take the test belongs to Argentine citizens. It is an absurd law, but a law nonetheless."

Test Costs

The costs associated with medical tests in Argentina are paid for by the boxer. Bisbal says that boxers are considered "professionals, or workers, and it is the boxers' responsibility to comply with the licensing requirements. There are some situations, however, where the Medical Council of the Federation can conduct tests. We provide medical services in the areas of ophthalmology, clinicians, cardiology, neurology, specialists in sports medicine, and even dentistry. The boxers can get their tests done through the Federation, in public hospitals, or in private health clinics. However, the cost of anti-doping tests is charged to the FAB."

Medical Council

The Medical Council of the FAB serves a series of functions. Bisbal explains that a Medical Council has been in existence at the FAB since 1968, when professional Argentine boxers began to be required to obtain licenses. Prior to that year, Bisbal says, only amateur boxers were licensed in Argentina.

> This was done by a national law that required a register of boxer records. The purpose was to avoid the possibility of boxers having two or three licenses from different provinces and thus potentially fighting in different provinces with different licenses. Prior to 1968, some boxers would fight in one province on a given Saturday, then travel to another province and fight one week later, possibly under a different name. There were a lot of problems with that. By having one single license in one country, the problem was solved. Now boxers cannot present themselves anywhere without their license from the FAB. This also enables local commissions to see all of the boxer's history. This is in addition to the information on our Web site and in our files. The fighters must present a license that can be analyzed by any commission that can read the results of the boxer's fights and if his medical examinations are up to date.

In this regard, Argentina's system of licensing resembles that of the United States, where a boxer is required to present his federal boxing ID to compete.

Bisbal notes, "When the boxer obtains his initial license, he must present medical records to the Medical Council and they determine if he will be licensed or not. The council can renew the license, or the boxer can have his license renewed in his province. We have our own office building, which includes an arena and a gymnasium. Thus, the Medical Council also serves the purpose, required by municipal law, that there are physicians present at the gymnasium."

Ambulance Presence

When asked about the requirement to have an ambulance present at boxing events, Bisbal replied that Argentina requires "two, not one. One ambulance is ready for the boxers, if necessary, while another is for the fans. Although the second ambulance is not obligatory, the owners of the site of the matches or the promoters can enter into legal problems if something happens, so the promoters that deal with the FAB normally have one ambulance for the boxers and one for intensive therapy. Two ringside physicians are also required at each boxing event." Principi concurs, saying, "There are ambulances present at the fights. That rule is followed."

Suspension Lists

Argentina has a national list of boxers who are suspended listed on its Web site. They also have the official records of all boxers licensed in Argentina, complete with their name, license number, national ID number, date and place of birth. The records for each boxer show the date, location, opponent (cross-linked with the opponent's record if he is Argentine), scheduled rounds, result, weight and title (if applicable). Unlike the U.S. federal suspension list or official records from Fight Fax, their list is freely available to anyone with an Internet connection. Bisbal says that the list is current, although he recognizes, "It's possible that someone has fallen through the cracks."

Standards for Competitive Fights

Principi suggests that "the FAB has a very good set of regulations, but the most important rules are not enforced, such as ensuring competitive fights, contract disclosures, and the redistribution of funds to the provincial commissions, who only receive old gloves." However, Bisbal claims that the FAB has standards for competitive fights. He says, "There is a rule that speaks to general equivalencies, based upon the boxer's capacities and results. There is a committee within the Federation that is exclusively dedicated to analyzing the parity of the matches. Sometimes the records don't show this, but one knows that the boxers can be evenly matched despite the differences in their records. We have a boxer, Omar Narvaez, who fought for the world title after just eleven fights. He is the reigning champion and is just a couple of title defenses away from breaking Carlos Monzon's record of title defenses by an Argentine boxer. Thus, there are exceptional cases." Narvaez is the World Boxing Organization flyweight champion. He is 26-0-2 (16) and has made 12 title defenses. However, it should be noted that Narvaez had a distinguished amateur career, representing Argentina in the 1996 and 2000 Olympics. He was the first Olympic boxer from the 2000 games to win a professional championship.

There is evidence that the FAB does indeed impose its regulation mandating the general equivalency of combatants. In 2002, the Argentine national news agency *Telam* reported that a fight between the popular, but utterly unskilled, heavyweight Fabio "La Mole" Moli, and Miguel Aguirre was not authorized by the FAB for this reason. Although the promoter and the local commission wanted the fight to go on, the fight was cancelled for fear of the boxers being suspended.[37]

Health Care and Insurance

In terms of health care, Argentina is quite different from the United States. In a chapter entitled *Reorganizing the Health Care System in Argentina*, Susana Belmartino explains the Argentine health services system known as *Obras sociales*: "*Obras sociales* are group insurance schemes based on the occupation of their beneficiaries. They function as sickness insurance funds, financing health care services for employees and their immediate families. *Obras sociales* are semi-public, because their creation requires authorization by the state, which has the means to intervene in their administration. The 281 *Obras sociales* at the national level are the central agents of the health insurance system and cover 48.21 percent of the population ensured under the compulsory insurance system (Local Office, World Bank). The 23 provincial *Obras sociales* cover 29.41 percent of the population, mainly employees of the provincial public sector and their dependents. Their source of financing is income-related contributions by employers and employees."[38]

Since 90 percent of Argentineans are covered by the national or provincial health care system, Boxers in Argentina do not receive any special or accidental health care coverage from promoters, as they do in many states throughout the U.S. Bisbal explains, "Boxers have *Obras Sociales.* The promoter is obligated to make a contribution to the *Obra Social* that the boxers belong to." While Argentina's health care system has its own set of problems, boxers can practice their trade without fear of bankrupting their families should they suffer serious medical consequences arising from their job.

Drug Testing

A national anti-doping law, *Ley Nacional 24.819*, and related resolutions were established in 1997 to preserve "fair play" with respect to the consumption of drugs by athletes.[39] This law created a National Antidoping Commission to oversee all facets of athletic drug testing in Argentina. Bisbal explains its implementation by the FAB saying, "We conduct drug testing based upon the National Antidoping Law, which requires all sports federations to practice antidoping tests under the direction of the National Secretariat of Sports. We are obliged to carry out drug tests, and we can do this at any boxing event, at any time and carry out surprise doping tests for boxers at any time, even at a gymnasium." The level of Argentina's commitment to anti-doping is remarkable for the boxing world, as drug tests can be required by the Federation during training sessions or by participants in non-championship fights.

5 • An Alternative Model?

Principi counters, "The anti-doping tests are not undertaken in the manner described by the FAB. Each time that they do carry them out, it is disorganized and unclear. When Frankie Randall fought Juan Martin Coggi in 1996, the urine specimens were sent to Las Vegas from Argentina, but the positive results weren't accepted due to irregularities in Randall's examination." Principi is referring to Randall's reported positive drug test for cocaine after his twelve round win over Coggi in a WBA junior welterweight title fight held in Argentina nearly a decade ago. The World Boxing Association reportedly rejected the positive test, due to irregularities in the way the urine specimens were handled.[40] As a result, Randall regained the WBA title.

Certification of Ring Officials

Ring officials, including referees and judges, are certified and licensed by the FAB. Bisbal notes, "We offer training courses, and we approve the officials. However, they are not in a dependent relationship with regards to the FAB. Here, the judges and referees are designated; however, they can decline an assignment, in which case another official would be assigned. The payment of the judges and referees' travel costs

Frankie Randall, 1994. Randall reportedly tested positive for cocaine after his 1996 fight with Juan Martin Coggi, but the result was upheld due to irregularities in the way the urine drug test was handled.

comes from the promoter." This system resembles the process used by the U.S.-based Association of Boxing Commissions, with the exception that payment of ring officials normally passes through the hands of the commission, creating a division between the promoter and the officials.

Related Ring Sports

Women's boxing in Argentina was legalized in 2001, but don't expect the FAB to regulate mixed martial arts, known as *Vale Todo* in Argentina, anytime soon. "We do not regulate mixed martial arts, and furthermore, we are against it. We do not consider it part of boxing, nor does it even bear resemblance to boxing. We are not in agreement with the sport. The institution is not in agreement with it. We are not aware of their regulations, at least in Argentina, nor of what type of controls exist. It is a spectacle that has only occurred a few times in this country, perhaps for television. It did not gain much of a following and at first glance, it appears to be rather lamentable. We do not want to have anything to do with that. While I am president of this institution, we will not assume regulatory responsibility for that sport."

On the Possible Formation of a U.S. Boxing Commission

When asked his opinion of the current U.S. legislation to adopt a national boxing commission, Bisbal says he believes it is a good idea.

> The level of boxing in Argentina is not at the level of the United States. We are well below that of the United States, I'm not sure if in quantity, but in quality in terms of the events themselves and the money involved. I would say that although there are a lot of fights here, in comparison to boxing in the United States, we are poor, financially speaking. However, in my opinion, the unification of rules is precisely what is lacking in the United States, in the sense that states have independence in their role of regulating boxing, and they are supposed to be there to enforce the rules. I believe that the state commissions should unite to establish standard regulations based upon the information of the expert professionals in the United States, especially in terms of health and safety. The rules should be the same everywhere in the country. The U.S. is not the country with the best system of regulating boxing; however, the United Kingdom has an excellent system of regulations.

Principi has mixed feelings about the U.S. attempts to form a national regulatory body for boxing. He says that if a national commission is established, "It should be formed by the appropriate people, and today in the

United States they do not exist. Senator John McCain has gained a lot of publicity with this. Yet he was not able to keep the WBA and WBC from introducing their secondary unofficial titles in the USA. It is an example of the lack of character and understanding. Today, the U.S. does not have boxing regulators that are talented and credible."

Conclusion

This case study of Argentine boxing regulations is useful for providing an example of both the positive and negative aspects of having a national boxing commission. Since Argentina's governmental structure resembles that of the U.S. and it possesses a rich boxing history with multiple boxers enshrined in the IBHOF, it is an appropriate selection for a comparative case study. The primary difference between the Argentine and U.S. systems of regulating boxing is that Argentina has a national federation that oversees the sport. The regulations of the FAB cannot be superseded by provincial or municipal commissions, and while the FAB's authority is not mandated by law, its legitimacy is maintained by its historical strength.

Since the Association of Boxing Commissions in the United States lacks legal and historical authority, state commissions will continue to regulate boxing within their jurisdictions unless a national commission is created by Congress. If one should be created, those appointed to lead the USBC can look to the Argentine system as a model to simultaneously embrace and avoid. Some aspects of the FAB are to be applauded, such as its authority to conduct drug testing of boxers at any point in time, not just before and after fights. In addition, the information provided on the Web page including a freely accessible and current database of boxer (and other) suspensions and official records should be adopted by such an entity in the United States. Furthermore, having two ambulances present at fight cards helps to ensure the safety of combatants and spectators. Also, the mandate that provincial and municipal commissions' rules not conflict with those authorized by the FAB is essential to maintain the supremacy of the national organization. Finally, the establishment of a permanent centralized headquarters, complete with a gymnasium and small arena, adds to its institutionalization.

While there are many aspects of the Argentine system that are appealing, there are also aspects of the FAB that could never function in the United States, such as having a television network be the primary funding source for

The Regulation of Boxing

HBO's broadcast team over the past several years consisted of George Foreman, Jim Lampley and Larry Merchant. One can only imagine the potential conflict of interest that would result if HBO was the primary funding source of a hypothetical U.S. Boxing Commission.

the national commission. One can only imagine the conflicts of interests that would ensue if ESPN or HBO or any other television network was responsible for funding the day-to-day activities of the national entity created to regulate the sport. Another limitation, which is not actually the fault of the FAB but rather that of the Argentine government, is the prohibition of mandatory HIV testing for boxers. There are clearly compelling reasons for requiring boxers to be tested for the virus that causes AIDS, including the protection of boxers, trainers, referees, judges, and everyone else sitting at ringside. Obviously, the boxers, and to a lesser extent trainers and referees, are the ones with the most potential risk; however, also at risk are those who have sat ringside had specks of blood reach their faces, hands, drinks, and clothes. While the probability of transmitting the virus in this manner is extremely unlikely, there is no compelling reason to allow HIV-positive boxers to potentially expose anyone to the virus. A third area in which the FAB is lacking is in requiring post-fight medical evaluations for all boxers. There have been many cases of boxers suffering the ill effects of their fights after leaving the ring or their dressing rooms. Some type of physical evaluation must be mandatory for all, not just those who suffered a knockout.

One aspect of the FAB's regulations, that of requiring the general equivalency of competing fighters, appears to be sporadically enforced. Fight cards broadcast from Argentina on TyC Sports regularly display mismatches where the winner can easily be predicted prior to the bout. This problem, however, exists in fight cards that take place in the United States and the world over. In theory, it is a good idea for regulatory bodies to prohibit such blatant mismatches, but in practice, with all of the challenges involved in putting together a fight card this is easier said than done.

In sum, a national boxing commission in the United States must be created by federal law in order to have any real authority to define and enforce national standards for boxing. If the USBC is ever created, its leaders can adopt those aspects of other national bodies that regulate boxing in countries throughout the world, and avoid the mistakes and challenges that face other national federations. The case of Argentina, and more specifically, the Argentine Boxing Federation is a useful case to examine for this purpose.

Conclusion

Historical Evolution of Boxing Regulations

The historical antecedents of professional boxing regulations have shown for centuries that regulatory changes come in the face of tragedy. The brutal origins of the sport in Ancient Egypt gave way to a still violent but more controlled version of the sport that emerged in eighteenth century England. Boxing-related deaths, even then, had effects on the sport, as they led to the adoption of extensive sets of rules that would lead the sport to become a gloved contest by the end of the 1800s. In the United States, federalism has become a double-edged sword for boxing. The system of state and federal government has allowed the sport to flourish in the United States, as there was not a federal ban on boxing and states were able to set their own standards for the legalization of the sport. Thus, as detailed in Chapter 1, boxers and promoters found creative ways to stage boxing events. The legalization and later legitimization of the sport in New York and Nevada would pave the way for other states to follow suit. However, as this study indicates, federalism also allowed for the creation of state athletic commissions that have resulted in imperfect regulatory implications for professional boxing that remain to this day. The federal government's minimal intervention in the sport has created a situation of great inequality, as boxing is regulated with great disparity across states. This policy challenge to the federalist system is on the verge of being rectified.

The timing of this research is critical as the U.S. Congress is (once again) reconsidering legislation to form a federal boxing commission to oversee the sport. As members of Congress deliberate the pending federal legislation, they will have the opportunity to read about the disparities in health and safety regulations for boxers across the states. Furthermore, if the legislation is passed and the president signs it into law, members appointed to the U.S. Boxing Commission will also have access to the results of this research.

Conclusion

Contribution to Political Science

This study advances the field of political science through its examination of a largely ignored policy area: professional boxing regulations. The reasons political scientists have ignored this area of research is unknown, as it is a salient policy area that affects people nationwide. It is regulated by state and federal laws, and legislation to help govern the sport has been introduced to Congress and state legislatures for over 100 years. One possible reason that this policy area has been shunned by political scientists is that the small number of cases makes quantitative analysis on this issue difficult for researchers. Nevertheless, the regulation of boxing involves politicians and legislation at both the state and federal levels and provides a perfect case for analyzing the difficulties posed when state governments exhibit great disparity in the way they regulate the same policy issue. The national scope of this study is the first of its kind. For the first time in history, athletic commission personnel, state legislators, governors, members of the federal government, and boxing aficionados have a resource that indicates how states regulate the health and safety aspects of professional boxing.

The study is grounded in state politics theory and methodology. Both quantitative and qualitative methodologies are used to analyze the differences in state boxing regulations and determine the causes of these differences. The innovative nature of this research necessitated the creation of an original analytical model to analyze this policy issue. Therefore, the formation of the Boxing Health and Safety Index (BHSI), which captures state variance on health and safety testing for professional boxers in the United States, is a pioneering technique to investigate this variance. The theoretical underpinnings of previous state politics and public policy research, especially that of political scientist John Kingdon (focusing events), political scientist Virginia Gray (state wealth), sports management professor Laurence Chalip and political scientist Arthur Johnson (gambling), along with political scientist Daniel Elazar (political culture) have guided the selection of the independent variables and the statistical processes that were conducted.

The multiple regression analysis significantly shows that the focusing events of boxing deaths and state wealth (as measured by median household income) positively affect the state score on the Boxing Health and Safety Index while controlling for gambling and political culture. This is a very significant finding, as it demonstrates that states that have experienced higher levels of boxing-related deaths and have higher levels of median income also conduct more health and safety testing for professional boxers. With the vantage point provided by the results of the statistical analysis, we can better predict whether a state will implement health and safety policies for boxing based on the knowledge of their experience with boxing-related deaths and the level of their median household income.

The test of the analytical model came with the creation of the state athletic commissions in Kansas and Minnesota. As described in Chapter 2, by plugging in the state's data into the multiple regression analysis equation, the model predicted each state's score on the BHSI reasonably well. Therefore, the model created in this study fulfils the aim of political science research: to help explain political phenomena and aid in the prediction of future political processes. The research also confirms two existing theories of state politics: Kingdon's theory of a focusing event's ability to motivate politicians to enact or improve a policy area is conclusively shown as boxing-related deaths proved to significantly affect boxing regulations in a positive direction. Also, the theory of state wealth affecting policy issues forwarded by Virginia Gray is also reinforced by the results of the current research.

This study also dispels many commonly held notions about the variance of boxing regulations throughout the United States. For example, most states (43 of 50) possessed a boxing commission in 2004. By 2008, this number had risen to 45. Thus, in 90 percent of the United States the sport has some official state regulatory oversight. In addition, this study shows that the number of boxing events held in a particular state does not necessarily mean that the state will have high levels of health and safety regulations. For example, four of the six states that received the highest possible score on the BHSI (New Jersey, Maryland, Oregon and South Carolina) are not ranked among the top-twelve states that hosted boxing events in 2004. Furthermore, all respondent states reported that they are consistent in requiring some basic health and safety standards such as pre-fight medical evaluations, standards for competitive match-ups, ensuring that an ambulance or emergency personnel and equipment are present at boxing events, health insurance for boxers, and boxing licenses of participants.

If one examines the preceding paragraph on only a superficial level, the sport may not appear to be in the dismal shape that most think it is in. However, as the qualitative analysis in Chapter 2 of this study indicates, state boxing regulations vary in their details. For example, there is a wide range of inconsistency on issues such as what tests should be included in pre-fight medical evaluations. The American Association of Professional Ringside Physicians State Medical Requirements database highlights the disparity among states on required tests, particularly with respect to MRIs and CT scans. In addition, as shown in this study, the number of first-round knockouts that take place in many states demonstrates the exaggeration of state officials that claim to have standards for competitive match-ups. The current loophole surrounding the issue of on-site medical personnel and equipment in lieu of requiring ambulances present at all times during a boxing event remains a troubling area. The longer that this federal requirement is not amended to explicitly state what constitutes "medical personnel with appropriate resuscitation equipment," or better yet, simply changed to require an ambulance on site, the longer boxers will be in peril. The minimal required amount of health insurance for boxers is not federally established, therefore the wide range of insurance policies described in the survey results will continue to exist, because promoters can get away with purchasing amounts that would barely cover the ambulance ride to a hospital and the check-in procedure at the emergency room. While all states require boxing licenses, the standards vary from being a living adult to requiring a battery of medical tests from would-be participants. All states are required by federal law to honor each other's suspensions, yet it is known that not all states do so. Two state officials actually reported that they "don't know" if they honor other states' suspensions on their responses to the BHS Survey. Finally, while approximately three-fourths of states require some sort of certification and approval for ring officials, several states continue to regulate the sport without any type of official required training.

As if the discrepancies noted above were not enough, the greatest disparities in state health and safety regulations in 2004 came in the form of neurological testing (only 30 percent required), HIV (only 55 percent required) and drug testing (only 65 percent required randomly or discretionarily in non-championship bouts). These tests (which compose the BHSI) are perhaps the most controversial yet crucial policy areas that can and should be reformed. However, the Professional Boxing Amendments Act of 2007 does not explicitly state that these tests will be required if the legislation is passed, as the U.S. Boxing Commission members will set the minimum required health and safety standards.

Nevada Case Study

Among the revealing insights of this research are the results of the Nevada case-study analysis. By tracing the major historical and legislative developments of boxing in the state, one gains insight into the evolution of the sport and the importance the state government gives to it. The legalization of the sport prior to the twentieth century as a means to increase the state economy, the establishment of the athletic commission in the 1940s to better regulate the sport, and the expansion of the commission in the 1980s to create a medical advisory board to help protect boxers could not have been possible without supportive state legislators and governors.

The extensive interviews with Marc Ratner, Dr. Margaret Goodman, Joe Cortez and Keith Kizer further reveal the level of expertise possessed by the administrators of the most important boxing state in the United States, and perhaps the world. The participant-observation of a boxing event held in Las Vegas highlights the application of the health and safety regulations detailed in the data analysis. It is also revealing of the manner officials place the law into action. The conduct of officials was certainly professional, but the cursory post-fight physical examinations and the mistake with the drug testing procedures described in Chapter 3 raise concerns as to how other states that may not be as sophisticated as Nevada carry out their duties.

Kansas Case Study

The state of Kansas, in its infinite wisdom, decided to establish a body to regulate boxing in 2004. Since then, a commission has been appointed, rules and regulations have been established, and boxers, ringside officials and others involved in the sport have been licensed by the state. However, Kansas does not currently conduct two of the three tests that form the BHSI. While having a commission is certainly an improvement over not having any regulatory body at all, the state is lacking in its health and safety examinations. Despite a genuine desire to increase testing procedures, as expressed by Boxing Commissioner Aaron Davis, Kansas will remain a step behind other states in terms of health and safety until it begins implementing HIV and neurological testing for boxers.

HIV testing can theoretically be implemented immediately by the commission through an administrative regulation. If the issue preventing the implementation of this test is the cost, then boxers who are low income or otherwise do not have (or cannot afford) private insurance can very easily go to a community health center in or near their hometown to obtain a free test. As long as the boxers can prove that the test results are actually theirs, this problem could be resolved. The boxing commission should also begin the process of pressing state legislators to provide more funding to the commission specifically to carry out neurological tests and (random) drug tests, while simultaneously establishing contact with medical testing laboratories that would be willing to establish cost-effective rates for these tests. Promoters can and should absorb some of these costs as well. The impending establishment of state-owned casinos in Kansas may provide an opportunity for the additional funding that the commission needs to require and enforce more stringent health and safety regulations.

Argentine Case Study

The Argentine Boxing Federation is a good example of the positive and negative aspects of having a national boxing commission. While the volume of boxing is much lower than that of the United States, one has to take into consideration that in terms of population and geography, Argentina is much smaller than the United States. Yet in terms of per capita boxing events, and per capita boxing matches, Argentina's average is actually higher than the United States, and therefore presents a legitimate model of comparison.[1] The positive aspects of the Argentine system include uniform regulations, free public disclosure of boxer records and suspensions, and its system of random drug testing at any time leading up to and after a fight. The negative aspects of the Argentine model include the federation's dependence on a television station for funding, a lack of mandatory HIV testing, and lack of a national law prohibiting competing national federations from arising. Despite having a solid set of regulations on the books, the consistent enforcement of the regulations is questionable. Furthermore, the control of the federation appears to have some oligarchic qualities.

The FAB's evident authority over provincial and municipal commissions can be seen as both positive and negative. On one hand, it imposes minimal standards of regulations that the local commissions must abide by. On the other hand, local commissions have virtually no power to change any regulations that the FAB imposes upon them.

Potential Effects of the Professional Boxing Amendments Act of 2007

If enacted, the Professional Boxing Amendments Act of 2007 would become the most far-reaching federal law to affect boxing in U.S. history. However, it would not provide a miracle cure for all of the sport's ills. While a United States Boxing Commission may be created to oversee the sport, it would not eliminate state or tribal boxing commissions. Rather, it would work in conjunction with these commissions and the Association of Boxing Commissions (ABC) to implement, enhance and enforce minimum national health and safety standards.

State or tribal commissions would not be prohibited from exceeding the minimum standards set forth by the Professional Boxing Amendments Act of 2007. The three-member commission under the advice of the ABC would determine the guidelines for such standards. In addition, contractual standards and mandatory disclosures would be established, as would objective and consistent criteria for sanctioning bodies to rate boxers (under the legislation, the USBC cannot rate boxers itself, nor can it promote events). The commission would require licensure of ring officials, provide licensing guidelines for boxers and would create a national medical registry of professional boxers.

Perhaps most importantly, the commission would have the federal authority to suspend boxers, launch investigations, obtain injunctions or restraining orders, enforce subpoenas, and pursue legal action against violators of the act. Furthermore, it is designed to produce annual reports and public reports of the progress made in raising health and safety standards for professional boxers.

One concern about a potential federal commission that has been raised by former Nevada Athletic Commission executive director Marc Ratner, current NAC director Keith Kizer and Kansas boxing commissioner Aaron Davis deals with the funding of the United States Boxing Commission requirements or activities. The legislation stipulates that it may collect fees through several means. The ambiguous writing in the legislation leaves room for interpretation that the implementation of this law might become a "states' rights issue," as Ratner put it (see Chapter 3). The commissioners would have to resolve this issue if indeed the bill eventually passes. Some commission executive directors, such as Armando Garcia of California, have already recommended that the commission contact Senator McCain's office to see if states that already implement the "equivalent standards" of the proposed regulations can be granted an exemption.[2] That begs the question: if a state commission is already implementing the standards called for by a federal law, why should it be exempted? But the funding of any federal mandates is a legitimate concern that is not currently specified in the legislation. This study shows that state wealth is already a significant factor in the level of state boxing regulations;

therefore it is essential that any mandates from the USBC explicitly designate who will be responsible for the costs so states can be in compliance.

The last point mentioned in my concluding thoughts on the Argentine Boxing Federation raises important questions about the same dynamic arising with a national boxing commission in the U.S. In order for such a commission to be effective, it would have to maintain a minimal set of regulations. But in light of Ratner and Davis's comments, what recourse would states have to change any imposed regulations that they did not agree with? To resolve such a case might take years of litigation and accumulate costs that would be far better spent on protecting boxers. Thus, any federal commission formed in the United States should implement a process to hear state commission recommendations, concerns and grievances. But if a federal commission is simply going to let states carry on their activities without having to change anything, then what is the point of having one?

In a related issue, the bill proposes "minimum levels" of health and safety regulations, yet it does not specify what those levels are. The three most variant policy issues that emerged in the results of this study, neurological, HIV, and drug testing, are not mentioned in the federal legislation at all. Only testing for "infectious diseases" is explicitly mentioned. There is no guarantee that states would be required to implement such tests, and if so, which types of tests would be required and who would fund them.

This study has already determined the areas in which the states are relatively consistent. If the existing state standards are considered to be the "minimum standards" implemented by the federal legislation, then there is not much of a need for a federal entity to regulate the sport. However, if the commissioners appointed to the USBC take a proactive stance toward truly *enhancing* the health and safety regulations for professional boxers and requiring the tests included in the BHSI nationally, then the United States will become a model for the sport, and the federal government will truly be doing its part to protect the health and safety of professional boxers.

If the Professional Boxing Amendments Act of 2007 passes both houses of Congress and is signed into law by the president, the appointment of commission members would make the difference as to whether this law will help clean up the sport or if we will have more of the same with just another level of bureaucracy. The federal government has an opportunity to enhance a policy area that states are reluctant to improve, as this study indicates. If the states, through their respective boxing commissions, are unwilling to improve health and safety standards for professional boxing, then federal involvement is long overdue, as has been the case with civil rights and interstate transportation issues.

Limitations

As with all research, this study has its limitations. While it would have been ideal to have received a 100 percent response rate to the BHS Survey, the 74 percent received is excellent, as it is a representative sample of the population, particularly since all of the top-twelve boxing states (where 84 percent of matches are held) replied. The augmentation of the data collected for the BHSI from the AAPRP State Medical Requirements is imperfect; however, it allowed me to analyze 93 percent of the cases. Since the three states omitted from the study did not reply to either the BHS Survey or the AAPRP, this research includes all cases for which data is available. While the findings can be applied to the entire United States, they cannot be applied to U.S. territories, the federal district or Indian reservations.

A second limitation is that this study is a snapshot in time. State boxing regulations were examined only for 2004, as were the number of boxing events. Boxing regulations are subject to change and a few states indicated that their regulations would be changed to require HIV testing in the future. As mentioned earlier, the state of Kansas passed a law to create a boxing commission in 2005 and Minnesota also followed suit. Thus, some states are making proactive efforts to improve their health and safety standards for professional boxing, but these efforts are not completely captured in this book.

Third, the findings of this study apply only to professional boxing. Amateur boxing in the United States is governed by the Amateur Sports Act of 1978 (36 USC 371). This federal law allows for the designation of a single entity to govern each Olympic sport. For amateur boxing, USA Boxing is the only recognized national governing body, with the sole authority to regulate the sport.[3] Many states, such as Michigan (mentioned in George Kimball's Foreword for this book), have laws on the books specifically stating that amateur boxers in the state must be registered with USA Boxing.[4] Other state laws are less restrictive, such as the Kansas law stating that amateur boxing will be "sanctioned by a nationally-recognized amateur sanctioning body approved by the commission."[5]

Finally, a verification of the state officials' responses was not independently carried out. Therefore it is possible that the state official who completed

Conclusion

the BHS Survey did not accurately respond to the questions. Nearly all respondents completed their name and provided contact information on the survey and indicated that they were willing to be contacted for a follow-up interview. Since each of these individuals is a state employee, it is unlikely that surveys were deliberately inaccurate as to make the state appear that it is carrying out a higher level of health and safety regulations than it actually does. Nevertheless, this study is based on a reading of the information provided by the athletic commissions themselves. It is also based upon information on the number of boxing matches and events that is compiled by boxrec.com and the collection of information on boxing deaths reported in the *Journal of Combative Sport*. Any inaccuracies in the data reporting are on the part of the state athletic commissioner (or designee) that completed the survey, the information posted on boxrec.com, or the data in the *Journal of Combative Sport*.

Future Research

The participant-observation of the Nevada Athletic Commission highlights one of many avenues for future research that this study may take. Further observations in Nevada would reveal if the activities that took place at the observed boxing event were typical or if they were an exception. As mentioned in Chapter 3, the boxing event observed was considered an evening of club fights, before any of the participants such as Sultan Ibragimov (who is the WBO heavyweight champion as of early 2008) reached the top echelons of boxing. Thus, it would be interesting to see if the standards of conduct by commission personnel are any different in major boxing events. In addition, comparative observations in several states would also enable the researcher to better determine the level of professionalism demonstrated by the various athletic commissions. It would further reveal the methods used by commission personnel to enforce the regulations on the books. Such research would of course require appropriate funding in addition to extensive time and travel.

Additional extensions of the current research could come in the form of examining the boxing regulations in U.S. territories such as Puerto Rico, the U.S. Virgin Islands, and the District of Columbia, all of which possess boxing commissions and host boxing events. The rise of boxing events held in casinos located on Indian reservations also raises the possibility of producing a comparative study that exclusively examines tribal boxing commissions. And of course, if the United States Boxing Commission is established, the regulations that it will enact can then be compared to those in the international sphere, as many nation-states across the globe already possess national boxing commissions, such as Argentina.

Final Thoughts

This study contributes to the political science literature by thoroughly examining an ignored policy area on a national level. It also contributes to the popular boxing literature by presenting a perspective on the regulatory side of the sport. Boxing fans, columnists in online and print publications, and even some members of the United States Congress often complain about the lack of regulations to protect the health and safety of boxers. This book provides at least some of the resources needed to make informed judgments about the current state of boxing health and safety regulations.

Between 2005 and 2008, a few states have improved their boxing regulations. Two state athletic commissions were created (Kansas and Minnesota), though Kansas carries out only one of the BHSI tests and Minnesota carries out only two tests included in the BHSI.[6] Six states included in the 2005 BHS survey added HIV testing to their pre-fight requirements (Connecticut, Hawaii, Iowa, Kentucky, Mississippi, and Missouri).[7] Five states included in the original study have started requiring neurological tests (Kentucky, Nebraska, New Hampshire, Ohio, and Texas).[8]

The federal bill introduced to the 110th Congress may create a national boxing commission to improve the health and safety standards of professional boxing in the United States. The overwhelming evidence presented in this study indicates that passage of this legislation would be a very positive step toward improving the sport, even if it is initially met with resistance by state athletic commissions. The health and safety of boxers throughout the country depends on it.

To conclude, I would like to refer the reader to the following images taken by Missouri-based photographer Bob Carson of Randie Carver's fatal bout with Kabary Salem. May the tragedy depicted in these photographs, appearing on pages 201 through 204, serve as a reminder of why boxing regulations in the United States must improve.

Above and pages 202, 203, and 204: Randie Carver died on September 14, 1999, as a result of injuries sustained in his fight with Kabary Salem two days earlier. This series of photographs captures moments from that fateful fight (photographs courtesy Bob Carson).

Conclusion

Conclusion

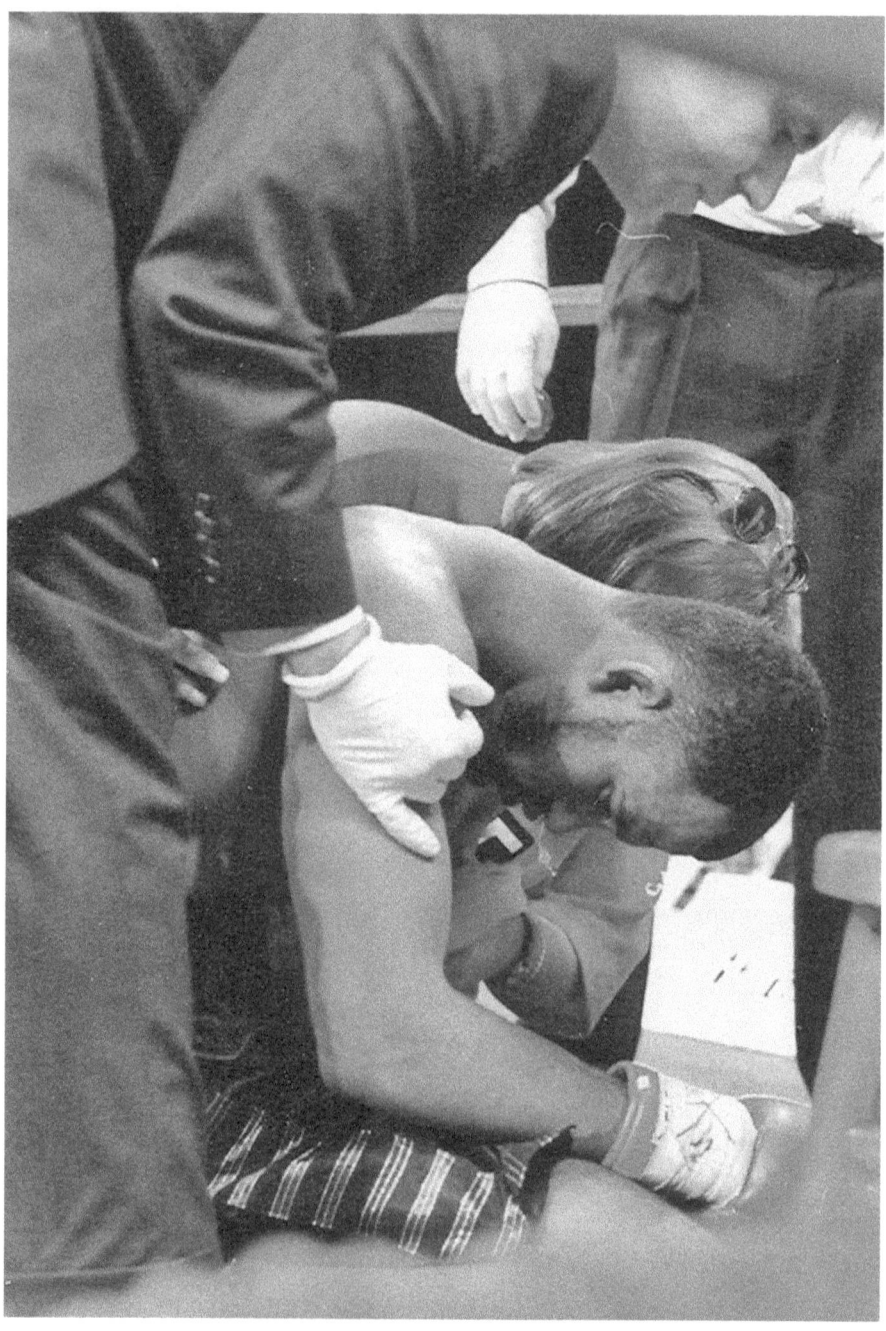

Chapter Notes

Preface

1. Cyber Boxing Zone. <http://www.cyberboxingzone.com/boxing/kd929991.htm.> Active as of February 13, 2008.
2. Public Law 104-272. Professional Boxing Safety Act of 1996. <http://frwebgate.access.gpo.gov/cgi-bin/getdoc.cgi?dbname=104_cong_public_laws&docid=f:publ272.104.>
3. David A. Lieb, "Supreme Court to re-hear case on brain-damaged boxer," Associated Press, December 7, 2004.
4. Supreme Court of Missouri Docket Summary. SC85747 Fernando Ibarra Maldonado v. Gateway Hotel Holdings, L.L.C., St. Louis City. <http://www.courts.mo.gov/SUP/index.nsf/fe8feff4659e0b7b8625699f0079eddf/643abeabc3a43ef286256e66006b3f61?OpenDocument.>
5. *Sports Illustrated*. <http://sportsillustrated.cnn.com/more/boxing/news/1999/09/14/carver_obit_ap/.> Active as of February 13, 2008.
6. GAO report number GAO-03-699, "Professional Boxing: Issues Related to the Protection of Boxers' Health, Safety, and Economic Interests." July 22, 2003. http://www.gao.gov/htext/d03699.html

Introduction

1. *Milwaukee Journal Sentinel*. <http://www.jsonline.com/sports/etc/ap/may02/ap-box-ali-congres052302.asp.> Active as of February 13, 2008.
2. The terms "state athletic commission" and "state boxing commission" are often used interchangeably to describe the same entity.
3. See Kansas Statute No. 12-5103.
4. For this study, only states will be analyzed. Federal territories and American Indian reservations may be examined in a future study.
5. *GAO Report to the Chairman, Committee on Commerce, Science, and Transportation, U.S. Senate*. July 2003.
6. S. 893 A bill to establish the National Boxing Commission, and for other purposes, sponsored by Senator Harry Reid (Nevada), and S. 2550 A bill to amend the Professional Boxing Safety Act of 1996 and to establish the United States Boxing Administration, sponsored by Senator John McCain (Arizona). See http://sports.espn.go.com/sports/boxing/news/story?id=1773025.
7. David M. Hedge, *Governance and the Changing American States* (Boulder, CO: Westview Press, 1998), p. 1.
8. Ibid., p. 3-5.
9. Virginia Gray, "The socioeconomic and political context of states," in Gray and Russell L. Hanson, *Politics in the American States: A Comparative Analysis* (Washington: CQ Press, 2004), p. 6.
10. Evan J. Ringquist and James C. Garand, "Policy Change in the American States," in Ronald E. Weber and Paul Brace, eds., *American State and Local Politics: Directions for the 21st Century* (New York: Chatham House, 1999), p. 268, 270.
11. Ibid., p. 270-272.
12. Ibid., p. 272-274.
13. Ibid., p. 275-278.
14. John W. Kingdon, *Agendas, Alternatives, and Public Policies*. 2nd ed. (New York: Harper Collins, 1995), p. 94-95.
15. Barrie Houlihan, *Sport, Policy and Politics* (London: Routledge, 1997), p. 67.
16. Laurence Chalip and Arthur Johnson, "Sports Policy in the United States," in Chalip, Johnson and Stachura, eds., *National Sports Policies: An International Handbook* (Westport, CT: Greenwood Press, 1996), p. 404.
17. Ibid., p. 406, 428.
18. Arthur Johnson and James H. Frey, eds., *Government and Sport: The Public Policy Issues* (Totowa, NJ: Rowman and Allanheld, 1985), p. ix.
19. Chalip and Johnson, p. 416.
20. Ibid., p. 418.
21. Houlihan, p. 100.

NOTES — CHAPTER 1

22. John Wilson, *Playing by the Rules: Sport, Society, and the State* (Detroit, MI: Wayne State University Press, 1994), p. 24.
23. Houlihan, p. 102.
24. The Association of Boxing Commissions Internet site lists all U.S.-based commissions that oversee boxing. <http://www.abcboxing.com/>
25. In Missouri, the boxing commission is called the Office of Athletics; in Connecticut, it is the Department of Consumer Protection; in Massachusetts it is the Department of Public Safety.
26. The survey is modeled after several health and safety issues presented in the 2003 GAO Report on Professional Boxing and the Professional Boxing Safety Act of 1996.

Chapter 1

1. Bert Randolph Sugar, ed. *100 Years of Boxing* (New York: Galley Press, 1982), p. 12.
2. Arthur R. Ashe Jr., *A Hard Road to Glory: The African American Athlete in Boxing* (New York: Amistad, 1993) p. 1.
3. Homer, *The Iliad*. Translated by Robert Fitzgerald. (London: Collins Harvill, 1985).
4. Ibid. p. 1. Other historians suggest that boxing entered the ancient Olympics in 688 B.C. See Peter Brooke-Ball, *The Boxing Album: An Illustrated History* (New York: Anness, 1995), p. 8–11.
5. See "Black-figured amphora" under "Etruscan sports" in <http://www.thebritishmuseum.ac.uk/compass/.> Active as of February 13, 2008.
6. See "Red-figured cup, attributed to the Foundry Painter" in <http://www.thebritishmuseum.ac.uk/compass/> Active as of February 13, 2008.
7. See "Theseus, the all-Athenian hero" and "Two terracotta figurines of African boxers" in <http://www.thebritishmuseum.ac.uk/compass/.> Active as of July 13, 2005. See also "Terra-cotta Lamp Modeled as a Gymnasium" in <http://www.eternalegypt.org.> Active as of February 13, 2008.
8. Brooke-Ball, p. 121.
9. For a description and illustration of these ancient handwraps, see Brooke-Ball, p. 8–11.
10. George Stevenson died from injuries sustained in a prizefight with Jack Broughton in 1741.
11. Brooke-Ball, p. 16–17.
12. Nat Fleischer and Sam Andre, *A Pictorial History of Boxing* (New York: Citadel Press, 1993), p. 39.
13. Ibid.
14. Brooke-Ball, p. 125.
15. Ibid., p. 124.
16. Elliott J. Gorn, "The First American Championship Fight," *OAH Magazine of History* 7, Summer 1992.
17. Ashe, p. 5.
18. Gorn.
19. Peter Arnold, *The Pictorial History of Boxing* (New York: Gallery Books, 1988), p. 22.
20. W. Russel Gray, "For Whom the Bell Tolled: The Decline of British Prize Fighting in the Victorian Era," *Journal of Popular Culture* 21, no.2 (Fall 1987): 59–60.
21. Sugar, p. 33.
22. An image of a ticket to the Sullivan vs. Corbett fight can be seen at <http://www.ibhof.com/ibhfhvy2.htm.> Active as of February 13, 2008.
23. Fleischer and Andre, p. 69–70.
24. Gray, p. 59.
25. The National Sporting Club of London renamed itself in 1929 as the British Board of Boxing Control, the organization that regulates boxing in the United Kingdom to this day.
26. Gilbert Odd, *The Encyclopedia of Boxing* (Secaucus, NJ: Chartwell Books, 1989) p. 203.
27. Jeffrey T. Sammons, *Beyond the Ring: The Role of Boxing in American Society* (Urbana: University of Illinois Press, 1990), p. 15.
28. Ibid. p. 16.
29. Ibid.
30. Ibid. p. 20–21.
31. Ibid. p. 22.
32. USC Annenberg School <http://www.usc.edu/schools/annenberg/asc/projects/comm544/library/images/413.html.> Active as of February 13, 2008.
33. Peter A. Adams, "Win, Lose, and Drawing Conclusions: Bellows, Boxing and Progressivism," *OAH Magazine of History* 7, Summer 1992.
34. James B. Roberts and Alexander G. Skutt, *The Boxing Register: International Boxing Hall of Fame Official Record Book* (Ithaca, NY: McBooks Press, 2002).
35. David K. Wiggins, "Peter Jackson and the Elusive Heavyweight Championship," *Journal of Sport History* 12, no. 2 (Summer 1985): 149.
36. Sammons, p. 24.
37. This data comes from fights listed by state and year on <http://www.boxrec.com.> Active as of February 13, 2008.
38. Sammons, p. 28.
39. Ibid., p. 37.

Notes — Chapter 2

40. Randy Roberts, *Jack Dempsey: The Manassa Mauler* (Baton Rouge: Louisiana State University Press, 1984) p. 24.
41. Ibid., p. 25.
42. Sammons, p. 62–63.
43. Roberts, p. 27–28.
44. William M. Tuttle Jr., *Race Riot: Chicago in the Red Summer of 1919* (Urbana: University of Illinois Press, 1996), p. 75.
45. Roberts, p. 28.
46. Ibid., p. 66.
47. Roberts and Skutt, p. 51.
48. Theodore Roosevelt, *An Autobiography* (New York: Macmillan, 1913), Bartleby.com, 1998. <http://www.bartleby.com/55/03/06/05.> Active as of February 13, 2008.
49. Roger Kahn, *A Flame of Pure Fire: Jack Dempsey and the Roaring '20s* (New York: Harcourt Brace, 1999), p. 204–205.
50. Sammons, p. 63.
51. Roberts and Skutt, p. 51.
52. Stanley Weston and Steven Farhood, *The Ring: Boxing in the 20th Century* (New York: BDD Illustrated Books, 1993), p. 52.
53. Benjamin J. Rader, *American Sports: From the Age of Folk Games to the Age of Televised Sports* (Upper Saddle River, NJ: Prentice Hall, 1999), p. 297.
54. Bert Randolph Sugar, *Bert Sugar on Boxing* (Guilford, CT: The Lyons Press, 2003), p. 120.
55. Sammons, p. 119.
56. Benjamin G. Rader, *In Its Own Image: How Television Has Transformed Sports* (New York: The Free Press, 1984), p. 41.
57. Sammons, p. 132–133.
58. Rader, *American Sports*, p. 233.
59. Garry Whannel, *Fields in Vision: Television Sport and Cultural Transformation* (London: Routledge, 1992), p. 166–167.
60. Rader, *In Its Own Image*, p. 41–42.
61. Ibid., p. 45.
62. *Ring of Fire: The Emile Griffith Story*, DVD, directed by Ron Berger and Dan Klores (Anchor Bay Entertainment, 2005).
63. Rader, *American Sports*, p. 234.
64. Sammons, p. 176–177.
65. U.S. Code Title 18, Part I, Chapter 11 #224. Bribery in Sporting Contests <http://www.law.cornell.edu/uscode/html/uscode18/usc_sec_18_00000224——000-.html.> Active as of July 13, 2005.
66. Bob Mee, *Boxing: Heroes and Champions* (Edison, NJ: Chartwell Books, 1997), p. 10.
67. Ibid.
68. Adidas. <http://www.press.adidas.com/DesktopDefault.aspx?tabid-70/96_read-318/.> Active as of February 13, 2008.
69. Edmund P. Edmonds and William H. Manz, *Congress and Boxing: A Legislative History, 1960–2003.* Volume 1, Document Numbers 1–2 (Buffalo, NY: William S. Hein, 2005), p. 1–22.
70. Charles Jay, "No Commission by Omission," *Boxing Digest,* December 2007, p. 43.
71. Sammons, p. 210.
72. Clay, aka *Ali v. United States*, 403 U.S. 698 Certiorari to the United States Court of Appeals for the Fifth Circuit No. 783 Argued April 19, 1971— Decided June 28, 1971.
73. Edmonds and Manz, p. 1–22.
74. Mee, p. 10.
75. The term "linear" in this context refers to the concept of a championship changing hands from one boxer to another only through a loss in the ring. Thus, Larry Holmes, the WBC champion, was considered the linear champion by virtue of his 1980 victory over Muhammad Ali. Meanwhile, the WBA heavyweight title passed through several boxers.
76. Arguello gave a guest lecture to a Latin American studies course at the University of Kansas on December 6, 2007.
77. *Champion*, directed by Kyung-Taek Kwak, DVD (First Look Home Entertainment, 2006).
78. Associated Press, "12-round limit for W.B.C.," *The New York Times*, December 10, 1982.
79. Thomas Hauser, *The Black Lights: Inside the World of Professional Boxing* (Fayetteville, AR: University of Arkansas Press, 2000) p. 24.
80. H.R.4167— Professional Boxing Safety Act of 1996.
81. Muhammad Ali Boxing Reform Act.
82. Library of Congress. <http://thomas.loc.gov/cgi-bin/bdquery/D?d109:6:./temp/~bdTHsd::×/bss/109search.html.> Active as of July 13, 2005.
83. The Sweet Science. <http://www.thesweetscience.com/boxing-article/4931/benn-mcclennan-boxing-game/.> Active as of February 13, 2008.
84. Margaret Goodman, "HIV: Boxing's Hidden Danger," *The Ring Magazine*, December 2007.
85. John Eligon and Duff Wilson, "Morrison Says Error in H.I.V. Test Hurt Career," *The New York Times*, July 22, 2007.

Chapter 2

1. Human Subjects Research approval from the University of Kansas was obtained for this project.

Notes — Chapter 2

2. BoxRec. <http://www.boxrec.com.> Active as of February 13, 2008.
3. Ibid.
4. The number of boxing events that took place in the United States is compiled by <http://www.boxrec.com.> Active as of February 13, 2008.
5. Kaiser State Health Facts. <http://www.statehealthfacts.org/comparemaptable.jsp?ind=449&cat=9&yr=1& typ=1&sort=n&o=d.> Active as of February 13, 2008.
6. Ibid.
7. American Association of Professional Ringside Physicians. <http://www.aaprp.org/Commission% 20Requirements.> Active as of July 13, 2005.
8. American Association of Professional Ringside Physicians. <http://www.aaprp.org/Pre-fight %20Washinton.> Active as of July 13, 2005.
9. BHS Survey.
10. Panella letter, January 26, 2005.
11. See appendix. Professional Boxing Safety Act of 1996 § 6306.
12. BHS Survey.
13. Ibid.
14. Association of Boxing Commissions. <http://www.abcboxing.com.> Active as of February 13, 2008; Fight Fax, Inc. <http://www.fightfax.com.> Active as of February 13, 2008.
15. BHS Survey.
16. Ibid.
17. Marc Ratner, interview, June 8, 2005.
18. BHS Survey
19. Ibid.
20. Panella letter, January 26, 2005.
21. BHS Survey
22. Ibid.
23. Ibid.
24. BoxRec. <http://www.boxrec.com.> Active as of February 13, 2008.
25. ESPN.com. <http://sports.espn.go.com/sports/boxing/news/story?id=2074559.> Active as of February 13, 2008.
26. Ibid.
27. The Professional Boxing Safety Act of 1996 (15 U.S.C. 6301 et seq.).
28. BHS Survey.
29. The Professional Boxing Safety Act of 1996 (15 U.S.C. 6301 et seq.).
30. BHS Survey.
31. Maryland Title 09 Department of Licensing and Regulation; Subtitle 14 State Athletic Commission; Chapter 04.08 Location of Contest to Emergency Medical Facilities. p. 401.
32. BHS Survey.
33. The Professional Boxing Safety Act of 1996 (15 U.S.C. 6301 et seq.).
34. BHS Survey.
35. Ibid.
36. Ibid.
37. Ibid.
38. Ibid.
39. Association of Boxing Commissions. <http://www.abcboxing.com.> Active as of February 13, 2008.
40. BHS Survey.
41. West Virginia, South Carolina, and Mississippi noted that they planned to implement such requirements in 2005.
42. BHS Survey.
43. Ibid.
44. North Carolina, Oklahoma, Hawaii and Missouri indicate on their survey responses that they are planning to implement HIV testing.
45. BHS Survey.
46. ESPN.com. <http://sports.espn.go.com/sports/boxing/columns/story?id=2052593.> Active as of February 13, 2008.
47. World Boxing Association Regulations and Rules Governing World Championship Contests, p. 10; World Boxing Association. <http://www.wbaonline.com.> Active as of February 13, 2008.
48. The state of Hawaii indicated on the BHS survey that it was "Currently in the process of changing the rules to allow testing."
49. BHS Survey.
50. Some states that conduct random or discretionary testing indicated "no" on the survey responses. Such replies were recoded as "yes" to capture all states that have mechanisms to conduct drug tests if necessary. Likewise, California indicated "yes" on this question, but it conducts drug tests only in championship bouts. The state does not indicate random or discretionary tests in non-title bouts, thus the reply was recoded as "no."
51. BHS Survey.
52. Pat Panella interview, January 25, 2005.
53. Bradley Wright interview, May 9, 2005.
54. ESPN.com <http://sports.espn.go.com/sports/boxing/news/story?id=2058197.> Active as of February 13, 2008.
55. ESPN.com <http://sports.espn.go.com/sports/boxing/news/story?id=2075444.> Active as of February 13, 2008.
56. State of Louisiana, Office of Inspector General. Follow up of Prior Audits 5/31/05–11/20/06. Released August 1, 2007.
57. Virginia Gray, "The socioeconomic and political context of states," in Gray and Russell L. Hanson, *Politics in the American States: A Comparative Analysis* (Washington, DC: CQ Press, 2004).

58. Evan J. Ringquist and James C. Garand, "Policy Change in the American States," in Ronald E. Weber and Paul Brace, eds., *American State and Local Politics: Directions for the 21st Century* (New York: Catham House, 1999).
59. Ibid., p. 275–278.
60. Laurence Chalip and Arthur Johnson, "Sports Policy in the United States," in Chalip, Johnson and Stachura, eds., *National Sports Policies: An International Handbook* (Westport, CT: Greenwood Press, 1996), p. 416.
61. Joseph R. Svinth, "Death Under the Spotlight: The Manuel Velasquez Boxing Fatality Collection," *Journal of Combative Sport*, February 2004.
62. National Conference of State Legislatures. <http://www.ncsl.org/programs/econ/00 gaming.htm.> Active as of February 13, 2008.
63. Gray, "The socioeconomic and political context of states."
64. In this study, an Ordinary Least Squares (OLS) Multiple Regression Analysis was conducted.
65. The interview with Thomas Hauser took place in June 2005.
66. Kansas's predicted score of 1.29 was calculated by multiplying Kansas's actual values on each independent variable, adding them, and then subtracting the constant from the total.
67. Minnesota's predicted score of 1.75 was calculated by multiplying Minnesota's actual values on each independent variable, adding them, and then subtracting the constant from the total.
68. Minnesota Statutes 2006 Chapter 341 Boxing Commission, <http://www.ros.leg.mn/bin/getpub.php?pubtype= STAT_CHAP&year=2006&section=341.> Active as of February 13, 2008.

Chapter 3

1. David Thomson, *In Nevada: The Land, the People, God, and Chance* (New York: Alfred A. Knopf, 1999), p. 41.
2. James W. Hulse, *The Silver State: Nevada's Heritage Reinterpreted* (Reno, NV: University of Nevada Press, 2004), p. 162.
3. Mella Rothwell Harmon, in John B. Reid and Ronald M. James. *Uncovering Nevada's Past: A Primary Source History of the Silver State* (Reno, NV: University of Nevada Press, 2004), p. 133.
4. *Statutes of the State of Nevada Passed at the Eighteenth Session of the Legislature 1897* (Carson City, NV: State Printing Office, 1897). I would like to especially thank Nevada state archivists Christopher Driggs and Mella Rothwell Harmon for obtaining copies of the Nevada legislation for me.
5. Ibid.
6. Ibid.
7. Theblackboardfreepress.com, <http://www.theblackboardfreepress.com/200305/outpast.html.> Active as of February 13, 2008.
8. Harmon, in Reid and James, p. 133.
9. Phillip I. Earl, *This Was Nevada* (Reno, NV: Nevada Historical Society, 1986), p. 169–171.
10. Ibid., p. 173.
11. Ibid.
12. James B. Roberts and Alexander G. Skutt, *The Boxing Register* (Ithaca, NY: McBooks Press, 2002), p. 628.
13. Ibid.
14. Earl, p. 174.
15. *Statutes of the State of Nevada Passed at the Fortieth Session of the Legislature 1941* (Carson City, NV: State Printing Office, 1941).
16. Ibid.
17. Tim Dahlberg, *Fight Town: Las Vegas—The Boxing Capital of the World* (Las Vegas: Stephens Press, 2004), p. 42.
18. Thomson, p. 41.
19. Hulse, p. 217.
20. Harmon, in Reid and James, p. 134.
21. Dahlberg, p. 47.
22. Ibid., p. 51.
23. Hulse, p. 217.
24. Dahlberg, p. 118.
25. Ibid. p. 52, 121, 129.
26. Nevada State Athletic Commission. <http://boxing.nv.gov.> Active as of February 13, 2008.
27. Ibid.
28. This interview with Marc Ratner took place on June 8, 2005.
29. This interview with Dr. Margaret Goodman took place on June 6, 2005.
30. I want to expressly thank Dr. Margaret Goodman and Marc Ratner for allowing me to observe the commission carry out its duties. I also wish to thank Barbara Barcenas for obtaining complementary tickets to the event, and Guilty Boxing, Inc., for providing a staff credential allowing me unrestricted access at the venue.
31. Sultan Ibragimov would go on to win the World Boxing Organization heavyweight championship on June 2, 2007.
32. ESPN.com. <http://sports.espn.go.com/sports/boxing/news/story?id=2099870.> Active as of February 13, 2008.

Notes—Chapters 4 and 5

33. *The Boxing Times.* <http://www.sweetscience.com/analyses/2005/050917chavez_johnson.html.> Active as of February 13, 2008.
34. Geoffrey Gray, "In debate over safety, no neutral corner," *The New York Times Online.* <http://www.nytimes.com/2005/12/03/sports/othersports/03ring.html.> Active as of February 13, 2008.
35. 2006 Nevada Advisory Committee on Boxer Health and Safety Report.
36. Kizer Memorandum to All Licensed Promoters and Matchmakers, July 24, 2006.
37. 2006 Nevada Advisory Committee on Boxer Health and Safety Report.
38. *Las Vegas Review-Journal.* <http://www.reviewjournal.com/lvrj_home/2005/Oct-28-Fri2005/sports/4038861.html.> Active as of February 13, 2008.

Chapter 4

1. Kansas Legislative Research Department. August 28, 2003. Joint Committee on Economic Development Minutes. <http://www.kslegislature.org/committeeminutes/03-04/interim_joint/joint/jtecodev8-12&13-03.pdf.> Active as of February 13, 2008.
2. Ibid.
3. Ibid.
4. Ibid.
5. Results were compiled from an analysis of boxrec.com records. <http://www.boxrec.com/.> Active as of February 13, 2008.
6. Ibid.
7. Kansas Boxing Commission. <http://kdoch.state.ks.us/boxingks/fees.jsp.> Active as of February 13, 2008.
8. Kansas Regulated Sports Act.
9. Minnesota Boxing Commission. <http://www.budget.state.mn.us/budget/operating/200809/nov/331155.pdf.> Active as of February 13, 2008.
10. *Arkansas Democrat Gazette.* <http://www.nwanews.com/adg/Sports/125549/print/.> Active as of February 13, 2008.
11. Ohio Athletic Commission. <http://www.lbo.state.oh.us/fiscal/budget/FiscalAnalysis/127GA/ATH.pdf.> Active as of February 13, 2008; Florida Office of Program Policy Analysis and Government Accountability. <http://www.oppaga.state.fl.us/profiles/4045/print.asp.> Active as of February 13, 2008.
12. Arkansas State Athletic Commission. <http://www.arkleg.state.ar.us/data/agency_budgets/0209.pdf.> Active as of February 13, 2008.
13. Colorado Department of Regulatory Agencies. <http://www.dora.state.co.us/boxing/about.htm.> Active as of February 13, 2008.
14. *Lawrence Journal-World.* <http://www2.ljworld.com/news/2008/jan/17/budget_gamble/.> Active as of February 13, 2008.
15. Association of Boxing Commissions. <http://www.abcboxing.com/.> Active as of February 13, 2008.
16. Stateline.org. <http://www.stateline.org/live/ViewPage.action?siteNodeId=136&languageId=1&contentId=43941.> Active as of February 13, 2008.

Chapter 5

1. An English version of the Argentine Constitution can be found online at the Argentine National Senate Web page. <http://www.senado.gov.ar/web/interes/constitucion/english.php.> Active as of February 13, 2008.
2. See, for example, the Constitution of the Neuquen Province at the Neuquen Provincial Government Web page. <http://www.neuquen.gov.ar/constitucion/constitucion2006.htm.> Active as of February 13, 2008.
3. Database Olympics. <http://www.databaseolympics.com/country/countrysport.htm?cty=ARG&sp=BOX.> Active as of February 13, 2008.
4. Centro de Documentacion Historica sobre Educacion fisica y Deportes. Boletin #28. <http://www.romerobrest.edu.ar/cdh/boletin28.htm.> Active as of February 13, 2008.
5. Society for Irish Latin American Studies <http://www.irlandeses.net/mccarthy2.htm.> Active as of February 13, 2008.
6. Víctor Lupo, *Historia Politica del Deporte Argentino, 1610–2002* (Buenos Aires: Corregidor, 2004), p. 94.
7. Society for Irish Latin American Studies.
8. Lupo, p. 95.
9. BoxRec.com. <http://www.boxrec.com/list_bouts.php?human_id=10607&cat=boxer.> Active as of February 13, 2008.
10. Info-Almagro.com. <http://info-almagro.com.ar/almagro2_1/historia/federaci.htm.> Active as of July 13, 2005.
11. Lupo, p. 78.
12. Info-Almagro.com..
13. Boxed-Boxing.com. <http://www.boxeo-boxing.com/Punoyletra/punoyletra32.htm.> Active as of February 13, 2008.
14. James B. Roberts and Alexander Skutt, *The Boxing Register: International Boxing Hall of*

Fame Official Record Book (Ithaca, NY: McBooks Press, 2002), p. 620.
15. Cyberboxingzone.com. <http://cyberboxingzone.com/boxing/w1002-bwjuneedition.pdf.> Active as of February 13, 2008.
16. Lupo, p. 191.
17. *Diario Clarin.* <http://www.clarin.com/diario/2005/01/13/conexiones/t-903512.htm.> Active as of February 13, 2008.
18. Ibid.
19. Ibid.
20. ESPNdeportes.com. Translated by author. <http://espndeportes.espn.go.com/news/print?id=287746&type=story.> Active as of February 13, 2008.
21. FAB. <http://www.fabox.com.ar/peleasyfestivales2005.htm.> Active as of February 13, 2008.
22. *Diario Misiones.* <http://misionesonline.net/paginas/noticiaPrint.php?db=noticias2005&id=18694.> Active as of February 13, 2008.
23. Ibid.
24. Ibid.
25. Government of Argentina. Author's translation. <http://www.argentina.gov.ar/argentina/portal/paginas.dhtml?pagina=298.> Active as of February 13, 2008.
26. *Diario Clarin.* <http://www.clarin.com/diario/2006/12/15/deportes/d-07801.htm.> Active as of February 13, 2008; *Revista Noticias.* <http://www.revista-noticias.com.ar/ed_1566/articulo.php?art=94.> Active as of February 13, 2008.
27. Pagina Argentina de Boxeo. <http://www.boxeo.org.ar/nota.php?noticia=1359.> Active as of February 13, 2008.
28. Consejo Argentino de Boxeo Profesional. <http://www.boxeocabp.com.ar/boletin.asp.> Active as of February 13, 2008.
29. Ibid.
30. *El Diario del Centro del Pais.* Author's translation. <http://www.eldiariocba.com.ar/anteriores/2006/07%20de%20abril%20de%202006/deportes/deportes.htm.> Active as of February 13, 2008.
31. Ibid.
32. *Diario El Chenque.* <http://elchenque.com.ar/dep/articulos/07/claulo.htm.> Active as of February 13, 2008.
33. ESPNdeportes.com.
34. *El Diario del Centro del Pais.* <http://www.eldiariocba.com.ar/anteriores/2006/15%20de%20abril%20de% 202006/deportes/deportes.htm.> Active as of February 13, 2008.
35. Municipality of General Villegas. <http://www.villegas.gov.ar/index.php?option=com_content&task=view&id =456&Itemid=253.> Active as of February 13, 2008.
36. Ley 23.798. Prevencion y Lucha contra el Sindrome de Inmunodeficiencia Adquirida (SIDA). <http://www.protecciondedatos.com.ar/ley23798.htm.> Active as of February 13, 2008.
37. *Diario Rio Negro.* <http://www.rionegro.com.ar/arch200203/d09j14.html.> Active as of February 13, 2008.
38. Susana Belmartino, "Reorganizing the Health Care System in Argentina." <http://www.idrc.ca/en/ev-35180-201-1-DO_TOPIC.html.> Active as of July 13, 2005.
39. Lealtad y Juego Limpio en el Deporte. Doping. Comision Nacional Antidoping. Sanciones Deportivas. Trafico de Doping. Doping de Animales. <http://www.aat.com.ar/Files/6.Ley%20Nacional%20Antidoping.pdf.> Active as of February 13, 2008.
40. *Diario Clarin.* <http://www.clarin.com/diario/96/09/12/t-91501d.htm.> Active as of February 13, 2008.

Conclusion

1. The number of professional boxing events in the United States in 2004 was 860 (4588 boxing matches) according to BoxRec.com. <http://www.boxrec.com.> Active as of February 13, 2008. The population of the United States in 2004 was 293,191,511 according the U.S. Census. By dividing the number of boxing matches by the U.S. population, the United States is calculated to have had .000015 boxing matches per capita in 2004. In Argentina, the number of boxing events in 2005 was 417 (871 boxing matches) according the FAB Web site <http://www.fabox.com.ar.> Active as of February 13, 2008. While this number is far less than that of the U.S., the population of Argentina is also far less at 39,537,943. The number of boxing matches per capita in Argentina is .000022, which is greater than that of the U.S.
2. California State Athletic Commission Meeting Minutes. August 6, 2007. <http://www.dca.ca.gov/csac/about_us/meetings/20070806_minutes.pdf.> Active as of February 13, 2008.
3. USA Boxing. "Statement on Amateur Boxing Safety," 2003. <http://www.usaboxing.org/579.htm.> Active as of February 13, 2008. USA Boxing requires an ambulance present on site for sanctioned bouts. If the bouts mentioned by Kimball in the forward to this book were

sanctioned by USA Boxing, Michigan erred by not having an ambulance present for the amateur bouts.

4. Michigan State Law. PA 403 of 2004.

5. Kansas State Law. Chapter 74, Article 50 (74-50-195).

6. This information is according to interviews with Kansas boxing commissioner Aaron Davis and Minnesota boxing commissioner Scott Ledoux, carried out in late 2007 and early 2008.

7. AAPRP Medical Requirements 2007. <http://www.aaprp.org/Commission%20Requirements.> Active as of February 13, 2008. Two states that were not included in the original analysis due to their failure to provide data on the BHS Survey or the AAPRP Web site have also begun requiring HIV tests according to the AAPRP Web site as of February 2008 (Louisiana and Rhode Island). Dr. Michael Schwartz, president of the American Association of Professional Ringside Physicians, granted the author permission to use the AAPRP data compilation for this study.

8. AAPRP Medical Requirements 2007. <http://www.aaprp.org/Commission%20Requirements.> Active as of February 13, 2008. One state that was not included in the original analysis due to its failure to provide data on the BHS Survey or the AAPRP Web site has also begun requiring neurological tests according to the AAPRP Web site as of February 2008 (Vermont). Dr. Michael Schwartz, president of the American Association of Professional Ringside Physicians, granted the author permission to use the AAPRP data compilation for this study.

BIBLIOGRAPHY

Adams, Peter A. "Win, Lose, and Drawing Conclusions: Bellows, Boxing and Progressivism." *OAH Magazine of History* 7, Summer 1992.
Arnold, Peter. *The Pictorial History of Boxing*. New York: Gallery Books, 1988.
Ashe, Arthur R. *A Hard Road to Glory: The African American Athlete in Boxing*. New York: Amistad Press, 1993.
Bernstein, Robert A., and James A. Dyer. *An Introduction to Political Science Methods*. 3rd ed. Englewood Cliffs, NJ: Prentice Hall, 1992.
Brooke-Ball, Peter. *The Boxing Album: An Illustrated History*. London: Anness, 1995.
California State Athletic Commission Meeting Minutes. August 6, 2007.
Chalip, Laurence, and Arthur Johnson. "Sports Policy in the United States." In Chalip, Johnson and Stachura, eds., *National Sports Policies: An International Handbook*. Westport, CT: Greenwood Press, 1996.
Dahlberg, Tim. *Fight Town: Las Vegas—The Boxing Capital of the World*. Las Vegas, NV: Stephens Press, 2004.
Earl, Phillip I. *This Was Nevada*. Reno, NV: Nevada Historical Society, 1986.
Fleischer, Nat, and Sam Andre. *A Pictorial History of Boxing*. Secaucus, NJ: Citadel Press, 1993.
GAO Report to the Chairman, Committee on Commerce, Science, and Transportation, U.S. Senate. "Professional Boxing." July 2003.
Gorn, Elliott J. "The First American Championship Fight." *OAH Magazine of History* 7, Summer 1992.
Gray, Virginia. "The Socioeconomic and Political Context of States." In Gray and Russell L. Hanson, *Politics in the American States: A Comparative Analysis*. Washington: CQ Press, 2004
Gray, W. Russel. "For Whom the Bell Tolled: The Decline of British Prize Fighting in the Victorian Era." In *Journal of Popular Culture* 21 no. 2 (Fall 1987).
Hauser, Thomas. *A Beautiful Sickness: Reflections on the Sweet Science*. Fayetteville: University of Arkansas Press, 2001.
_____. *The Black Lights: Inside the World of Professional Boxing*. Fayetteville: University of Arkansas Press, 2000.
Hedge, David M. *Governance and the Changing American States*. Boulder, CO: Westview Press: 1998.
Homer. *The Iliad*. Translated by Robert Fitzgerald. London: Collins Harvill, 1985.
Houlihan, Barrie. *Sport, Policy and Politics: A Comparative Analysis*. London: Routledge, 1997.
Hulse, James W. *The Silver State: Nevada's Heritage Reinterpreted*. Reno: University of Nevada Press. 2004.
Jennison, Keith W., ed. *The Concise Encyclopedia of Sports*. New York: Franklin Watts, 1970.
Johnson, Arthur, and James H. Frey, eds. *Government and Sport: The Public Policy Issues*. Totowa, NJ: Rowman and Allanheld, 1985.
Joslyn, Mark R., and Steve Ceccoli. "Attentiveness to Television News and Opinion Change

in the Fall 1992 Presidential Campaign." In *Political Behavior* 18, no. 2 (June 1996): 141–170.
Kahn, Roger. *A Flame of Pure Fire: Jack Dempsey and the Roaring '20s*. New York: Harcourt Brace, 1999.
Kingdon, John W. *Agendas, Alternatives and Public Policies*. New York: Harper Collins, 1984.
Manheim, Jarol B., and Richard C. Rich. *Empirical Political Analysis: Research Methods in Political Science*. 3rd ed. White Plains, NY: Longman, 1991.
Mee, Bob. *Boxing: Heroes & Champions*. Edison, NJ: Chartwell Books, 1997.
O'Connor, Karen, and Larry J. Sabato. *American Government: Roots and Reform*. Brief ed. New York: Macmillan, 1994.
Odd, Gilbert. *The Encyclopedia of Boxing*. Secaucus, NJ: Chartwell Books, 1989.
Rader, Benjamin G. *American Sports: From the Age of Folk Games to the Age of Televised Sports*. Upper Saddle River, NJ: Prentice Hall, 1999.
_____. *In Its Own Image: How Television Has Transformed Sports*. New York: The Free Press, 1984.
Raimondo, Henry J. "State Budgeting: Problems, Choices, Money." In Van Horn, Carl E., ed. *The State of the States*. 3rd ed. Washington: CQ Press, 1996.
Reid, John B., and Ronald M. James. *Uncovering Nevada's Past: A Primary Source History of the Silver State*. Reno: University of Nevada Press, 2004.
Ringquist, Evan J., and James C. Garand. "Policy Change in the American States." In Ronald E. Weber and Paul Brace, eds. *American State and Local Politics: Directions for the 21st Century*. New York: Chatham House, 1999.
Roberts, James B., and Alexander G. Skutt. *The Boxing Register*. Ithaca, NY: McBooks Press, 2002.
Roberts, Randy. *Jack Dempsey: The Manassa Mauler*. Baton Rouge: Louisiana State University Press, 1984.
Roosevelt, Theodore. *An Autobiography*. New York: Macmillan, 1913; Bartleby.com, 1998.
Sammons, Jeffrey T. *Beyond the Ring: The Role of Boxing in American Society*. Urbana: University of Illinois Press, 1990.
Smith, Kevin R. *Black Genesis: The History of the Black Prizefighter 1760–1870*. Lincoln, NE: iUniverse, 2003.
Statutes of the State of Nevada Passed at the Eighteenth Session of the Legislature 1897. Carson City, NV: State Printing Office, 1897.
Statutes of the State of Nevada Passed at the Fortieth Session of the Legislature 1941. Carson City, NV: State Printing Office, 1941.
Sugar, Bert Randolph, ed. *100 Years of Boxing*. New York: Galley Press, 1982.
_____. *Bert Sugar on Boxing*. Guilford, CT: The Lyons Press, 2003
Thomson, David. *In Nevada: The Land, the People, God, and Chance*. New York: Alfred P. Knopf, 1999.
Tuttle, William M. Jr. *Race Riot: Chicago in the Red Summer of 1919*. Urbana: University of Illinois Press, 1996.
Van Horn, Carl E., ed. *The State of the States, Third Edition*. Washington: CQ Press, 1996.
Weston, Stanley, and Steven Farhood. *The Ring: Boxing in the 20th Century*. New York: BDD Illustrated Books, 1993.
Whannel, Garry. *Fields in Vision: Television Sport and Cultural Transformation*. London: Routledge, 1992.
Wiggins, David K. "Peter Jackson and the Elusive Heavyweight Championship." In *Journal of Sport History* 12, no. 2 (Summer, 1985): 149.
Wilson, John. *Playing by the Rules: Sport, Society, and the State*. Detroit: Wayne State University Press, 1994.

INDEX

References in ***bold italics*** are to pages with illustrations

ABC Sports 42
Adams, Peter 32
Adidas 41
Advisory Committee on Boxer Health and Safety (Nevada) 133, 142
African American 16, 25, 28, 32, 33, 161
Aguirre, Miguel 183
Alabama 19, 64
Alamo, Dr. Tony 117
Alaska 19, 64, 66
Ali, Lonnie 56
Ali, Muhammad 7, 41, 42, 56, ***57***, 99, 114, 116, 164; Boxing Reform Act (2000) 3, 55–56, 146
Ali vs. Bonavena 164
Ali vs. Liston 41
Ali vs. Spinks 7, 116
Allred, Steven 71–72, 75
Amateur boxing 1, 154, 198
Ambulance, presence of 1, 2, 10, 15, 21, 54, 57, 67, 73, 106, 130, 182, 187, 192, 193
America Sports (Argentina) 177
American Association of Professional Ringside Physicians (AAPRP) 20, 21, 68–69, 77, 80, 82, 92–99, 102, 106, 123, 158, 159, 192, 198
American Indian reservations 13, 20, 54, 55, 57, 88, 159–160, 196, 198, 200
American Medical Association 53
Ancient Egypt 23, 24, 62, 190
Ancient Greece 23–24
Ancient Mesopotamia 24
Ancient Olympics 23, 24
Andretti, Mario 144
Anifowoshe, "Kid" Akeem ***59***, 60, ***168***
Argentina 22; boxing gyms 172; boxing history 166–171; boxing in 19, 163–189, 195; boxing regulations 12, 19, 22; *Chubut* Province 175; *Club Huracán* 172, 177; *Club San Carlos* 172; *Comodoro Rivadavia* 175; Congress 178; *Córdoba* Province 172; current boxing outlook 172–189; *Entre Rios* Province 170; *General Villegas* Municipality 177; *Gimnasio Coral de Palos* 172; governmental structure 163–164; *Inspección General de Justicia* 175; *Ley de Deportes 20.655* 171; *Ley Nacional 23.798* 181; Mixed Martial Arts 186; National Day of the Boxer 167; National Secretariat of Sports 178; *Obras Sociales* 184; Olympians 164; Olympic Boxing 173, 175–176; *Parana* Boxing Club 170; *Polideportivo Municipal* in Caseros 172; prominent boxers 164–166; rival commissions 174–175; *Torneo Evita* 171; women's boxing in 186; world champions 164–166
Argentine Boxing Federation (FAB) 4, 167, 170, ***171***, ***173***, 172–189, 197; certification of ring officials 185–186; drug testing 184–185; funding 179–180; health insurance 184; mismatches 183; structure 176–177; suspensions 183
Argentine Boxing Federation (FAB) *Consejo Directivo* 176
Argentine Boxing Federation (FAB) Medical Council 180–182
Argentine Olympic Committee 173
Argentine Professional Boxing Council (CABP) 174–175, 177, 178
Arguello, Alexis 47
Arizona 56, 107
Arkansas 41; boxing in 31
Arkansas Athletic Commission 155
Armstrong, Henry 37
Arum, Bob ***61***, 103, 113
Aryan Supremacy 37
Asia 47
Asian Pacific Heavyweight Title 130
Association of Argentine Boxing 167
Association of Boxing Commissions 2, 13, 55, 59, 64, 65, 70, 75, 101, 114, 118, 122, 128, 140, 147, 158, 159, 160, 186, 196
Athenian Games 24
Athens, Pennsylvania 32
Atlantic City, boxing in 88, 98, 116
Australia 33
Austria 37

215

INDEX

Avansino, Skip, Jr. 117, 134
Avilas, Carlos 8

Baer, Max 38
Baer vs. Nova 38
Bailey, John R. 117
Baldomir, Carlos 166, 172
Baltimore 32
Barcenas, Barbara 131
Bare-knuckle boxing 24
Barrera, Marco Antonio 46, 148
Barrios, Jorge 166
Baseball 38, 146
Basketball 153
Battle of the Long Count 36
Beasley, Tom 25
Beckman, Connie 74
Beddes, Larry 70, 73
Bejines, Francisco "Kiko" 48–50
Bejines-Davila 48–50, 53
Bello Diaz, Luis 175
Bellows, George 32, 164
Belmartino, Susana 184
Benn, Nigel 46, 60
Benn vs. McClellan 60
Berliner, Dr. William 133
Berry, Dave 36
Bill, "Brighton" 26
Bisbal, Osvaldo 172, 175–187
Black, William 28
Blanco, Gov. Kathleen 83
Bonavena, Oscar 164
Bosch de Sartori, Irene 174
Boston 31, 32
Bowe, Riddick 9
Bowe vs. Holyfield II 9
Bowen, Andy 31
Boxer records 54, 131
Boxer registry 54
Boxing: contemporary television 47; equipment 134; genesis 23–24; gloves 28, 141, 144; gymnasiums 135; licenses 4, 21, 54, 57, 67, 74–75, 106, 111, 192; media coverage 46–47; number of events 65–67; ring size 26; scandals in the 1980s 46–48; suspensions 14, 20, 54, 57, 69, 71, 74, 106, 132, 193; trainers 135; weight categories 29, 30
Boxing commissioners, lack of diversity 160–161
Boxing commissions in the United States 192
Boxing Day 33
Boxing Health and Safety Index (BHSI) 22, 83–86, 92–99, 106–107, 126, 191, 192, 194, 197, 198

Boxing Health and Safety Survey (BHS Survey) 20–21, 63–85, 105–107, 109, 117, 121, 180, 193, 198
Boxing regulations: historical evolution 190; political science research 191
Boxing-related deaths 22, 86–87, 92–99, 106–207, 144, 190, 191
Boxing Writers Association of America 99
Boxrec.com 65, 67
Boyle, Dr. Joseph 53
Braddock, James J. 37
Bredahl, Jimmy 48
Brinkley, Jesse 102
British Board of Boxing Control 41, 60
British Commonwealth 41
Brooklyn, New York 32
Brooks, Leroy 131
Broughton, Jack 24, 87
Broughton vs. Stevenson 87
Broughton's Rules 24–26, 62
Brown, Joe W. 117
Buenos Aires 170, 172
Buenos Aires Boxing Club 166, 167
Burchfield, Jimmy 3
Burns, Tommy 33
Burns vs. Johnson 33
Burroughs, Tom 151

Cabrera, Delfo 171
Caesars Palace 116
Caestus 24
Cairo 23
California 30, 33, 67, 196; boxing in 32, 65, 66, 87
California Athletic Club (San Francisco) 32
California Athletic Commission 13, 14, 20, 70, 71, 72, 77, 84, 102
Cambridge 28
Campanna, Dr. Albert 118
Canada 64
Canastota, NY 169
Carbo, Frankie 39
Carpentier, Georges 36
Carson, Bob 200, *201–204*
Carson City, NV 31, 112
Carver, Randie 1–2, 9, 72, 73, 200, *201–204*
Carver vs. Salem 1–2, 9, 200, *201–204*
Carville, Gov. E.P. 113
Castle, John 61
Castro, Jorge 166
Cermesoni, Jorge Roque 166
Certification and approval for ring officials 21, 67, 75–76, 159, 193

216

Index

Chalip, Laurence 17, 18, 86, 88, 191
Chambers, John Graham 28
Champion 47
Chapman, Dr. Todd 118
Charles, Ezzard 38
Chavez, Jesus 133
Chavez, Julio Cesar 51, 108, *110*
Chavez vs. Johnson 133
Chavez vs. Kamau 51
Chavez vs. Taylor 108
Chicago 32
Chile, boxing in 167
Civil War, US 28
Clancy, Gil *40*
Clinton, Pres. Bill 3
Coggi, Juan Martin 166, 172–173, 185
Cole, Laurence 104
Collins, Walter 114
Colorado 157; boxing in 65
Colorado Athletic Commission 11, 79, 81, 153, 155
Columbia, Missouri 151
Conn, Billy 38
Connecticut, boxing in 2
Connecticut Athletic Commission 69–70
Consejo Argentino de Boxeo Profesional see Argentine Professional Boxing Council (CABP)
The Contender 102
Contreras, Ruben 72
Cooney, Gerry 7
Corbett, James J. 30, 111
Corbett vs. Fitzsimmons 31, 111–112, 149
Cortez, Joe 12, 109, 131, 136–142, 137, 150, 194
Court of Appeals 42
Cribb, Tom 25
Cunningham, Milton J. 31

Dahlberg, Tim 114–116
Dallas 104
Darnell, Steve 7
Davidson, Dr. Jeff 133
Davila, Albert 12, 48–53, *51, 52*
Davila, Alyssa 53
Davis, Aaron 4, 19, 101, 107, 153–161, 194, 196, 197
Decima, Pedro *168*
De La Hoya, Oscar 46, *48,* 116, 149
De La Hoya vs. Mosley II 103
Delaware 19, 64
Dempsey, Jack "The Nonpareil" 29
Dempsey, Jack (Heavyweight Champion) 36, 41, 112, 113, 149, 164

Dempsey vs. Firpo 164, 167
Dempsey vs. Fulljames 29
Dempsey vs. Tunney 36, 113
Denny, Cleveland 2
Denny-Hart 2
Denver 32
DeRienzo, Charlie 103
Detroit 32; boxing in 1
Diaz, Miguel *168*
District of Columbia (Washington, D.C.) 13, 31, 147, 199
Dominican Republic 79
Don King Productions 42
Douglas, John Sholto 28
Drug testing 15, 21, 68, 80–82, 83, 84, 92–99, 106–107, 124–128, 132, 143, 145, 150, 157, 161, 174, 193, 194, 195, 197
Dundee, Angelo *117*
Dunes Hotel and Casino 116
Duran, Roberto 2, 47, *49*
Duran vs. Leonard 2, 7
Duva, Lou *100*

Earl, Phillip 112
Egypt 23, 24; *see also* Ancient Egypt
Elazar, Daniel 91, 191
Elazar Scale 22, 86, 91–92, 96
Electrolyte drinks 26, 134, 143–144
El-Minia Governorate 23
Ely, NV 112
Embanato, Anthony "Buddy" 83
England 24, 25, 30, 62, 190
ESPN 179, 188
ESPN Classic 47
ESPN Deportes 172
ESPN.com 72
Etruria 23
Europe 47
European Boxing Union 38

Fangio, Juan Manuel 171
Farhood, Steven 36
FECARBOX 130
Federal Boxing Board 42
Federal sports policy 18
Federalism 11, 13, 17, 190
Federación Argentina de Boxeo see Argentine Boxing Federation (FAB)
Fenech, Jeff *137*
Ferro Carril Oeste 170
Figg, James 24
Fight Fax, Inc. 65, 70, 74, 128, 158, 183
Firpo, Luis Angel 164, *165,* 167
Fitzsimmons, Bob 31, 111
Fleischer, Nat 5, 30, 41, 113

INDEX

Florida 64, 123; boxing in 65
Football 38, 146, 153
Ford, Duane 103, 131
Foreman, George 42, *43*, 116, **188**
Formula 1 171
Fox, Richard Kyle 29
Fox Sports 47, 174
Frawley Law 33
Frazier, Joe 42, 164
Frazier vs. Bonavena 164
Frey, James 18
Fulljames, George 29
Fulmer, Gene 115

Gagliardi, Joe 104
Galindez, Victor 165
Gambling 22, 88–89, 92–99, 106–107, 116, 156, 162, 191
Game, Dr. James 131, 132
Gans, Joe 32, 112, 113
Gans vs. Nelson 112, 113
Garand, James C. 16, 17, 86, 87, 90
Garcia, Armando 102, 160, 196
Garcia, Jimmy 2
Garcia vs. Ruelas 2
Gatica, Jose Maria 171
Gatti, Arturo 116
Gavin, William A. 36
General Accounting Office 14, 64
Georgia 42
Georgia Athletic Commission 42
Germany 37
Gillette Friday Night Fights 38
Golden Age of Sport 36
Golden Age of Television 38
Golden Gloves 136
Goldfield, Nevada 112
Gonzalez, David 138–139
Goodman, Dr. Margaret 12, 81, 109, 118, 124–134, 140, 150, 194
Gorn, Elliott 28
Gould, Jack 38
Gray, Virginia 16, 86, 90, 91, 191, 192
Graziano, Rocky 38
Great Depression 36–37
Great Western Forum 7, 8, 27
Great White Hope 34
Greece 23, 24; *see also* Ancient Greece
Greenwich Village 35
Griffith, Emile 39, *40*
Griffith vs. Paret 39

Hagler, Marvin 108
Hagler vs. Hearns 108
Hagney, Frank 167
Hamed, "Prince" Naseem 46
Harmon, Mella Rothwell 111, 112
Harris, Rep. Oren 41
Hart, Gaetan 2
Hart, Marvin 33, 112
Hart vs. Root 112
Hatton, Ricky 148
Hatton vs. Mayweather 148
Hauser, Thomas 12, 99–105, 125
Havana 34
Hawaii 66, 69
Hawaii Athletic Commission 69, 75, 77
Hazzard, Larry 160
Health insurance 15, 21, 54, 67, 74, 104, 106, 192, 193
Hearns, Thomas 7, *45*, 46, 108
Hearns-Roldan 7
Hearns vs. Kinchen 46
Hedge, David M. 16
Hill, Virgil 165
Hilton Hotel and Casino 116
Himantes 24
Hinckley, Wayne 114
Hispanic (Latino) 16, 67, 135, 161
Hitler, Adolf 37
HIV testing 15, 21, 57, 60–61, 68, 69, 78–80, 83, 84, 92–99, 100, 106–107, 123, 124–128, 131, 145, 150, 157, 161, 174, 181, 188, 193, 194, 195, 197
Hockey 146
Holmes, Larry 7, *44*, 46, *77*
Holmes vs. Cooney 7, 108, 116
Holmes, Lindell 7
Holyfield, Evander 9, *43*, *77*, **100**, 108, 116, 125
Holyfield vs. Holmes *77*
Holyfield vs. Tyson 108
Homansky, Dr. Flip 117, 125, 130
Home Box Office (HBO) 179, **188**
Homer 23
Hopkins, Bernard 165
Horton Law 32, 35
Houlihan, Barrie 17, 90
House Committee on Education and the Workforce 15
House Committee on Energy and Commerce 15
Hulse, James W. 111
Hyde Park 24
Hyer, Jacob 25
Hyer, Tom 28, 35

Ibragimov, Sultan 130, 132, 199
Ibragimov, Timur 130, 132, 133

218

Index

Idaho Athletic Commission 70, 73, 74, 75, 76
Iliad 23
Illinois, boxing in 65
Illinois Athletic Commission 75, 79
Indiana, boxing in 65
Indiana Athletic Commission 75
Indianapolis 104
International Boxing Club 4, 39
International Boxing Club (Buenos Aires) 167
International Boxing Federation 43, 44, 46, 48, 164
International Boxing Hall of Fame 164, 165, 169, 187
International Boxing Union 35
Iowa 107
Iraq 23
Irish immigrants 29
Italy 24

James, Bill 5
Jeffries, Jim 33, 112, 113
Jernigan, Wally 70
Jofre, Eder 169
Johnson, Arthur 17, 18, 86, 88, 191
Johnson, Jack 33, 112, 113, 167
Johnson vs. Jeffries 33, 112, 113, 149
Johnson, Leroy 42
Johnson, Levander 133
Johnson, Pres. Lyndon 39
Jones, Roy, Jr. 116, **118**
Jordan, Don 114
Journal of Combative Sport 22, 86, 199

Kahn, Roger 35
Kamau, David 51, **52, 168**
Kansas 1, 8, 20, 22, 62, 64, 130, 157; amateur boxing 198; boxing in 14, 152, 153, 194–195; licensing fees 152
Kansas Athletic Commission 4, 12, 13–14, 19, 22, 107, 151–162, 192
Kansas City 151, 153; boxing in 1, 2, 9, 10, 156
Kansas City Police Department 9
Kansas City Sports Page 8
Kansas Department of Commerce 154, 155
Kansas Division of Travel and Tourism 156
Kansas Expo Center 155
Kansas Professional Regulated Sports Act (2004) 151, 152, 154
Kansas State Legislature 14
Kefauver, Sen. Carey Estes 39
Kellison, W. 114

Kelly, Ray 103
Kennedy, Rep. Ambrose J. 37
Kennedy, Att. Gen. Robert 39
Kerik, Bernard 103
Kilrain, Jake 29
Kim, Duk-Koo 47, 138
Kimball, George 1–5, 198
Kinchen, James 46
King, Don **44,** 113
King, Martin Luther, Jr. 33
King, Rep. Peter 15, 56
King George I 24
Kingdon, John 17, 86, 87, 191
Kirchner, Pres. Nestor 174
Kizer, Keith 101, 109, 135–136, 142–150, 155, 194, 196

Laciar, Santos 165, **167,** 172
Lampley, Jim **188**
Lane, Mills **109,** 137
Las Vegas 110, 156, 185; boxing in 2, 88, 98, 108, 114–116, 130, 150
Las Vegas Convention Center 115, 149
Latin America 40, 47, 166, 178
Lato, Anthony, Jr. 132
Lavigne, George 31
Lavigne vs. Bowen 31
Lecture, Jose 169
Lecture, Juan Carlos "Tito" **168,** 169, **170**
Ledoux, Scott 107, 155
Lee, Bob 43
Lembo, Nicholas 75
Lennon, Jimmy, Jr. 27
Leonard, "Sugar" Ray 2, 47, **49**
Leonard vs. Duran II 47
Lewis, Lennox 11, 99
Lewis, William 114
Lewis Law 32
Lexis-Nexis 20–21, 63
Liston, Charles "Sonny" 41, 114, 115, 116
Liston vs. Martin 116
Livera, Esteban 169
Llambias, Dr. Joaquin 167
Lobo, Rogerio 130, 132
Locche, Nicolino 164, **166,** 172
London 24, 30
London Prize Ring Rules 26–28, 62
Long, John 35
Lonsdale, Lord 30
Lonsdale Belts 30
Lopez, Claudia 175
Los Angeles 8, 110
Louhis, Dean 71, 72
Louis, Joe 37, 41
Louis vs. Conn II 38

Index

Louis vs. Schmeling 37
Louisiana 123; boxing in 30, 31
Louisiana Athletic Commission 83
Lueckenhoff, Tim 2, 64, 70, 74, 101–102, 122
Luna Park Stadium 167–170, **168**

Mack, Luther 134
Madison Square Garden **40**, 108, 113, 114, 167, 169
Major League Baseball 5, 15
Maldonado, Fernando 10
Mancini, Ray "Boom Boom" 47, **50**, 138
Mancini vs. Kim 49, 138
Mandalay Bay Hotel and Casino 116
Mann Act 34
Manon, Leocadio 60, 79
Manuel Velazquez Boxing Fatality Collection 86–87
Maradona, Diego 171
Mares, Abner 79
Marquis of Queensberry Rules 28–31, 62
Marsden, Reuben (Andy) 87
Martin, Leotis 116
Maryland 64, 69, 85; boxing in 28
Maryland Athletic Commission 69, 71, 73, 79, 81, 192
Mason, Joseph 160
Massachusetts 29
Mastaba Tomb 23
Mayweather, Floyd 148, 149
McCain, Sen. John 3, 13, 15, 53, 54, 56, 146, 187, 196
McCarthy, Paddy 166
McCarthy vs. Robassio 166
McClellan, Gerald **59**, 60
Medical Advisory Board (Nevada) 118, 119, 121–122, 124–134, 135, 147
Medical Advisory Board (WBC) 47
Mee, Bob 41, 43
Mendoza, Daniel 25
Mendoza, Gilberto Jesus 177
Merchant, Larry **188**
Mery-Ra, tomb of 23
Mesi, Joe 3, 100, 148
Mesopotamia 23, 24; *see also* Ancient Mesopotamia
Mexico 62
Mexico City 40
MGM Grand Hotel and Casino 116
Michigan 64; amateur boxing 198; boxing in 1, 65
Michigan Athletic Commission 11, 74, 75, 79, 82
Midwest 8, 32, 64, 85, 162

Minker, Chuck 137
Minnesota 64
Minnesota Athletic Commission 20, 107, 155, 192
Mismatches 14, 15, 21, 57, 67, 71–73, 106, 189, 192
Missouri 122, 157; boxing in 10, 65, 151
Missouri Athletic Commission 2, 9, 10, 20, 72, 153
Mixed Martial Arts 146, 148, 152, 157–158
Moli, Fabio "La Mole" 183
Molineux, Tom 25
Montana Athletic Commission 69–70, 74, 75, 79
Montilla, Miguel 136
Montreal, boxing in 2
Monzon, Carlos 164–165, 172, 183
Moore, Archie **169**
Morris, Darrin 105
Morrison, Tommy "The Duke" **61**
Morrissey, John 28
Muhammad, Robert 102
Muhammad Ali Boxing Reform Act (2000) 3, 55–56, 146
Munford, Harvey 134
Murray, Jack 167

Narvaez, Omar 166, 172, 183
National Basketball Association (NBA) 104
National Boxing Association 36, 40
National Conference of State Legislatures 22, 88–89
National Football League 104
National Police Gazette 29
National Registry of Boxing Personnel 58
National Sporting Club 30
Nave, Dr. Jim 134
NCAA 53
Nebraska Athletic Commission 70, 71
Nelson, Azumah **137**
Nelson, Oscar "Battling" 112, 113
Nelson vs. Fenech **137**
Neurological testing 14, 21, 68, 76–78, 83, 84, 92–99, 100, 106–107, 123, 124–128, 131, 134, 145, 148, 162, 174, 193, 194, 195, 197
Nevada 22, 33, 62, 64, 67, 85, 88, 100, 103, 108–150, 193; boxing in 31, 32, 190, 193–194; boxing regulations 119–121; early boxing history 111–113; legalization of boxing 31
Nevada Athletic Commission 3, 4, 11, 12, 19, 22, 47, 70, 75, 81, 82, 99, 100, 103, 105, 108–150, 158, 196, 199; participant-observation 20, 109

220

Index

New Britain, Connecticut 32
New Hampshire 107
New Jersey 85, 123, 136
New Jersey Athletic Commission 75, 77, 79, 80–81, 192
New Orleans, boxing in 30, 31
New York 31, 32, 33, 40, 62, 64, 67, 85, 100, 101, 102, 123; boxing in 28, 35, 65, 87, 108, 190; legalization of boxing 32
New York Athletic Commission 33, 36, 41, 70, 77–78, 82, 99, 100, 101, 103
New York City 32
New York Times 61
Newberry, Jorge 166
Newspaper decisions 34
Norris, "Terrible" Terry **109**
Norris, James A. 4, 39
North American Boxing Federation 9
North Dakota Athletic Commission 69
North Kansas City Hospital 2
Nova, Lou 38
Nunn, Michael **117**

Obama, Sen. Barack 3
Oberlin College 53
Ohio, boxing in 65
Ohio Athletic Commission 74
Oklahoma 157
Oklahoma Athletic Commission 71, 77
Olympic Auditorium (Los Angeles) 170
Olympic boxing 130, 183; *see also* Ancient Olympics
Olympic Club (New Orleans) 31
Oregon 85
Oregon Athletic Commission 70, 77, 192
Orleans Hotel and Casino 130, 133
Ortiz, Carlos 169
Owen, Johnny 50

Pace, Domingo 167
Pace, Ismael 169
Pacheco, Ferdie 2
Palermo, Blinky 39
Palombo, Eduardo Juan 174
Panella, Pat 69, 71, 81
Pankration 23
Paret, Benny 39, 114
Paret vs. Jordan 114
Paris 35
Parker, Dr. Jeffrey 118
Parkinson's Syndrome 56
Patterson, Floyd 103, 115
Patterson vs. Liston 115
Pennsylvania 33, 123; boxing in 65
Pennsylvania Athletic Commission 71, 77

Percy, Hugh 25
Perez, Pascual 164, 171, 172
Peron, Evita 171
Peron, Juan Domingo 170
Peterson, Roxane 73
Pharaohs 23
Philadelphia 32
Physical examinations: post-fight 14, 21, 67, 70–71, 132, 133, 180, 188, 194; pre-fight examinations 20, 54, 67, 68–69, 106, 130, 156–157, 180, 192
Physicians, ringside 54, 122, 124–129
Pintor, Lupe 49–50
Pintor vs. Owen 50, 53
Political culture 22, 91–99, 106–107, 191
Political science 11, 15, 191
Pollard, Dr. Anthony 118
Post-fight physical examinations 14, 21, 67, 70–71, 132, 133, 180, 188, 194
Potenza, Maria del Carmen 175
Prairie Band Potawatomi Nation 160
Pre-fight physical examinations 20, 54, 67, 68–69, 106, 130, 156–157, 180, 192
Pregnancy test 68
Principi, Osvaldo 175–187
Prine, Kim 72
Private boxing clubs 31, 32–33
Professional Boxing Amendments Act (2007) 56–60, 62, 104, 123, 195, 197
Professional Boxing Organizations 40
Professional Boxing Safety Act (1996) 3, 4, 54–55, 56–58, 64, 73, 74, 146
Prohibition 34
Proliferation of World Championships 46
Providence, Rhode Island 32
Pryor, Aaron 47, 136
Pryor vs. Arguello II 47
Ptah Hotep 23
Public policy 18
Puerto Rico 20, 46, 199
Purity Crusade 31

Quiroga, Robert 60
Quiroga vs. Anifowoshe 60

Rader, Benjamin 38
Rader, Benn 37
Randall, Frankie **185**
Randall vs. Coggi 185
Ratner, Marc 4, 70, 105, 109, 117, 121–124, 125, 129, 133, 142, 150, 194, 196, 197
Referee 26
Reid, Sen. Harry 146
Reno, Nevada 33, 112
Revolutionary War, American 25

INDEX

Rhode Island Athletic Commission 3–4, 83
Rhone, Bradley 101
Richardson, Rep. Bill 3, 43, 53
Richmond, Bill 25
Rickard, George Lewis "Tex" 112, 113, 149
The Ring Magazine 8, 30, 41, 113, 124, 125
Ring of Fire 39
Ringquist, Evan J. 16, 17, 86, 87, 90
Ringside physicians 54, 122, 124–129
Riviera Hotel and Casino 116
Roaring 20s 36
Robassio, Abelardo 166
Roberts, James 34, 35
Roberts, Randy 33, 34
Robinson, "Sugar" Ray 38, 115
Rodriguez Papini, Dr. Hugo 173
Rogich, Sig 134
Roldan, Juan Domingo 7, 165
Romans 24
Roosevelt, Pres. Franklin 37
Roosevelt, Pres. Theodore 35
Root, Jack 112
Roth, Sen. William 53
Ruddock, Donovan "Razor" **115**
Ruelas, Gabriel 2
Ruggeroli, Dr. Charles 134
Ruiz, John 82
Ruth, Babe 36
Ryan, Paddy 29

Sac and Fox Nation 160
Saddler, Sandy 169
Sadler, Gov. Reinhol 111
St. Joseph, Missouri 151
St. Louis, boxing in 10
Salem, Karabary 1–2, 9, 200, **201**
Sammons, Jeffrey 31, 36, 37
Sample, Andy 130
San Francisco 31, 32, 33, 104
Sanchez, Martin 133
Saqqara 23
Schmeling, Max 37
Schwartz, Dr. Michael 69, 102, 123
Sebelius, Gov. Kathleen 14, 151, 160
Senate Committee on Commerce, Science and Transportation 15
Skutt, Alexander 34, 35
Slaves 28
Smith, Gov. Alfred E. 35
Smith, Jem 29
South Carolina 85, 123
South Carolina Athletic Commission 74, 192
South Dakota 20, 123

Southard, Mel 103
Spinks, Leon 7, 116
Spinks, Michael 116, 165
Sports in the United States 18
Sports policy 17–19
State athletic commissions, creation of 19–20
State athletic commissions, funding for 154–155
State policy 16–17
State wealth 22, 89–90, 92–99, 106–107, 191, 196
Statistical results 92–99, 105–106
Stearns, Rep. Cliff 56
Steele, Richard 137
Stevens, Ron Scott 102, 103
Stevenson, George 87
Strada, Ross 9, **201, 203**
Subdural hematoma 73, 100
Sugar, Bert Randolph 37
Sullivan, James "Yankee" 28, 35
Sullivan, John L. 29, 30, 41
Sullivan vs. Corbett 30, 31
Sullivan vs. Hyer 28
Sumerians 23
Supreme Court 42
Svinth, Joseph R. 86
Swift, Owen 26
Sydney 33
Syria 23

Taylor, Jermain 155
Taylor, Meldrick 108, **109**
Telefutura 47
Television, early boxing broadcasts 38
Ten Point Must System 36
Tennessee 39, 100
Tennessee Athletic Commission 11, 99, 100
Texas 67, 123; boxing in 31, 65
Texas Athletic Commission 11, 71, 104
Thomas and Mack Center 116
Thomson, David 111, 114
Tiberi, David 53
Tilden, Bill 36
Tinch, M.C. 114
Tintetti, Dr. Noemi 180
Toledo, Ohio 34
Tomb of Mery-Ra 23
Toney, James 53, **55**, 82, 139
Toney vs. Ruiz 82
Toney vs. Tiberi 53
Toney vs. Williams 139
Tonopah, Nevada 32, 112
Topeka, Kansas 154
Torricelli, Rep. Robert 53

Track and Field 153
Trenton, New Jersey 32
Tunney, Gene 36, 113
Tuttle, William J. 34
TyC Sports 47, 175, 176, 179, 189
Tyson, Mike 11, 26, *27,* 99, 108, *115,* 116, 125
Tyson vs. Ruddock II *115*

Ultimate Fighting Championship 121, 134
Union Hispana 8
United Kingdom 186
United States. Attorney General 54
____. Congress 15, 18, 37, 39, 41, 42, 43, 53, 54, 56, 60, 190, 191, 197, 200
____. Department of Commerce 56
____. Department of Justice 39
____. Supreme Court 42
United States, first prizefight in 25
United States Boxing Commission 56–60, 128, 187, 189, 190, 196, 197, 199
United States Census American Community Survey Summary (2003) 22
University of Kansas 10–11, 20
Universal Boxing Council 175
University of Nevada Las Vegas 116
University of Southern California 53
US Census American Community Survey Summary (2003) 90
USA Boxing 198
USA Boxing News 8
Utah Athletic Commission 79, 99, 107

Vasquez, Julio Cesar 166
Vermont 66
Vermont Athletic Commission 83
Viale, Cesar 167
Vietnam War 42
Viloria, Brian 72
Viloria vs. Contreras 72, 102–103
Virgin Islands (US) 20, 199
Virginia Athletic Commission 70–71

Walcott, Jersey Joe 38, 41, 136
Walker, James J. 35
Walker Law 35–36
Wangila, Robert 138–139
Wangila vs. Gonzalez 138–139
Washington, D.C. *see* District of Columbia
Washington State 69
Weisharr, Matt 62
West Virginia, boxing in 65
West Virginia Athletic Commission 61, 71–72, 75
Weston, Stanley 36
White House 37
Willard, Jess 34
Willard vs. Dempsey 34
Williams, Charles 139
Williams, Ike 8, *39*
Wilson, John 18
Wisconsin 64
Wisconsin Athletic Commission 72, 73, 74, 79
Women 16
Women's International Boxing Association 164, 175
Women's Suffrage 34
Woods, Tiger 104
World Bank 183
World Boxing Association 40, 43, 44, 47–48, 80, 82, 105, 136, 164, 185
World Boxing Council 34, 40, 43, 44, 47, 49, 164
World Boxing Organization 46, 60, 61, 105, 164, 183
World War II 37–38
Wright, Bradley 82
Wyoming 20, 66

Zale, Tony 38
Zerlentes, Becky 60

www.ingramcontent.com/pod-product-compliance
Ingram Content Group UK Ltd.
Pitfield, Milton Keynes, MK11 3LW, UK
UKHW041950140426
5217IPUK00014B/731

9 780786 438624